I Love
This Game

I Love
This Game

THE AUTOBIOGRAPHY

Patrice Evra

with Andy Mitten

**SIMON &
SCHUSTER**

London · New York · Sydney · Toronto · New Delhi

First published in Great Britain by Simon & Schuster UK Ltd, 2021

Copyright © Patrice Evra, 2021

The right of Patrice Evra to be identified as the author
of this work has been asserted in accordance with the
Copyright, Designs and Patents Act, 1988.

1 3 5 7 9 10 8 6 4 2

Simon & Schuster UK Ltd
1st Floor
222 Gray's Inn Road
London WC1X 8HB

www.simonandschuster.co.uk
www.simonandschuster.com.au
www.simonandschuster.co.in

Simon & Schuster Australia, Sydney
Simon & Schuster India, New Delhi

The author and publishers have made all reasonable
efforts to contact copyright-holders for permission, and apologise
for any omissions or errors in the form of credits given.
Corrections may be made to future printings.

A CIP catalogue record for this book
is available from the British Library.

Hardback ISBN: 978-1-4711-7084-3
Trade paperback ISBN: 978-1-3985-1402-7
eBook ISBN: 978-1-4711-7085-0

Typeset in Bembo by M Rules
Printed and bound by CPI Group (UK) Ltd, Croydon, CR0 4YY

CONTENTS

CHAPTER 1

Running Wild

I switched my bedroom light off and pushed the door shut. Each night I followed the same ritual before climbing into bed. I kept my underpants on and knotted the laces of my football boots together to make a long string, tied tightly around the waist. Then I pulled my pyjama trousers on, fastening their cord as securely as I could, before climbing into bed.

I knew what was coming. There would be the click of the catch, which I couldn't lock, a chink of light around the door frame. I'd watch closely as the figure of my head teacher entered and crept slowly towards my bed. I was 13 years old and staying at his house because my own home was too far away from my new school, a school which offered greater opportunities for a young footballer.

The head teacher, believing I'd gone to sleep, would put his hands under my bedcover and try to touch me. I knew what he was doing was wrong, so I tried to push him away and punch him. I was tough, but I was scared too, although I couldn't show him my fear. This could go on for ten or 15 minutes, like a fight. He wasn't joking; he was going hard trying to get my pants off. There were no words spoken in the dark, but he was touching

1

himself and getting sexually excited by what was happening, by the aggression.

I didn't tell anybody. I was too ashamed to speak to my mother and I didn't know if anyone else would believe me. I haven't told anybody the full story until now. My wife saw me crying one day watching a programme about child abuse and she asked me what was wrong. I told her a little bit, but I still felt ashamed.

I'd become exhausted making the long journey to my new school each day from Les Ulis. Les Ulis does not even have a train station and I'd take a bus and then a train. Sometimes I'd fall asleep on the train and wake up at the end of the line and then be late for school. I was also tired mentally and waiting only for lessons to finish so that I could play football.

The head teacher offered a solution: 'You can sleep at my house three nights of the week. You won't need to travel and you can rest.' He lived inside the school grounds, alone. It seemed like a smart idea, until he came into my bedroom.

I now recognise that he'd tried to groom me. He let me play on a Nintendo. He helped me do my homework and cooked really good food for me. Not as good as my mother's African food – her rice and chicken – but still tasty. And then he tried to abuse me.

I would get butterflies in my stomach when I was due to sleep over as the end of the school day drew near. It couldn't go on, and after a few months I told my mum that I didn't want to stay with him any longer. I didn't give any reason. By that time, my would-be abuser had become tired of the situation. I was a fighter; I was not going to give in. He didn't even ask why I was leaving. He knew.

On the last night at that man's house, when he knew that I was going back to my family, he finally succeeded. He put my penis in his mouth.

2

Years later, when I was playing for Monaco, the police called me. Some kids had complained about this man and the police wanted to know if he'd ever tried to do something to me. Because I was famous and worried about the reaction, I lied and said no. They asked me if I was sure and I assured them I was. I have lived with that lie for many years. I can't tell you how much I regret that.

If you are a child reading this and you are being abused, you must talk. Don't carry your shame because there is no shame. Deal with your nightmare by talking about it. I look at my own son and think, 'If something happens, I hope he would tell me.'

A lot of shit things happened in my childhood. The people I know and love will read this and I don't want to put them through more pain, but it's important that I tell my story honestly. I'm 40 years old and telling the truth. Why now? I met someone very special, Margaux, who helped set me free from these demons. I am free to cry now. I am a free man. I am not a coward. I feel less guilty and I am not ashamed to share those dark parts of my life because I was hurt, badly hurt. Margaux asked me if I'd considered getting professional help, but I said no. I don't open up easily, especially not to strangers. My therapist is myself – and Margaux. What else can I say? This is me and what made me. You might cry, but you will laugh too, I promise. There has been a great deal of love and light in my life. In the country of my birth, Senegal, the people are sweet. They don't want war, they are generous, they smile and laugh. I have inherited that, though you may not think it from the stories I am going to tell you about growing up in France. When I dance around in my online videos, the happiness that you see is genuine. I love life, but it has been tough, especially before I became a professional footballer.

My father, Cyprien Evra, did not enjoy watching television.

Instead, he made children: between them, my parents had 24 children. I have a large and complicated extended family. My mum, Juliette, had 11 children, eight of them with my father: Marie 'Duchesse' Dalouze, Dominique, Charlotte, Marthe, Christiane, Florentine, Mado and me, Patrice, the youngest. She also had three children before she met my dad: Claude, Albert and Youssoufa. My father had another 13 children not with my mother: Pierre 'Pierrot' Francois, Marie Louise, Joachin 'Ouzin', David 'Dave Colver', Annette, Max, Fatima, Anne Marie, Elizabeth, Betty, Benji, Casper and Etienne. So we had enough for two football teams with substitutes.

I was born in the capital of Senegal, Dakar, on 15 May 1981, but my family moved to Belgium when I was one. My father is usually described as a diplomat. When people think 'diplomat', they also think 'comfortable middle-class lifestyle', but that's not true. Dad had a job working with the Senegalese embassy and won a three-year contract to help promote Senegalese culture in Belgium and so we were transferred to Brussels. I can remember very little but I'm told it rained a lot.

When the contract was up, we moved to Les Bergères near Paris in 1985 to live briefly with relatives before moving to Les Ulis, 23 kilometres south-west of Paris, which at that time was this newish settlement of concrete towers between six and 14 storeys under the flight path to Orly Airport. Les Ulis had a bad reputation. In many people's eyes it was a black ghetto where crime and drugs were rife, but it was the place where I grew up and I loved it. To this day, I consider myself Ulissien and not Parisian. The communal areas between the blocks were my playground, the trees and benches my goalposts.

There is a long history of Senegalese settlement in France, as Senegal was a French colony before it gained its independence in 1960. In the First World War, 200,000 'Senegalese Tirailleurs', Senegalese infantrymen and men recruited from the other

French African colonies, went to the Western Front to fight in the name of France and many remained in the country after the war was over.

My background is Senegalese, but I consider myself a human being first before any nationality. I grew up in France and played for France – a decision for which I was criticised by some Senegalese people. I also feel sometimes like I'm a Mancunian after the time I spent in Manchester. I am a chameleon who adapts to its environment.

Initially, my parents lived in my mother's younger brother's apartment in Les Bergères, with my six sisters and my half-brother Albert, who was the oldest and born in 1964. It was generous of our relatives to take us in. With their own children, it meant that 15 of us had to fit into a three-bedroom apartment. The children had to sleep three to each mattress. Two kids lay on the outside of the mattress with their heads at one end, and the person in the middle lay the other way up, but wherever you lay you always ended up getting feet in your face. For a whole year we managed in these cramped circumstances, until we found an apartment of our own in Les Ulis – with four small bedrooms.

Although my childhood was difficult, we were never poor. My father always made sure we had food to eat. Once settled in our new apartment, I became friends with a neighbour, César. Like me, he was proud to be from Les Ulis, but it could be a bad quartier (district) to grow up in. I had friends who were shot or who died young from violence or drugs, like my close friend Issaka's brother.

We were at a party in Le Radazik, a club in my quartier where concerts or parties were usually held, and I was enjoying myself when I heard the blast of a shotgun. As we ran towards the noise to see what was happening, I saw a pool of blood spreading towards me and looked into the face of Issaka's brother sprawled out on the cold, tiled floor. There'd been an argument and someone had shot him. He died.

There were bad people around, but they were not representative of the majority of my area of Les Ulis, Les Hautes Plaines. I felt as if we belonged to a big family, like we were untouchable, and we made sure we looked after each other. I was in a gang called 'Maaf', named after our street, with Tshimen (my best friend who later had three kids with one of my sisters), Issaka, Mahamadou, Guillaume, Gaye, Patrick, Billey, Oliver, Romaric, Yedi, Yassine and Hakim. The gang gave me protection. The area was no-go for outsiders. If the police came, we would throw rubbish bins across the road to stop their cars getting through. It was our castle to defend.

My friends were mainly from an African background: Congo, Cameroon, Gabon, Senegal, Mali. I did have one white friend, Dani. He was rich but pretended he was poor. We discovered his secret when we visited his house. One of the gang compared it to the Palace of Versailles, but I'd never been to Versailles. Why would I?

Dani wanted to slum it with us on the street and when we confronted him he admitted he'd lied because he was embarrassed that his family was wealthy. I once saw him get beaten up really badly. He wanted to prove he was part of the gang and picked a fight one day when he shouldn't have done. He had a big wooden stick and pepper spray and approached two guys he had a problem with in a car park. The spray came back into his face and the guys grabbed his stick and gave him a terrible beating. They were jumping on his head. Although we wanted to intervene, we stood back. We had rules. If you picked a fight, it was your fight. With fists. We were shouting for Dani to get up, that he could be like Rocky Balboa, but he was unconscious, so we took him to the hospital in a car, terrified that he was dying.

Dani opened his eyes, looked at me and asked: 'Where are

we? Is it Christmas?' I laughed out loud with relief. After that, he never came back to the gang. He realised that it was our life, not a game anyone could join in. He'd lived a lie because he wanted to be part of the gang and not be rejected by us. We also called ourselves the ZSP – Zulus Sans Pitié, which means 'Zulus without pity' – because we wanted to be thought of as hard men.

I joined the gang after my dad left home when I was ten. He and my mother argued too much and so they separated, Dad moving to Saint-Quentin, closer to Paris, to live with a friend. Until that point, I was a well-behaved kid. Dad was well educated and strict – I couldn't get away with lying to him. He would ask me: 'Have you done your homework?' I would always answer yes, but with a little hesitation when I hadn't done it, which Dad spotted every time, demanding: 'Bring me your homework now.' Then the interrogation began. He would open my book at the first page and fire questions at me. 'But, Dad,' I'd protest, 'that page was from a long time ago.' He wasn't impressed and would close my book and say: 'You need to know all your book, Patrice.'

I should have done better at school. I started brightly enough and even jumped a class to be with people one year ahead of me but, when Dad left, my schooling suffered.

I didn't enjoy reaching the age of ten. Just before Dad went, my mum took me to Senegal to be circumcised – a tradition in my family. They think it's cleaner; that was the accepted belief in my quartier. I was being sent to Senegal to become a proper man. Although people had told me it was a straightforward operation, I didn't want to go, didn't want it to happen – and I was right.

I got to the hospital with my cousin, who screamed so loud that I became scared and ran away down the corridor. The nurses chased after me and a doctor caught me, dragged me back and gave me a local anaesthetic. I felt nothing from it, it did not work. They pinned me on the bed, put something on my penis, then I saw the doctor get some scissors. He started to cut away at my penis. The pain was acute; I'd never felt pain like it and never have since.

My suffering was not over. Shortly afterwards I was horrified to see my penis balloon in size. I stayed in Senegal for two weeks, two weeks of infection and pain. Back in France, I went to see another doctor about the infection. He shook his head. My circumcision had been botched. I needed more surgery.

My trouble was not confined to my penis. I started to be a bad boy after Dad left and I believed that I could do whatever I wanted. I began to steal things from shops. I began to sell marijuana. I also begged outside the local bread shop. One old man looked at me one day and said: 'Do you think money comes from the sky?' I remember that now as a lesson that you don't get money for nothing, but it didn't stop me. I was actually begging to have enough money to buy a kebab. Kebabs were my dream food. It was difficult for my mother even to provide basic meals after Dad walked out. She worked in a shop which sold cheap clothes and she didn't earn much money.

In France, poor parents are paid money when their children go to school. So Dad had brought some of his other children from previous marriages over from Senegal to take advantage of those grants. The money was supposed to be used to buy school clothes, travel and books, but it didn't always get to the intended destination. Instead, he sent it to my half-brothers and sisters, some of them in Senegal, because he thought they would need it more there. He felt we lived like kings in France.

As Dad no longer took that money, Mum started offering it to us as pocket money. I told her to keep it, explaining that one day I would have so much money I wouldn't need it. I wanted her to use the money herself, for essentials – and besides, I thought

I'd found my own source of income selling weed, which seemed the easiest way of earning money.

I was lucky because my brother Dominique worked at McDonald's in the local shopping centre. If I was ever hungry, I could go there for some food because he would give me some for free. Not that he got free food; he gave me his own lunch instead. We would also wait by the door until McDonald's closed and they threw out their leftovers. I started to like a cold Big Mac.

Our gang wandered around getting into trouble. I liked to fight alongside my friends. We would go to the neighbouring housing estate to show that we were better than them. It would start with a football game and end in a fight. Because we were too poor to go away on holidays, we just stayed in our quartier and had a great time playing football until midnight, fighting and making our own barbecues from food we had stolen. I didn't know anyone who had been to a beach. In summer, we begged the man who looked after the gymnasium to keep it open late so we could play football. Sometimes he would, other times he would refuse, but we'd threaten to smash everything up unless he kept it open until midnight.

We lived on the edge of the urban sprawl of Paris, yet our world was completely different to the Paris that tourists visited. The centre of the city wasn't far away and we'd get there by jumping on the RER B line train without a ticket. When the ticket collectors came we'd run away from them, a game of cat and mouse through trains and tunnels. Looking back, I realise we lived a dangerous life, but it brought me so much happiness. And it never felt dangerous; to me it was normal.

Our one-hour journeys to Paris weren't to visit the Louvre or Champs-Élysées; instead we went to Châtelet, a place popular with tourists in the centre between Notre-Dame and the Pompidou Centre. A shop there sold the best kebab in the world. Only my mother's cooking was better than the kebab in Châtelet. It was like heaven, with ketchup, mayonnaise and spices. We would sit on the street, eating the kebab and thinking, 'This is Paris, we've made it in life.' Even now, I'll try one once a year. We'd also go to a market where they sold nice trainers, Nike and Adidas, not that we could afford them. If we had enough money, we would go to Montmartre for crêpes.

We began to drift ever closer into low-level, petty crime. In Les Ulis there was a big Carrefour store close to where we lived, and we'd go there to steal things. I remember seeing a football computer game advertised on television and decided that I wanted it, so we went to the store to shoplift one. Security were suspicious of us, but our tactics were well prepared.

The football game came in a big box. We broke one open, removed the game and hid it among the garden furniture. Security came over to see what we were up to, but we pretended that we'd dropped the box with the football game in. They were unconvinced: 'Come on, we saw something,' they said, but when they searched us they couldn't find anything. Two days later, we returned with enough money to buy bread. We went to the garden section, retrieved the game, which was small enough to fit in my pants under a belt, and paid only for the bread.

By the time I was 15 I'd picked up the nickname 'Leef' – meaning a baton in Senegalese – and this is why. We had gone to a shop to steal a Sega Mega Drive, but this time we were caught by security and they told us that we were going to jail. The police said they'd call our parents, which was a bigger worry for us than the police themselves. They rang the father of one of my friends and he came to the store.

'Do you know his parents?' they pointed to me.

'Yes, he lives in my quartier,' replied the father, who was entrusted to take me home. I thought I'd got away with it and that my mother would never find out.

'Patrice,' he said. 'I'm going to explain to your mother what happened. Where exactly do you live?'

'Oh, no,' I thought. 'Should I run and escape when the car stops?' But I respected him enough not to run. My friend's father knocked on the door. My mother had been extremely worried because it was late and I wasn't home and she was relieved to see me, but her expression changed quickly when she heard the word 'police'. When I saw her eyes tighten, I thought 'I'm dead.'

'What have you done?' she screamed at me.

'Nothing, Mum!' I replied. 'I didn't steal anything. I was just an accomplice.'

'Accomplice!' she raged, before hitting me with a big stick – a 'leef'. My brothers and sisters were laughing as my mother chased me around, swiping at me. I realised at that point just how physically strong my mother was. She frightened me so much with that stick that I was too scared to steal again. Well, at least big items. I would still steal chocolate or sausages. Let me explain.

Our barbecues needed sausages. They also needed a barbecue, but a broken trolley from Carrefour made an ideal grill. We needed to steal the rest: the coal, the lighters, the bread, the drinks and of course the sausages, which tasted nearly as good as the Châtelet kebabs. We'd hold the most fantastic barbecues in a park near our home, digging out a hole in the ground for the charcoal. Each of us was assigned something to steal. The sausages were the trickiest and I used to put them up the sleeves of my jacket, which was awkward but I had fast hands as well as fast feet.

I didn't consider myself a gangster, and I never wanted to make a life from crime. I knew that what I was doing was wrong, but it was just a way to survive. I'm not proud of what I did, and I don't want my own children to live that sort of life. Soon, it went beyond petty theft: I began to deal marijuana. I didn't sell drugs for long, only three months, but I made enough money to buy my girlfriend some shoes. And a pager, so I could do my drug deals. My friends wouldn't have understood if I didn't sell drugs, but I should have known better as I'd seen from my early years the reality of what drugs could do.

When I was a small child, I'd woken up needing to go to the toilet in the apartment in Les Ulis. The door was slightly ajar and the light was on. I pushed it open to find my brother Albert sitting on the toilet, staring into space. A needle was hanging from his arm. I didn't understand what was happening, but I knew it was something very bad. I closed the door and went back to bed. Albert eventually died from the drug addiction which had already taken over his life when I found him that night. Crack cocaine was the cause of his death. He would be very aggressive when he ran out of drugs and he'd demand money, which I didn't have as I was only a child. If we didn't give him what he wanted he would beat us.

It was tragic to see another human in this condition, a man so desperate for money to feed his habit that he would later travel to Africa to sell all his French papers so that they could be used by someone who wanted to get into France illegally. My mother received a call to say that he'd died in a bathroom out there from an overdose. She was distraught, as any parent would be, to lose her child. But that was in the future – what stopped me selling drugs at the time was the danger to my own life. I never used them myself – I have Albert to thank for that.

And I also need to thank football. I was obsessed with it, like all the boys in Les Ulis. We always had a football and there were many places where we could play in the quartier between the various tower blocks. After school finished, Tshimen and I would break into the school playground and play football on the artificial surface. I was a tricky little player. I taught myself on the street, playing against older boys. A teacher saw that I came to school with holes in my shoes as I was playing so much I wore them out. He bought me some blue trainers. I never forgot that.

'You have talent, Patrice,' he said. 'You should be a footballer.' I felt like the king of the world when I heard that.

Les Ulis has become a football factory. Thierry Henry, Anthony Martial, Yaya Sanogo, Moussa Marega and I all grew up there. We are probably the only town in the world with players that have won every major trophy in football – the World Cup, Champions League, Europa League. The lot. Henry has paid for a football pitch which is well used. There are another 15 professional players from my generation, though Martial is from the generation below.

People want to know the secret of why such a tiny area, a *banlieue* of only 24,000 people, turns out so many top-class footballers. It's no mystery. First of all, the kids are outside playing football at all hours. Second, it's an escape – it was for me – from violence and crime. When they opened a synthetic pitch near my school we hung around there and played football rather than go to Carrefour to steal things. Third, the mixture of genetics because of the immigration. There are big players from Africa, small Arab players from Morocco. Fourth, from the age of six onwards, there are great teachers in the school and qualified coaches – like my friends Tshimen and Mahamadou who both coach in my old quartier – who try to support and develop the whole child, not just his football. Walk around the area with them, and young boys of 13 or 14 come up to them, ask them politely how they are doing and go on their way. I'm proud that they are so well respected in the streets of where I grew up.

Next, there is an excellent structure of teams through which talented kids can progress. They receive top-class coaching from the age of six from coaches who are close to them. Those coaches want them to be a success at school and on the football pitch. They tell them to eat well, sleep well, brush their teeth twice a day, wash well and be a good person.

As a result, Martial and the younger generation are nice boys. Their Les Ulis is different from mine. The area has improved a lot, the tower blocks have been smartened up and there is less trouble. It was tougher for my generation of second-generation West Africans, even tougher for the generation above me. So many of my elder brothers' friends went to jail. But what hasn't changed is the determination to succeed that the young footballers of Les Ulis and the other settlements around Paris have, which comes from their immigrant background, whether they are the black Africans like me from the old French colonies or those with roots in North Africa. This is the last and, for me, the greatest reason. In Les Ulis, you start to live football when you are in the womb and you have access to properly qualified coaches.

At the age of six, I joined the young team CO Les Ulis, which is also where Henry and the other guys I mentioned started out. I wanted to be a footballer, a striker like Romario. There are hundreds of young footballers there below the first team at Les Ulis, who play in the regional seventh tier of French football. Paris is surrounded by social housing projects that breed brilliant footballers. Add to the list above Paul Pogba, Kylian Mbappé, Benjamin Mendy, Riyad Mahrez, N'Golo Kanté, Lucas Digne, Nicolas Anelka, Moussa Sissoko, Blaise Matuidi, Adrien Rabiot, Kingsley Coman – all grew up around Paris.

At 13, I left to join CSF Brétigny, the best team in the area. Tshimen had encouraged me to link up with him there. My best friend gave me a great deal to live up to, telling the manager Didier Brilliant: 'We have a phenomenon and his name is Patrice.' It worked. Brilliant invited me for trials along with about 70 other kids. The balls were set up in the centre circle and we were told to walk up to the ball and then score a goal as quickly as possible. There was one defender and a goalkeeper to stop us. I walked up, ran at the defender, beat him and scored straight into the bottom corner. I missed with my second effort and scored with my third. I'd never been tested like that before.

The trial games started across five pitches. After five minutes, the coach said: 'Come here and sit down.' That was it, nothing more. I was worried I'd done something wrong. At the end of the games, the coach stood up and said: 'These players will sign for CSF Brétigny: Patrice Evra . . .' Mine was the first name he mentioned and I was excited beyond belief. CSF Brétigny was like a professional club to me, an escape from the street, but also a chance to join a better team than Les Ulis. Brétigny had national status, they played against the young teams of Paris Saint-Germain.

There was a problem, though. Their ground was 30 minutes from my house by car – but we didn't have one. By public transport, it was far more complicated. But it was possible for me to go to school nearby and play football there afterwards and to do extra training. Unfortunately, I had to get up at five in the morning. It was a nightmare. I took a bus and then two trains, then had a further walk to school, on Saturdays as well as weekdays. Unsurprisingly, I quickly became exhausted, and my situation at home didn't help.

My brother Dominique was a DJ and he would organise Zouk parties at our home on a Friday or Saturday night. Zouk is music from the French Antilles in the Caribbean islands. Around 100 people would come to these parties, cramming into our tiny apartment of 70 square metres. My brother would take the sofa and the chair out of the main room where the party would be, and I would sleep under the sofa. People would wander by accident into the room where I was trying to sleep and stand on me. I didn't sleep well.

That combination of long journeys and disrupted sleep was

why I went to stay with the school head teacher, the man who tried to abuse me. But, as I said before, I realised it was safer to go back to the two-hour journeys to school. Sometimes I had a train ticket, but sometimes I didn't pay and the ticket inspector would chase me. I lost many bags full of my school books while running away.

In the end, it all became too difficult, so, after just one year, I moved back to a school close to my home in my quartier. It didn't work out for me at my new school either. I was never the most academic member of my class. I had too many friends to concentrate on my studies, so instead of listening, I showed off. The teacher would tell me something and I would say: 'Turn the volume down, you're not my parent.' It was horribly disrespectful.

When the teacher sent me out of class, I would go off to Carrefour and steal things. Later in life, I apologised to some of the staff. The head teacher at this school was not like the other one. He tried to help me as much as possible. He would say: 'Patrice, when you are going to misbehave and argue with the teacher, just come here instead and sit in my office.' He loved me – and he also knew I was good at football. He'd brought football back onto the curriculum at school, but he introduced a new rule for me – I was not allowed to score, because he said I found it too easy. He also encouraged me to take up athletics and I think that's one reason I can jump so high. Without him, my life may have been very different. Rather than focusing on what I wasn't doing, he helped me build on my strengths and created new opportunities for me.

Meanwhile, my football was going well. I had become Brétigny's best player and, thanks to a teammate, Sebastian Vamellis, I had a beautiful yellow kit to train in. Sebastian was a blond guy from a middle-class background, a different world from mine. Most of the boys in the team seemed posh to me.

Their trainers were nice; they had shin pads when I didn't. They looked like models, and the girls wanted guys like Sebastian. When I went to his house, I saw they had a nice car, and he had his own bedroom with posters and a desk to do his school-work. Luxury.

In those days, I thought I was Romario, my idol. I played as a striker and wore an old Barcelona shirt – I have no idea where I got it. It was so small it fitted me like a bikini. I was 14 and it was for a child of eight. Sebastian felt sorry for me and gave me the yellow shirt, socks and shorts. I felt like an amazing player when I was kitted out properly. I was the guy from the street but middle-class guys sometimes like to be friends with the boys from the hood and I was good at football too, so I was not unpopular. And I loved the yellow kit Sebastian gave me – it was Nantes FC's strip. I was a little canary in it. Years later, my boss Alex Ferguson would say that left backs are like canaries – rare. Sebastian also passed on his old boots, and they worked because we often had the best team in the Île-de-France for our age. He may not have been in the first team, but in a sense he was because I was wearing all his clothes! I scored so many goals in that kit, playing as a fast little forward.

But even on the football field, my past could sometimes catch up with me. One day, CSF Brétigny played a game in a rival quartier to Les Ulis against guys we used to fight with. I felt fear descend upon me during the game when I heard an opponent shout: 'You're from Les Ulis.'

'No, I'm not,' I lied. While the game was going on, I could see more people along the side of the pitch pointing at me. By this time I was 14 and had a reputation for being the best player in my quartier for my age. I kept myself fit. Alcohol was off limits and so were cigarettes, as I considered even normal cigarettes to be drugs and I realised they would be harmful to my stamina. People remember my style – I was small, skilful and dribbled, never passing the ball. I was not much of a team player, but I could win games for my team and felt that playing football was easy. I had good technique, a low centre of gravity and I was quick. All those matches against older boys had helped my development. I was usually scared of nobody, but that afternoon I was very, very frightened when the people at the side of the pitch started shouting: 'We're going to break your legs.' My friends from Les Ulis, who were watching, saved me, shielding me until I got back to the changing rooms and I left the pitch with them, not my coach as I was supposed to. I felt safer with my friends.

Brétigny had a relationship with Rennes, an established Ligue 1 team. Rennes would recruit some of the best young players from Paris: Sylvain Wiltord, who played for Arsenal, came through there. So did Mikaël Silvestre, who'd later go to Manchester United and Arsenal. Brétigny usually sent their best players to Rennes for trials each year and I was always chosen to go. I always played well, too, yet I was never selected by the club. For four years they told me that they'd let me know, but they never did. It seemed very strange to me that I wasn't being chosen to make the step up; I felt as if Didier, who was an excellent coach, didn't want me to leave. Years later, I'd find out that was more than a hunch. But not every player from Brétigny went to Rennes, and Jérémy Ménez – who played for several top clubs and 24 times for France – would go from there to Sochaux before Monaco, Roma, PSG and AC Milan.

I'd had other trials before joining Brétigny. I went to PSG when I was 12, only to be told that I was too small to play football. A coach also said – to my face – that as I came from the street they had doubts that they could trust me in the dressing room, where they thought I could be trouble. I was paying the price for growing up on the street, especially as Les Ulis had a bad reputation, but it also made me who I was and I was proud to be from there. As for PSG saying I was too small – what could I do about that?

I also had trials at Toulouse, but with nothing coming of it there or at PSG and Rennes, it was back to the quartier. My mother was in an association that organised day trips for African people in the area, people who would otherwise never leave Les Ulis.

I would sometimes see girls at these parties, but in the quartier it was shameful to have a girl, to be seen holding hands with her. That was a sign of weakness. Even if you were seen just talking to a girl, you would be mocked as her slave. The reason for this was jealousy that you would leave the gang for a girl and that the gang would be weaker without you. The gang is family.

At home, there was always a fight around the television. My sisters wanted to watch a movie and I wanted to watch football. I loved to watch Arsène Wenger's Monaco because I liked George Weah, Glenn Hoddle, Jürgen Klinsmann and Youri Djorkaeff. Their youth team produced Thierry Henry and Lilian Thuram, players who would win the World Cup with France. There was much to like about Monaco.

Most of the people where I lived supported PSG, but there wasn't a culture of going to an actual football match. We played football and would pretend to be PSG, Monaco or Marseille, but we never found our way to the Parc des Princes, so the first time I went there to watch a game was when I was 15. I got my match ticket and guarded it carefully, putting it down my socks for safe keeping, but then I got into a football game. I sweated a lot and the ticket details washed off. My friends were laughing, as nobody could read the ticket. I still went to Parc des Princes, but we didn't leave enough time to get there because we didn't know how long the journey would take.

I arrived at the stadium with something that had once been a ticket. There were 30 minutes of the game left and security actually let us in. Our afternoon would not be easy as some of the PSG ultras were racist. My older friends knew this and warned us that we had to leave the stadium early as otherwise we would get beaten up by the skinheads who didn't like black people. I watched maybe 15 minutes of the game and then we left early, but we still saw the cops fighting with the Boulogne Boys, one of the ultra groups, in the street. It was a shambles, with all the fighting.

But by then I had heard the roar of the stadium as I walked towards our place in the stand. It was intoxicating. I looked at the pitch, it was more beautiful and green than the ones I played on. I saw the players. 'Wow!' I thought. 'This is what it must be like when you are a professional player.' And by my mid-teens that's where I knew I would end up, even if I hadn't yet signed for a professional team.

CHAPTER 2

Marsala and Monza

The summer of 1998 heralded the start of some much-needed changes in my life. By the age of 17, I was going nowhere in school and my exam results were terrible, with one pass in electronics. Life had started to become more dangerous in Les Hautes Plaines and I had been let go by PSG Youth because they still considered me too small.

Those changes began with me leaving France for the first time ever to go on a package holiday. I had a girlfriend and she had been badgering me: 'Why do you always spend your holiday round here where bad things happen? Can't we go away on an aeroplane?' I thought I was ready for something different and our flight was booked from Paris Orly Airport. Talk about taking me out of my comfort zone. When I arrived at the hotel in Tunisia I felt lost and I blamed my girlfriend for taking me away from my home and my friends. Maybe they were right – women were only there to steal me from the gang!

I was convinced someone was going to kidnap me, that I'd never go back to my apartment. I was suspicious of the food they put out because it was different from home. And yet, despite my initial paranoia, we had a good holiday and my confidence grew each day. I saw women wearing bikinis for the first time. Wow! My girlfriend was laughing at me, she said it was normal.

But I still didn't talk to anyone but her when we were in Tunisia. I had struggled to speak with people from outside my quartier when I was young because I was tense and aggressive. In any case, they would not have been able to understand me because my accent was so strong. We spoke in French, but we used our own version. We changed 'Bonjour' to 'Jourbon' – in English it is called 'back slang' – so that our parents could not understand us. 'Crazy' is 'Zycra'. My reticence and suspicion continued even when I moved away properly to Italy a few months later.

That summer was also a great one for France. The country staged the World Cup and Tshimen and I went to celebrate France's victory on the Champs-Élysées. His father Buhanga had been voted the African Footballer of the Year in 1973, playing for TP Mazembe and Zaire, and was known as the 'Black Beckenbauer'. Joining the national celebrations might seem the natural thing to do, but when I grew up on the street I didn't feel French, I just thought I lived in France, although I did admire some of the stars of the national team: Thierry Henry, Zinedine Zidane, Marcel Desailly, Fabien Barthez and the captain, Didier Deschamps. Tshimen even had the flag of Brazil, who were also very popular in France, and I loved them because of Romario.

But now I wrapped myself in the tricolour as we celebrated France being world champions because this France team was multi-ethnic, it was white and black, rich and poor. It was more than just a football team. The whole of France rejoiced and images of the players were projected onto the Arc de Triomphe. 'One day I will be one of them,' I told Tshimen, before we went for a kebab – from Châtelet, naturally.

Then that summer I was given the chance to make a bigger,

more permanent move and, as I said, it couldn't have come at a better time. I had started to see guns in the quartier, which had been smuggled out by people who were doing military service. One of my friends had a gun, which he used when some boys from a rival area came to a party in our quartier, and a guy ended up in a coma. I didn't leave to escape the guns, though, but because of football. I was offered a trial with Torino – a chance to be a professional footballer.

Until that point I was still attached to Brétigny but, apart from that, I hadn't been picked up by the national academy at Clairefontaine and hadn't been given the option to progress through the youth set-up at PSG where the best young French footballers went. I just knew in my heart that I was going to be a footballer; I had absolutely no doubts. I was single-minded and while I knew I was very good at football, I believed that if you really put your mind to something, you could achieve your dreams. I was also motivated to prove people wrong, like those who said I was too late to make it as a professional player. While I was – and still am – of a very positive mind, actions spoke louder than any thoughts. I trained alone every day and my friends would tell me: 'What are you doing? It's time to go out and find a nice, rich, white woman. Don't waste your time on football, they will never pick you because of your colour or where you come from.' I kept on going to school, kept on train-ing and persuading my friends to play football with me, even if they were not talented. I could train by myself at running, but I couldn't play football alone.

The trial came about through the intervention of my friend and one-time kit provider Sebastian. He invited me to play in a five-a-side tournament which a friend of his family, Onofrio Giammarresi, was going to attend. Giammarresi owned a famous restaurant and was well connected in Italian football, and a friend of Sebastian suggested that I might get a trial through him. I gave a good performance and Giammarresi asked for my number and said he'd be in touch. He called my mum the next day and told her: 'Your son is very talented. I want to take him to Italy for a trial.'

She was wary. 'No chance. You are a stranger, you don't know him.'

My big brother Dominique, who had become something of a father figure to me because he was ten years older, told our mum straight that she had to let me go because otherwise I would end up in jail or get killed if I carried on leading the life I was living, so Mum relented.

I flew to Turin with Giammarresi and I did the trial with their young players. I stayed in Torino's academy for a couple of weeks, but I quickly became homesick, missing my home, my friends, my street. I honestly thought that it was better that I trained badly so that Torino didn't want me. I started to pray and ask God for things to go better for me because I knew I could not carry on living in Les Ulis either.

My salvation came from an unexpected direction. I played in several different trial matches, one of them watched by a scout from Marsala, a small third-division club in Sicily, who told Giammarresi that I was a genius. Torino wanted me to sign as a youth player, but Marsala offered me a professional contract and the chance of first-team football. I was confident in my own ability and wanted to play with men, not kids. Giammarresi advised me that we should go back to France and decide there.

I was keen to go to Italy and become a professional footballer, but I also had to tell my girlfriend. I'd lied to her, saying that my trial was at Rennes, because if I'd revealed I was going to Italy she would have been very upset. Even my mum was in on the lie.

My girlfriend found my Alitalia toothpick from the flight and was furious until my mum explained that I'd lied to protect her. Then I told her about Sicily. My girlfriend looked at a map and decided that Marsala, in Sicily, was at the end of the world. When she asked me to choose between her and Marsala, I replied: 'I was playing football before I knew you and that's my destiny.' She was very upset and quickly decided that our relationship was at risk and she couldn't promise that we'd stay together. In hindsight, she was young and she wanted to scare me, but her threat didn't work – I decided to join Marsala.

I was to hook up with the team for their 1998–99 pre-season. This time, I travelled alone with a set of written instructions from Giammarresi about my journey. At the Gare de Lyon in Paris, Mum and Dominique waved me off from the platform. After a journey of eight hours, I arrived in Milano Centrale, but the train was late. I went to look at the big departures board for my connection. The destinations were moving quickly, too fast for my eyes. I was thinking, 'What the hell is going on here?' I could not see my next destination, nor could I speak Italian. I had no phone, only a piece of paper with my home phone number back in France written on it.

I began to panic and became tearful. I could see a black guy staring at me who came over and asked in French: 'What's the matter, my brother?'

When I showed him my ticket, he shook his head, saying: 'Your train has gone. There is not another until the morning.' I couldn't believe it, but he reassured me: 'Don't worry, you will be safe. You can stay at my house and take the train tomorrow.' I said no but asked him to call my mother. My mother was also very mistrustful and started to cry when the man explained that he was with me. She thought I was going to be kidnapped, but he assured her that he was from Senegal like me. My mum wouldn't listen and told him to put me on the next train back to Paris because I was causing her too much pain. He managed to persuade her that he would look after me and she told me to call her in two hours. Mum agreed to contact Giammarresi so he could inform Marsala that I would be delayed. I was still very apprehensive, but what other options did I have?

The stranger took me to a house very close to Milan's vast train station, where he invited me to eat with his friends, the food laid out on the floor. I then slept on a mattress on the floor. The next morning, he walked me to the station and I caught my train. I have never seen that man again, but he is one of the guardian angels who seem to pop up regularly in my life.

I was still unsure about the travel arrangements as I finally caught the train south towards the town of Nursia in the mountains near Perugia in the middle of Italy, where Marsala were doing their pre-season training because it was much cooler there in July than Sicily. There was a group of nuns on the train and I showed them my ticket. They gesticulated that I was to get off in three stations, but after only two stops, they left the train and I followed them. They pushed me back on board and said I should get off at the next station. I really didn't know if this was right, but I did what I was told. I was the only passenger and the station was so small that there wasn't even a bench to sit on, only the sign to say where it was.

I waited for five minutes to be picked up. Then ten minutes. Half an hour. An hour. Ninety minutes. I was in the middle of nowhere, with no phone. After two hours, I saw a car approaching with two men in it. They were from Marsala and they were talking, as you would expect, in Italian. I managed to understand enough of what one was saying: 'We came here yesterday but you were not here. We drove by in case you got this train.' The message from my mum had not got through. They took me to the team hotel. I walked in and saw 25 men sitting around a table, all of them white, all of them Italian.

Before I could say hello, I was told to go up to my room and change. A Marsala tracksuit lay on the bed, with flip-flops and trainers from Galex, an Italian sports company. I quickly changed into the blue tracksuit and then looked at myself in the mirror. Honestly, it was one of the greatest moments of my life. I was a professional footballer and I stared at myself for a full five minutes before I went downstairs to meet the team. I was not nervous. When I walked into the dining room, my new teammates applauded me. What a feeling! The captain, Valerio Leto, gave me a seat next to him. They made a few jokes which I didn't understand and they taught me some basics in Italian.

Then it was time to eat. I looked at the plates and cutlery in front of me. There was two of everything and I thought it must be a mistake. The players laughed and showed me that the small fork was for the starter. People came to serve me food, something I'd never had before because I'd never been to a restaurant. I felt like a king. The players were immediately friendly to me, they saw me as their little mascot.

The director gave me his mobile phone and told me to call my mother to let her know everything was fine. When I told her I was in heaven, that people were serving me food, my mother began crying again, saying: 'God bless you.'

At training the next morning, I marvelled at how the balls were new and shiny. I was earning a little money, not that I was told the figure or received anything like that because an agent – not even someone I knew – was taking a cut. But, to be honest, I would have been willing to play for free.

I got my first opportunity as a forward against Perugia in a pre-season game. My manager Agatino Cuttone encouraged me, told me I was good and that he'd bring me on for ten or 15 minutes. It was a huge thrill playing in front of a live crowd on beautiful grass pitches.

When pre-season finished we flew to Sicily and on to my new home in Marsala, a town of 85,000 on the western tip of Sicily by the Mediterranean and closer to Africa than the Italian mainland. The town had been badly bombed by the Americans during the Allied invasion in the Second World War and was considered a backwater, yet the people there were so friendly and invited me into their homes to eat.

Instead of being a dream move, life in Marsala became complicated immediately. Club officials told me that I couldn't play until they had my release forms, which Brétigny held. I assumed, as did the club, that it was a minor delay, but after a month of training I still couldn't play. The football side was fine, I was comfortable with the players and they gave my new nickname, the Black Panther. The great Eusebio had had the same nickname, so I liked it.

I slept in the academy where the players trained and ate before matches. There were a few rooms for players upstairs, but the conditions were spartan and it was not homely. I had been told by Giammarresi that I would have an apartment and a car, so I complained to him and he helped find me an apartment, but it was worse than the room I'd been staying in. The sofa would have been overpriced if it had cost €10, the TV was so small that it was difficult to watch and there was only one public phone box in the entire area. My mother came to visit me with my sister Charlotte and she cried once more when she saw my accommodation. She was right when she said our quartier in Les Ulis was better, though I did at least have my own bed in Marsala.

I'd feel sad at the end of training because I knew I had to go back to that grim apartment. I'd stand alone on the tiny balcony, unhappy. Not being able to play hardly helped me feel better, so I decided to do something about it. I rang Brétigny but they avoided my calls. Then they finally contacted my mother and said that I was to join the Rennes academy. The academy director phoned me and said everything was ready for me. I didn't understand why they had waited until I'd asked to leave

Brétigny. I was angry, told the director that I was staying in Italy, and he warned me that I was making a big mistake.

I wasn't going to leave it at that. I flew home and went to Brétigny personally with Dominique and Tshimen to find the coach responsible for the debacle. We tracked him down to his office and confronted him. He was visibly startled and said that in order to play for my team in France, we needed to pay for my licence and annual subscriptions, which covered insurance and proof of identity. They were four years in arrears. I hadn't paid my subscriptions because when I joined Brétigny I was told that I could play for free and never have to worry about paying. Then he said that I had to sign for Rennes because of their agreement with the club. I explained I was not going to Rennes, that I was in Italy and wanted the release form. Things got very heated, but he told us to calm down and eventually gave us the form.

The coach disappointed me. I don't even want to name him in my book. He was a fine coach for our team, but did he have his players' best interests at heart or his own? It seemed that it only became essential that I joined Rennes when I'd found myself another club. Okay, I hadn't told them what I was doing but, because of their complete lack of interest in me until then, I had assumed they wouldn't be the slightest bit bothered to see me go. He upset me deeply because I'd trusted him and I resisted his later attempts to contact me after I'd become a professional.

With my release form finally sorted, I had permission to play for Marsala but it was already January, halfway through the season. Soon there was a change of manager, with Cuttone replaced by Gigi Carducci, a coach who lived locally and had played for the *Biancazzurri* of Marsala, a team started by the English who'd come to the town at the start of the century to trade in the local wine of the same name. Carducci had been in charge of Marsala's youth system and was promoted. Cuttone had been charming and taken me to Italy; Carducci was different. He was a shouter who could intimidate some players, but the shouting would usually be followed by a smile. He gave me my professional debut and invited me to his house to eat with him and his wife. He even took me out on a boat for a barbecue at Easter and we visited a nice island; I'd never been on a boat before. I felt that he cared for me and I needed that, especially after all that had happened before.

I began to enjoy life in Marsala as I got to know the town better. I'd drop into Bar Vito, usually by myself, for a cappuccino. My teammates were really friendly, especially Egidio Ingrosso, a defender, and Filippo Pensalfini – they were my two best friends. Marsala had won Division C2, the fourth tier of the Italian league, the previous season and been promoted to C1 for the first time in 21 years, a big achievement for a small club. I was soon in the side, but there were problems with paying wages, and the players went months without any pay, even those who had families. The most forceful players, the ones the directors were scared of, got their money. I begged for €500 from the president accompanied by Dominique who had come to visit me in Italy. The president was receptive and handed over the cash, but I felt it helped that my brother was a big guy.

Marsala were struggling in the higher league but I was playing well and had done so right from my debut, when I'd come on as a substitute against Nocerina in a 1-1 draw. I felt that I'd done enough to show my skills and trouble the opposing defenders, and I was then told I would start the next game, so my mother and Dominique flew to watch me. I was playing as a third striker on the left side of a front three in a 4-3-3. I played 24 times for Marsala and scored three goals, including one straight from kick-off against Savoia. My first goal as a professional wasn't a bad one either, a strike from outside the box at home to Acireale.

I soon got myself a mobile phone, a StarTAC flip phone better than any of my teammates'. Tshimen acquired it for me in Les Ulis and my teammates would say: 'Are you sure you know how it works?' when I got it out. It wasn't racism, just ignorance.

The fans, who created a fantastic atmosphere even though there were only 4,000 of them, were happy with me and often told me so, but they didn't feel the same way about the team as a whole. Some angry fans surrounded the players after one game, just as they were about to leave in their cars. One of the players' wives came out to remonstrate, but she was slapped across the face, pushed back into the car and told where to go. It was horrible to see, and things were in danger of turning even more ugly when a man who always hung around the team – a kind of supporter who all the players knew – calmed the situation down. How? By pulling a gun out. Those angry fans started running.

I also quickly realised that I was one of the only black players in the league. People called me Nero – it means black in a friendly way, but I said: 'Guys, my mum didn't call me Nero, she called me Patrice. If you keep calling me Nero, then I'll call you Bianco.' Again, it was just ignorance. Once, in Palermo Airport, a boy shouted: 'Daddy, Daddy, look at the *nero*.' He'd never seen a black man before and asked for a photo with me.

While that was innocent curiosity, I was on the end of a lot of racist abuse and behaviour during matches. In one away game at Avellino, a player said to me: 'Negro, today I'm going to break your legs. You are not going to do your circus tricks with me because I will break your legs.' 'Negro' also means black, but it is not a respectful term.

After 15 minutes, the player tackled me so hard that he broke my shin pad. The pain was awful. The physio ran onto the pitch and I saw him flinch when he looked at my leg. He shouted: 'Don't look! Don't look!' But I couldn't help myself and I saw the white of my leg bone. I was taken to a really shit hospital where they cleaned it but didn't even put in any stitches. I still have a large scar on my shin from that tackle.

We lost the game, and the following day a director came up to me and accused me of giving up on the team. He blamed me for the defeat, pointing out that I didn't even have any stitches. He was being stupidly harsh on me, yet his words struck a chord and I learned that I needed to be a warrior.

The racism continued, especially in the derby against Palermo, the biggest team on an island with several big teams including Catania and Messina. Football mattered in Sicily. I heard monkey noises whenever I touched the ball and I even saw someone throw a banana. It was difficult to concentrate on the game and I wanted to climb into the stands and punch them, but when my anger came out like that I played better. So I began to think: 'If you abuse me then I'm going to play better', and I put everything I had into that derby.

I should stress that I am talking about a minority here and, even then, I don't think they were all genuinely racist, more ignorant or doing what was considered 'normal' among their friends. One of my own teammates even made a monkey noise at me. He didn't realise how offensive it was until we came close to having a fight. We had to be separated because I was going to punch him.

The Italian people I met while out and about were not racist but very friendly. When I walked the streets they would shout, 'Evra! Evra! Come, come!' and invite me into their homes. They were so kind to me, offering me food and laughs. This was also the country that gave me my opening into professional football, something I'll never forget.

I learned Italian, but I wouldn't advise anyone to start the way I did. The first phrase I learned was: 'Can I come in without paying?' I learned this for when my brother came over and I wanted to take him to a bar. If there was a long queue I walked straight to the front and asked to get in for free. The security told me to wait for 15 minutes. I was not famous, but as the only black player at Marsala maybe they recognised me and they eventually let me in. That was a little bit stupid of me and I wouldn't blame them if they were thinking, 'Who is this idiot?' After two or three months of watching Italian TV and listening to my teammates, I began to string sentences together, and I was doing interviews after three or four months as I didn't find Italian difficult.

Word soon spread about me, at first locally and then regionally, then from Sicily onto the Italian mainland. I picked up another flattering nickname – the Black Gazelle. *L'Equipe* even printed a small article about me in France, so I knew people would be reading about me. I was shining in a struggling team and as the season reached its end, we had to win one more game to stay up. Before the match, a player came into the dressing room with a box. It was full of blue plastic needles. The image remains vivid years later.

'Guys,' he said. 'I've got these. We can use them or not. If a player wants to use them, put their hands up.'

I couldn't believe what I was seeing. Two players raised their hands.

'And if you don't want to use them, put your hands up.' Fifteen hands went up. The box was thrown away without anybody using whatever was inside those needles. We won the game without cheating and we stayed up, finishing 15th.

I wasn't the best player at Marsala, that was the number 10 Nino Barraco, an equally small local boy who had played in Serie A, but I was the attraction, a curiosity. I was fast, skilful – and I stood out because of my skin colour. Despite Marsala's survival, I knew I was unlikely to be at the club the following season. Lazio were interested in me and their representatives came to see me in Sicily and they spoke to my agent. He had become more than an agent, for I'd signed a piece of paper which effectively made me his property. When I started to become famous he claimed in an interview to be the man who'd discovered me, which I resented greatly.

Lazio wanted to sign me; they said they would give me a nice salary. So I went to Rome with my family and saw the training ground and the Olimpico stadium. My mum was so happy, but after two days I'd heard nothing more from them. And then they called and said they didn't want to sign me because too many people were claiming to represent me and they didn't want the hassle. There were other agents trying to muscle in on the deal. I was angry, especially when I found out that some of my salary was going to another agent I'd never even met, which made me feel like I'd been passed along and sold like a slave. It was all very shady. In the circumstances, I felt it was time to change agents; Giammarresi was very upset when I told him so.

My mum was worried I might get myself into trouble. When a lawyer approached me and told me he could put me in touch with all the big clubs in Italy, this seemed to be the answer. I was inexperienced and listened to him. I expected to hear of interest from Juventus or Milan. But when the lawyer called, he told me it was Monza. 'Who the fuck are Monza?' was my reply.

This was May 1999 and my most vivid memory of that time is watching Sammy Kuffour punching the floor in the Champions League final against Manchester United after this crazy English team had scored twice in the last minute to beat Bayern Munich and become European champions. 'You should join a team like Monza,' the lawyer said. 'There's more money, they play in Serie

B, but it's effectively Milan's second team. You can live in Milan too, which is a great city.'

What he said was not unreasonable and it wasn't as if I had any other offers. I moved to Monza and an apartment in the town 20 minutes from Milan. I had more money, around €2,000 a month. I was also given an apartment that a former player had vacated in a hurry, I was told, because of a dispute over money. He left a large, new Bang & Olufsen television, so that made me smile.

Having money for the first time in my life turned me into a bit of an idiot, a bit big time. Someone who was starting to believe that I really was the man because I was a second division footballer in Italy. My girlfriend called me and asked about coming to visit. I told her that I thought it was better if we ended our relationship because we were too far apart. I explained that I could have any model I wanted in Milan, which was full of models, and that I was sick of her moaning. What a dickhead I was, but I was taking out my frustration on those closest to me because I wasn't getting in the Monza team. The finest models of Milan? They hadn't all rushed to my apartment either.

I couldn't understand why I wasn't playing, though. I'd got myself very fit and I felt really fast. I started the season on the bench but by November I wasn't even in the match-day squad. I believed I was the best forward at the club, but an older Italian played instead, even when he was injured. So I went to confront the manager, Pierluigi Frosio, and his response was merely: 'What's the matter? I always see you angry. You should smile.'

'Why should I smile? It's not my birthday,' I replied. 'I need to play. You always play the same team, we're shit and we draw or lose every week. Why don't you try me?'

He told me that he considered me at the same level and status as a couple of the other players who were training with the youth team. That made me furious. 'If I don't play then

I'm going to break the legs of another player in training,' I said wildly – of course, I had no intention of carrying out my threat.

'That's your problem, you're too aggressive,' Frosio replied. 'You think you are the best.'

'I'm good enough to play in this team. I signed to play for the first team.'

He started laughing. I knew then that my chances were finished, and I played only 24 minutes of league games in the entire season. He was later criticised in Italy for not seeing my potential – something others at the club could see.

It seemed that my career was stalling before it had even got properly started, but then came an opportunity from another unlikely source. An insurance representative kept coming to see the Monza players, advising us to take out a policy. The amount they wanted was huge and I said no, but this guy kept watching me train and he called an agent he knew, Federico Pastorello. He came to see me with a young colleague, Luca. They met me and my brother Dominique who, as I've said, is big while I am small. We joke that my father must have been in good shape when he made Dominique and tired when he made me.

I think the two agents were a bit intimidated by us when we met up in a car park, but we had a fruitful discussion. They took me to get some football boots and I naively thought they'd get me a sponsor and the latest boots. Instead, they went to a Decathlon sports shop and bought me a pair that were too big.

I was really down during that period, but I started to build a relationship with the two agents and they suggested I move on immediately. I still had two years left on my Monza contract, but the club were delighted to let me go for free as they had decided that I was trouble and a Monza director told my agents that I would never make it as a professional footballer. They even lied and said that I'd trashed the apartment I had been staying in. That wasn't true, but I was angry and frustrated in

Monza. I was immature and I'd retreated into a bubble and people were scared to talk to me. Looking back, had I been more mature about the situation I could have helped myself, but I was too headstrong, too touchy. When I felt threatened the instincts of the street came back and I didn't care who I upset with my complaints and aggression. My bad behaviour meant I was treated badly and, while I had the talent to play for Monza, I needed to focus my energy on improving and listening to the manager rather than being angry with the world.

Fortunately for my state of mind, Pastorello lined up a move to Nice in France's second division, where he had excellent connections. Nice had been acquired by AS Roma chairman Franco Sensi as a satellite club. I would earn less money than at Monza, but I would be back in France with a chance of play-ing football again. And that's all I wanted – to be a professional footballer who actually made it onto the pitch.

CHAPTER 3

Nice

Nobody knew who I was when I arrived in Nice in the summer of 2000 – not the players, the fans or the media. My first view of Nice, France's fifth-biggest city and the largest on the French Riviera, wowed me with its grand houses and expensive hotels overlooking the Promenade des Anglais and the Mediterranean. It was a different France from Les Ulis, to be sure. I was ready to play every week for OGC Nice in the French second division, Ligue 2, but I couldn't break into their settled team. My Monza nightmare seemed to be repeating itself as I played in only five first-team matches in that first season and the rest for the reserves, where we'd be lucky to have 100 people watching us.

I was then still a centre forward and I was going to be the next Romario, don't forget, except Romario played first-team football and I didn't. I started only two of my five games for the first team in 2000-01, playing in a 7-2 October defeat at LB Châteauroux, where I was booked after 33 minutes. So my first professional game in my own country was a humiliating hammering in which I was taken off after 69 minutes when the score was 5-1.

Sandro Salvioni, an Italian who was working outside Italy for the first time, was the first-team boss, a strong character who spoke his mind. He told me that I was arrogant and that I wore my yellow Nike cap too much so that he couldn't see my eyes. It's true that I was so angry I didn't make the squad one time that I ran a key down the paintwork of his car. When I looked up, I could see him in the distance, but I don't think he saw me doing it and I think I got away with it. I hated Salvioni, yet he was very direct and pulled no punches about why I was not featuring in his team.

'I don't play you because you don't listen to me,' he'd say. 'You are incapable of listening to instructions and yet you arrived here and demanded the number 7 shirt [which belonged to the best player]. Who do you think you are?'

Salvioni was also very critical of me to my agent, complaining that I was 19 and had done nothing in football and yet I thought I was the best and knew best. And you know what? He was right. I had started one league game at two different clubs in two seasons. Something had to change. Salvioni did give me a chance, playing me for 90 minutes in our final, meaningless game of the season at Le Havre, one of our furthest away matches at the other end of France. We lost 1-0 and finished 12th, but I didn't feel like 'we' in my first season at Nice because I was very much on the fringes.

I returned for pre-season training in 2001 with my agent urging me to work hard and listen to the coach. I agreed to do this and put everything into my training as well as improving my manners. I took my cap off and said 'good morning' to Salvioni each day. Guess what? He said 'good morning' back to me, although he was not convinced I had genuinely reformed.

'You pretend you like me, but you hate me,' he'd say. 'I know your game. All I ask is that you are polite with me.'

And polite I was and continued to be so and my mood began

to lift, especially when I was named in the starting line-up for the first game of the season against Stade Laval. Just under 5,000 fans came to watch that game in Nice's old ground, the Stade du Ray with its big main stand and three smaller open stands and a capacity of 18,000. I started in left midfield and played for the whole 90 minutes. We won 2-1, but with 15 minutes remaining I was moved into the defence as our left back had been injured. That was fine – I was happy to cover for a teammate so long as I stayed on the pitch.

For our away game at Strasbourg the following week, Salvioni told me that he wanted me to stay at left back because of another injury which meant our regular left back had to move to centre half. We had an argument, which he won, because I did what he wanted. Nice lost 3-0, but I had an excellent game and Salvioni said I was the best player. When he picked me as left back for the following game and I told him again that I was not a left back, he took my bib off me and said, 'Okay, you don't play then. You don't decide who plays where.' I backed down.

Finally, I was beginning to learn to shut my mouth and this helped me a lot. A manager deserves the right to talk without a player interrupting him with his point of view in front of the others. This can be done in private. I also began to respect his authority and even to like him. After a while, Salvioni had my full respect which he earned by telling me what he thought about me face to face. Others had tried to do that and I'd ignored them, but I was younger. Now I was starting to realise that I wasn't always right. Salvioni used a carrot-and-stick approach, giving me something that I wanted – first-team football – then threatening to take it away if I didn't listen to him. He didn't praise me, but he asked questions that made me think, like: 'When are you going to start to love defending?'

Salvioni wasn't the first Italian to appreciate the art of

defending and I admired his enthusiasm for it. He would stop training and tell me how to receive the ball from other players as a defender rather than as a forward. He gave me personal attention and individual training sessions, so much so that I started to look forward to learning from him, when previously I had thought he was wasting my time.

I also felt that he understood my personality, especially when he told me to keep hating the idea of playing left back because I was doing just fine with that attitude. He knew that I had a struggle going on in my mind between accepting that I was a left back and still thinking I wasn't. Salvioni could have told me to play as goalkeeper and I would have accepted this from him. What a man! What a turnaround!

I kept my place in the team at left back and, although we lost five of the first eight games, I was playing 90 minutes every week. I was slight, only 63 kilos, but so fast with a low centre of gravity. I could jump high to head the ball, I could cross it and I was so fit that I could fly up and down the wing to contribute to the attack. Results picked up, we beat eventual champions Ajaccio 3-1 at home, and we were in contention for promotion. We got the better of Strasbourg, who finished second, at home, too. It felt wonderful – to be a professional in a winning team, to be in the routine of playing every week and, as the season went on, to wear the Nice tracksuit and to feel a valued part of a squad. At last, I was a real professional footballer.

That season we lost 12 games, which may sound a lot and was why we finished in third place, but between February and the end of the season we lost only once and our stadium became a fortress. For four months we had a winning team and the Nice fans were on fire every week. They were so passionate and this helped us on the pitch, no doubt about it. We picked up many points because both our fans and players intimidated our opponents. It started in the tunnel where there were no cameras like there are nowadays. The lights would be turned off 'by accident' to disorientate our opponents before the teams went onto the pitch. We'd slap them in the dark, shouting: 'We're going to fucking kill you, sons of bitches.' My teammate Noé Pamarot, who later played for Portsmouth and Tottenham in the Premier League, was huge. He was built like an American footballer, one of his legs was wider than two of mine, and he only needed to stand there to unsettle people. The referee could hear the com- motion but couldn't see what was going on because the lights were off. I felt that I was still on the streets of Les Ulis, but with a professional club. I loved it.

Salvioni kept telling me that I was channelling my anger at not being in my preferred position into being a better foot- baller. Our team spirit soared – my reputation too. With so many newspapers talking about me, Nice realised that they could sell me for a lot of money, but I would be out of contract at the end of the season when I could leave for free. If they had me under contract I was worth millions to them, but I hadn't signed a new deal and I was being advised not to by my agent. Nice hoped to persuade me to sign a new one, but I began to have other ideas.

On a free afternoon I went to watch nearby Monaco play at home with my teammates Janick Tamazoute and Christophe Meslin. Monaco's stadium looked like a big hotel from the outside, but when I walked in and saw the pitch I heard a voice say: 'You will play here.' I turned to Meslin and announced: 'I will play for Monaco one day.' He laughed at me, crazy Patrice.

I was close friends with those two and we'd go to a beach bar in Nice where I'd order what locals called a 'Monaco' – a beer and lemonade with a dash of grenadine. It was a red- dish colour, even mine, which I asked for without beer as I still didn't drink any alcohol. I was enjoying my football and the lifestyle in Nice; I'd go to a record shop to buy mixes of hip-hop music in Vieux Nice, the beautiful old town full of little shops. I'd have my hair cut there and eat out in restaurants with my teammates.

There were some interesting characters in the Nice team including Majid Ben Haddou, who was from the roughest quartier in the north of Nice. He was intelligent and friendly, but some of his friends could be intimidating and would tell the manager that he had to play him otherwise they would beat him up. Salvioni was clever; not only did he become friends with Majid but also with Majid's mates, so they were less likely to turn on the manager when he left Majid out. Their threats stopped, which was a relief because these were not the type of people you wanted against you.

There were a lot of crazy fans around the club and again it reminded me of playing for my quartier. There are two versions of Nice: one, the rich tourist town with swanky apartments, and the other with the estates that weren't by the sea and which I felt an empathy with. It's a big city of around a million people and there has long been an association with right-wing politics, but I never felt any problems there as a black man.

I should have had problems with the police because I spent most of my time in Nice driving without a licence. Okay, so I had matured in my dealings with the manager, but that's as far as it went. It wasn't that I had failed my driving test, but that I had never taken it. According to Patrice's Law, I knew how to drive and so didn't need a piece of paper to tell me that I could. I'd managed to buy my first car by bluffing that I'd left my licence at home in Paris and would send it on later.

Then I bought an Audi A8 but, in true Les Ulis style, I didn't like the wheels on it because I considered them too small. Some friends in the quartier managed to get me bigger wheels from another car, which naturally didn't fit and so the car didn't drive well. So I took it to the Audi showroom to get it sorted out and when they asked for my papers I gave them Tshimen's driving licence – two black men, who could tell the difference? They didn't spot the fraud, but they did say that the wheels made the car too dangerous to drive. I told the man at Audi that the wheels were perfect and I wasn't going to change them.

He was right, of course, and a few days later the wheels stuck fast. My solution was to buy another car. Alphonse Tchami was my teammate from Cameroon, where he'd been a striker in their national team for 14 years. He'd played in World Cups and all around the world from Denmark to Argentina, where he was at Boca Juniors with Maradona. Tchami played in Germany, Russia and China and joined Nice from Dundee United. He was coming to the end of his career and I loved listening to his stories about his life. Even more, I loved his car, a blue VW Golf with cream leather seats and arm rests. The Mediterranean sun bounced off the shiny silver wheels and the car even had its own TV.

When Tchami announced in the dressing room that he was going to sell his beloved car I vowed that I would be the only person to buy it. But he wasn't exactly thrilled.

'There's a rumour that you don't have a licence, Patrice,' he said, knowing full well that it is illegal to sell a car to someone without one.

What Tchami didn't know was that by then I'd seen enough sense to actually take my driving test. The 18 hours of driving lessons were a complete pain in the ass because I already knew how to drive, which the driving instructor recognised immediately. I was soon booked in for my test and was so confident that I reclined my seat, unclipped my seat belt and reverse parked with only one hand on the wheel – at speed. I was so competent at driving that I could do that, but the examiner looked shocked. The two other students in the car who were also taking their tests took a different approach. They put both hands on the wheel and had the driving seat upright, which didn't make them look relaxed at all. In Les Ulis, you can't drive like that – you have to put the seat down and chill. You're not cool otherwise.

The examiner passed the other two students and I waited for him to do the same for me.

'You are a danger to other road users,' he said. 'You are too confident and I know you've been driving without a licence. And I thought I had seen everything in this job . . .'

I booked the test again and promised myself that I'd be a model student and not a street gangster. I passed no problem and it was that proof that I slammed on the table in front of Tchami.

'So they lie about you, Patrice. You do have a licence!' he said, delighted that someone was going to buy his dream machine. I was soon cruising the streets of Nice with the sunroof open, so impressed with the sunroof that I'd even drive standing up with my head poking out of it.

I had some competition in the 'cool car' stakes at Nice because Didier Angan had a Porsche, though it didn't have a TV inside like mine and he never cleaned it. That car deserved better than Angan driving it too fast and smoking in it. Yet when Angan walked onto that pitch he turned into a soldier of whom General Joffre, the French commander who refused to retreat in the First World War, would have been proud.

Angan was a hard man who would speak his mind. 'If you pass me then I'll break your legs,' he'd say, even in training. It was that never-say-die spirit which drove us on, along with our playboy Dominique Aulanier, with his beautiful long hair and captain's armband. Dominique was so confident that he was convinced he was the best player in the world. He had a fine technique and was hugely popular among the fans because he loved the club so much. At night, he wore his shirts open so that you could see his gold chains. He looked like a star to me.

Dominique and I were the two who played the most minutes in 2001–02, and I was named as the best left back in Ligue 2 at the end of the season. I didn't care as I still didn't consider myself a left back, but promotion was a beautiful feeling. Dominique cried when we won promotion, it meant so much to him. The season finished with Salvioni telling me that I would be a champion at the highest level one day ... before he moved back to Italy to become the head coach of Cosenza in Serie B. He left because of the criticism he was receiving in Nice, where the fans never fully accepted an Italian being in charge. The Italian influence on the board and a tie-up with AS Roma had caused resentment among fans. It was a shame Salvioni left for he was a very good manager, but I never did tell him that I'd scratched his car. Sorry, boss.

I was receiving a lot of attention and knew AS Monaco, who I'd liked as a kid, were interested. Guy Roux, the famous Auxerre coach who was in charge there for 44 years, left me a message inviting me to Auxerre. He said his wife made a fantastic beef bourguignon and that we had to eat it with them. I was excited that this legend of French football was calling me and it was a genuine touch for him to invite me to his house, but Nice had absolutely no intention of letting me go.

With Salvioni gone, we had a new German manager, Gernot Rohr, who had taken Girondins Bordeaux to the 1996 UEFA Cup final with a young Zinedine Zidane. They'd knocked out AC Milan on the way to the final, and Zidane had gone on to much better things since then. Ruhr told me that he would see that I signed for Barcelona, that he had a fine record with young players, but first I had to sign a new four-year contract with Nice.

Nice were desperate for me to stay. The new owners gave off an image of having money, but in reality didn't have as much as fans thought they had. I was one way they could make money, but I was going to be a free player because I was coming to the end of my contract, which, because I was playing all the time and getting appearance money, was now worth €7,000 per month – but only €3,500 after taxes.

Nice put me under a lot of pressure to sign. They said I would have a big increase in my salary and I was still not earning a huge amount.

Nice also told me that Barcelona had been in touch and wanted to sign me. They even showed me a fax from Barcelona, which I'm not convinced was genuine. They said that if I signed the new contract and stayed one more season, I could then move directly to Barcelona, but how many players go from French second-division clubs straight to Barcelona? I found their interest hard to believe.

My agent told me not to sign anything. He knew that Monaco wanted me and that I could go there for free if my contract had come to an end, which would put me in a far stronger position when the time came for me to negotiate a contract with them. He also knew that Nice's owners would put me under a great deal of pressure as they were so desperate. I was told to hide in my agent's apartment in Monaco. I moved a car full of clothes there and hid. It was scary, but fun and exciting in an odd way.

Nice's owners tracked me down to my hiding place. They invited me to a meal without my agent and stressed that I had to sign a new contract for the future of the club. I said that I wouldn't sign as my agent wasn't there. One of the owners punched the table in anger. The other one looked at him and said: 'Calm down, if you do that then he won't sign.'

I agreed: 'Look, I can see that you're getting aggressive. That's not going to work with me. I won't sign.'

I left the restaurant, but waiting by the door was a heavy guy who looked like a gangster. 'You have to sign what they ask you and if you don't do that then I'm going to break your leg,' he said. He wasn't French, but from Eastern Europe or Russia. I was scared – with no legs there is no football. I went back into the restaurant and asked the owners what was going on.

They insisted that they knew nothing about him, but repeated how keen they were for me to stay.

'Just sign, Patrice,' they said. 'If you sign everyone will be happy.' I signed one paper and a second, but I was supposed to sign seven or eight copies. However, once I'd done a couple I got up and left.

When I called my agent Luca's business partner to tell him what I'd done, he was furious. 'I told Luca to take you to Monaco and hide you there until you had signed for Monaco.'

'I was in Monaco, but I had to come back to Nice to get some things from my apartment,' I said. 'Someone saw me and I had a call off the club owners and went to meet them. Maybe I should not have done that.'

Luca came round to see me.

'Patrice, what have you done?'

'Nothing,' I lied.

'Patrice, I know you have signed. You were going to sign for free for Monaco.' With that he got his pen out and drew a castle and a tent next to it. 'You could have bought your mum a castle, now you can buy her a tent. Congratulations.' The bastard! Then he got serious. 'What did you actually sign?'

'Two forms,' I said.

'Only two? Not six? Are you sure?'

I was sure. He smiled, because he knew there would not be enough signed papers to register the move. The transfer was incomplete and I was told not to answer the phone – at all. I switched my phone off and hid in Monaco until it was time to meet Didier Deschamps, Monaco's coach, and complete my move. Nice never did get the money they would have made from selling me, but they had a great season out of me and won promotion to Ligue 1, where they stayed, despite having to appeal twice against demotion to Ligue 3 because of alleged financial irregularities. It would have been nice to stay with that team and to see how we fared, but Monaco are Monaco. They had some great players and I wanted to be one of them.

CHAPTER 4

Monaco

I should have been full of confidence when I arrived for a medical in Monaco after travelling south from Paris. Tshimen and I had put my car on the train and had booked couchettes so that we could get a night's sleep rather than make the long drive south. But I was messing around and jumped up in the carriage, cutting my toes badly. There was blood everywhere and it hurt. I became very anxious, believing I would fail my medical and that my big chance to play for Monaco would be lost. I'd soon find out. The doctor carrying out the medical examination asked me to take my socks off.

'What's wrong with your toes?' he asked, pointing at the fresh cuts that covered them. I explained to him that I'd been jumping around on a train. He stared at me, confused, but said no more. I passed the medical, but I would have liked to have known what he told his partner about Monaco's new player that night.

After that hurdle was over, I was on a high, convinced I could steamroller everything before me, even though I had yet to play a game at the highest level in France, Ligue 1. With my new contract and the signing-on fee, I had big sums of money for the first time in my life. I did two things with it. First, I bought a house for my mum in Senegal. She was thinking about moving back there, but didn't in the end.

I also went to the Porsche showroom in Monaco and bought a new car. This did not go down well with my new captain, Ludovic Giuly, who wasn't slow to tell me what he thought about it: 'Hey, Evra. Who do you think you are to buy a Porsche? You've not even played a game in the first team.'

'I didn't steal it,' I replied. 'I didn't kill for it. I just ran like a bastard and I will prove to you that not only do I deserve to drive a Porsche, I deserve a Ferrari.'

Giuly just laughed – I quickly found out he had a good sense of humour and was a very funny guy – but he also told me I was arrogant and crazy.

Pre-season proceeded without any problems, though I was surprised at the poor facilities at Monaco's La Turbie training ground, where the dressing rooms were prefabricated huts.

In my first game we won 4-0 at Troyes and I played really well. Deschamps was proud of me – he'd taken a risk starting me because he had two more experienced left backs at the club, not that I had yet accepted that I was a left back when I signed. But managers played me in this position and I had to live with it.

I felt that the game was easy and life was wonderful. I stayed living in Nice – Monaco was only an hour away by car. Monaco have long had great football teams, but it's not a big football city. The Stade Louis II could be so quiet that I could pick out mobile phones ringing in the stands for the first time as a footballer. I found that very odd and unsettling at the start, but the lack of atmosphere didn't affect our performances, though we could be confused by league crowds averaging 10,000 but as low as 7,000.

In my first season, 2002-03, we finished agonisingly second by only one point to Lyon, who had won Ligue 1 seven times in succession. They had top players and because they were so good they also attracted a great deal of envy. They didn't care; Lyon was a winning machine, with Juninho and Sonny Anderson. Yet we beat Lyon, in our best result of the season.

I was playing every week, injury free, becoming a better left back with every game and also becoming friends with several of my teammates like Giuly. I learned by coming up against world-class footballers such as Ronaldinho, who was with PSG. He was a magician – I was convinced he could dribble with his hair if he needed to. Watching him was like seeing someone dancing, with the ball stuck to his feet like a magnet. I had to concentrate because he could kill you so easily if you didn't.

Everyone respected Didier Deschamps, who had stopped playing and immediately became a manager at the age of 33. Deschamps had some trouble with Marco Simeone, the famous Milan striker, when I first arrived and I don't think they got on, but moments of tension were rare. Our team was young, crazy. We played together and partied together. Rafa Marquez was a classy centre half who'd captain Mexico and would eventually go, like Giuly, to Barcelona where they'd become Champions League winners. Marquez could pass the ball through three lines of players and was so calm on the pitch. He could strike the ball with the inside of his foot with power.

My first trophy in football was the Coupe de la Ligue, which we won in 2003, beating Sochaux in the Stade de France. It wasn't a big deal to me because we won the final so easily, 4-1, but it was the first time that Monaco had won the competition. I was also voted the best left back in Ligue 1. This time I was very happy to receive that award. It meant more to me than winning the Cup because I was getting proper recognition.

We also qualified for the Champions League. To touch the star on my shirt and hear that Champions League music before my first game made me think: 'I've made it, now I'm a big player.' Not only that, we beat PSV Eindhoven away 2-1. It was a significant victory because French teams had a poor record against Dutch sides, and it was a good start to our 13 Champions League games in 2003–04.

Monaco were young, carefree and didn't feel any pressure. There were no expectations that we would do anything in Europe. Deportivo de La Coruña, one of the best Spanish teams, were in our group. Deschamps went through the video of their team before the game and picked out Juan Carlos Valeron, their playmaker, describing him as the Zidane of Spain.

'I've never heard of him,' I told him, just being honest, in the team meeting. Deschamps went mad and ranted at me in front of the other players, saying I needed to watch more football, know more players and pay more attention. The others were laughing, but how was I supposed to know who Valeron was when I watched almost no football on television? I think most footballers did watch football on television, but I was not one of them, especially when I became a father. I played football every day and wanted to listen to music or see friends in my free time when we weren't travelling.

We went to La Coruña and lost 1-0. Juan Carlos Valeron was everywhere and I certainly knew who he was then. The return leg at home was unforgettable. It was the birthday of the Croatian Dado Prso, our big striker and the warrior of the team. I was in the hotel room next to him and all I heard was *bang! bang! bang!* I went in to find out what was going on. In between drinking coffee and heading the ball against the wall, he told me: 'It's my birthday, I have to score.' He had a knee injury but he was not going to miss the game. We went 1-0 up after two minutes, then 2-0 after only 11, then 3-0 with a Prso header. Prso got another header – 4-0. His hotel room practice had paid off.

We were flying and it was a joy to be part of this fast, young team, but we took risks too and could be punished. Deportivo grabbed two goals back at the end of the first half. Whatever Deschamps said at the break after six first-half goals, we took absolutely no notice. We flew out straight back at Deportivo and scored three stunning goals in the first four minutes of the second half, two of them from Prso. He was on fire on his birthday and, at the end, the scoreboard flashed up '8:3. Joyeux Anniversaire, Dado'. We were so entertaining to watch and French people loved us, just like I'd once loved Monaco as a child. The game finished 8-3, the highest-scoring Champions League game ever.

Jérôme Rothen was one of the stars of the team – he loved himself and wanted to be like David Beckham and even bought an England shirt with 'Beckham' on the back. Jérôme and I were friends and played together on the left side. We argued because I would do a lot of running and overlap him, but instead of giving me the ball back he'd cross it. I'd shout at him and say, 'If you don't give me the ball next time then I'll kick the ball to the other side of the pitch and you won't see it.' It irritated me so much I went to see Deschamps and told him that I was ready to fight Rothen. I told Rothen too but he just laughed. He told me face to face what he thought of me, which I respected as he wasn't a snake who said things behind your back. He's now a journalist.

We reached the last 16 but lost the first-leg game 2-1 in Moscow against Lokomotiv, despite playing well. 'If we don't go through, it will be a catastrophe,' I told a journalist afterwards. Deschamps called me into his office.

'Why did you say this, little man?' he asked. 'It's the first time we're in the Champions League and you're saying it will be a catastrophe if we don't reach the last eight. You're putting pressure on us.'

'Come on, boss!' I smiled. 'You can rely on Patrice!'

'I hope so,' he said, shaking his head.

It was the toughest of games in the return leg. Lokomotiv were excellent and created so many chances, but we managed to grab a goal and keep a clean sheet to win 1-0, which secured our passage to the next round.

My respect for Deschamps was huge, though we didn't always agree. He was not a flash man and he called me arrogant when I put the collar of my shirt up like Cantona. 'It's my style,' I said. 'I will do whatever I want.' I half listened to him, to please him.

I had another problem with Deschamps – my mother loved him and she would always side with him if we had an argument. Mum would say: 'He is a good man.' She even asked for a picture with him and told him: 'I can see that you love my son!' Mum couldn't believe that I was playing for Monaco. She'd seen me fighting with my sisters when I wanted to watch Monaco on television as a child. Now this man, the captain of France when the country won the World Cup, was my coach. He was a winner, yet Deschamps never praised me. He would always look for areas of my game that I could improve. It was his way of keeping my feet on the ground.

But I was lucky. Salvioni had been the key to my success at Nice and now I had Deschamps. They both knew how to motivate me. I was fortunate that I'd go on to play for two more of the greats, Sir Alex Ferguson and Massimiliano Allegri.

We had a filmmaker travelling with us that season. As Real Madrid were next up in the Champions League, it was starting to become very interesting for him, and I'd recommend the *Périple Rouge* documentary he made which captures the utter *joie de vivre* and fearlessness of that campaign. I was asked by a journalist: 'What is it like to play against Roberto Carlos, Luis Figo, David Beckham and Zinedine Zidane?' before we played in the Bernabeu.

'Ask them what it's like to play against Patrice Evra,' I replied. I was back in Deschamps' office very soon.

'Pat,' he'd say. 'I know you are confident, but be careful. Your teammates read the papers and your comments can put pressure on them and pressure on me.'

We played 4-5-1. I was at left back, with Flavio, a calm and intelligent goalkeeper, behind me. Rodriguez and Sébastien Squillaci were the centre backs with Gaël Givet at right back. Fernando Morientes, who'd been popular at Real Madrid, played up front with Giuly.

Madrid had Ronaldo, Raul, Figo, Beckham, Casillas, the real Galacticos. Deschamps said to Givet before the game: 'When Ronaldo runs at you, don't look at his legs, just look at the ball. Look at his legs and he'll beat you.'

The game started. Beckham hit long diagonal passes that didn't swerve at all. I'd not seen that before. Beckham was beautiful to look at and watch playing football. But all the Real Madrid players looked like models, superstars. I tried to get close to Ronaldo, not just to mark him, but because I wanted to be in the pictures with him the next day in the newspapers. Years later, Ronaldo would come up to me in Ibiza, call me a legend and say that he loved my Monday video which I'd start doing on Instagram much later in my career.

Those Madrid players passed the ball so well that they made us run like crazy, yet we went ahead through Sebastien Squillaci. At half-time we were leading 1-0 in the Bernabeu and the home team were booed by their own fans. Deschamps urged us to calm down, to relax, and stressed that we hadn't won anything yet, that we needed to focus.

Then Ronaldo ran at Givet, his legs doing exactly what Deschamps had warned us about. *Boom, boom, boom!* Madrid equalised and went up through their gears: 2-1, 3-1, 4-1. It was bewildering to play against them, they were just so superior to us. We were dazzled, but Morientes – the quiet, focused gentleman with a first touch as good as Dimitar Berbatov's – scored a wonderful header in the stadium where he'd once been a star. It would prove to be vital.

We flew back to Monaco, really disappointed, a bit dazed and star-struck. Giuly even bought shirts with some of the Madrid players' names on at the airport. We were like tourists in Disneyland. The disappointment soon dissipated and, because we were crazy, we began to think that we could beat Real Madrid 3-1 which would see us go through on the away goals rule. We heard that some Madrid fans were already talking about who they'd like to play in the semi-final.

Madrid came to Monaco. My friends in Les Ulis drove me mad asking me to get them Ronaldo's shirt after the match. Another asked me for Roberto Carlos's. Édouard Cissé, our midfielder, did an interview in which he said that if Madrid scored first, then it was game over. Now this is where Deschamps was a genius. He read the Cissé interview out loud in front of the players and then said: 'If Madrid score the first – and they *will* score the first goal – it doesn't matter because we will win 3-1.'

Cissé felt bad because Deschamps made him feel that he should trust himself more, but Deschamps was right. Raul scored after 36 minutes, making it 5-2 on aggregate. I crossed for Giuly to equalise just before half-time. Giuly came in the dressing room and said: 'I've just seen Zidane and Figo arguing.' He told us that Zidane had said that Madrid were tired, information that Giuly gleefully passed on to us – and he also told the media this after the game, which Zidane got strongly criticised for.

I crossed again for Morientes after 48 minutes. He scored. 2-1 and the quiet stadium came alive; you couldn't hear the phones any more. We needed one goal. Ibarra crossed, and an audacious Giuly back-flick – *bang!* – made it 3-1. It was my greatest moment as a Monaco player. Our unity was tight. We were young, angry men, a band of brothers. Deschamps was scared by how confident we were; I don't think he thought we could do this against Madrid. I was proud of my performance. I found myself getting a lot of space on the wing and set up two goals. Carlos Queiroz, Real Madrid's coach, would not forget me.

Chelsea were next in the semi-finals. This was the game when I got the full respect of my teammates as a man, but before the match, I did a stupid video in the hotel where I said, in English, 'You motherfucker, Hasselbaink! Lampard, suck my pussy!' I didn't speak English or realise how strong the words like 'fuck you' or 'motherfucker' were. I was just repeating phrases I'd heard watching Hollywood films, like 'suck my pussy', without even knowing what it meant until it was broadcast in the *Périple Rouge* documentary and picked up in the UK.

We beat Chelsea 3-1 at home in the first leg. Monaco's Akis Zikos was sent off when the score was 1-1 and Marcel Desailly sarcastically applauded the referee. I saw that and thought that it was now 10 against 12 because the referee was not going to help us. But I also knew we were going to beat Chelsea, no matter what. Morientes made it 2-1 near the end, then Shabani Nonda, our tough Congolese warrior who'd just come back from injury, made it 3-1. Nonda was born in Burundi but his family escaped and he grew up in a refugee camp in Tanzania. He later played for DR Congo in international football. He was so tough, yet I saw him crying in an ambulance when he got his injury. My thought then was: 'If he's crying then it must be really, really bad.' But he came back, while Rothen was amazing that night. We were no longer wanting to fight with each other, but close friends.

We arrived at Stamford Bridge for the second leg. It was my first game in England and I loved the atmosphere, with every seat taken, the fans close to the pitch and always supporting their team. The first 20 minutes it was all Chelsea, they were killing us and my ears were hurting with the noise made by the

English fans. Jesper Gronkjaer scored as I was getting treatment by the side of the pitch after Jimmy Floyd Hasselbaink shot then followed through on my ankle. I still have a big scar because of that challenge. Monaco's doctor was horrified when he took off my sock and saw the wound, signalling to the manager that I was to come off. I grabbed his arm and said: 'If you take me off then I'll kill you.' I was serious.

'Patrice,' the doctor said calmly. 'If you go back on and get another kick, you could lose your foot.'

I wouldn't listen and repeated my threat, so he signalled reluctantly to Deschamps that I was okay and started to strap up my ankle. It was 2-1 at half-time; Frank Lampard had scored. He was clearly not prepared to suck my pussy! During the break the doctor undid my dressing and stitched the gash up. The pain, without any numbing injection, ran my circumcision close as the worst I have ever felt. I gripped the massage table and screamed as my horrified teammates watched.

The doctor asked me: 'Are you sure you want to play?'

'It's the semi-final,' I said. 'I am playing.'

I went back out, Morientes made it 2-2 and we now led 5-3 on aggregate. We were going to the final.

While we celebrated, I saw that the doctor was down after the game, quiet and alone and detached from the rest. I'd threatened him and upset him. I apologised to him and I meant it.

'I respect you as a man, Patrice,' said the doctor, 'but you threatened to kill me.' I was wrong to do that to a very good professional doing his job, but I couldn't leave the field. And I had won the status of warrior among my teammates. This was a wonderful time for Monaco. Everyone thought Lyon would be the French team to do well in Europe, not our young side.

I'd become friends with Prince Albert and had his private phone number. He would text me after matches to offer his feedback like a fan. We had a dressing room full of characters, but Albert took a shine to me. Later, he even came to see me in Manchester.

And what of the other characters? Givet and Julien Rodriguez, two French defenders, used to slap each other across the face in the dressing room before matches to psych each other up. 'I don't feel the pain!' they would shout as they whacked each other. Then they took the machine from the doctor's bag and gave each other electric shocks. They even wanted to put war paint on their faces like American footballers, but were told it would be illegal. We really did think we were warriors going out to battle.

Euro 2004 was approaching and my performances meant I was named in the French 31-man squad for the championships, without ever having played a full international game. The squad was trimmed to 23 and I didn't make the cut, but I'd already decided to play for France rather than Senegal and had been a regular for the under-21 team under coach Raymond Domenech, a decision which caused me a lot of criticism in Senegal where some called me a monkey who pulled my trousers down for the whites.

My father received some comments going to the market from Senegalese people who asked him why his son hadn't chosen Senegal. My parents didn't put me under any pressure when I chose who to play for. Both France and Senegal approached me via Deschamps, who told me that he hoped I would play for France but that it was my choice. I chose France because, while I was born in Senegal, I only spent one year there. I grew up in France and it wasn't a difficult choice for me, but when I go to Senegal to visit the charitable shelters that I have set up where vulnerable children can stay, people still ask me why I didn't play for Senegal. I think Senegal is better served by 400 children having access to a shelter that I pay for than being able to cheer me on in a football stadium.

As well as reaching the Champions League final, Monaco

were also chasing the Ligue 1 title. It was a tight competition as Lyon and PSG were also going for the title, although we'd lost fewer games than any team in the league. We'd won 4-2 away at PSG, who'd sold Ronaldinho to Barcelona, and we got the better of Lyon 3-0 at home, though we lost away.

The league went down to the wire. Perhaps with our minds on the Champions League final, we stumbled and drew with Strasbourg in our 36th game and lost 1-4 at home to Rennes in the 37th, a terrible result. If we'd won both of those games we would have finished with the same points as champions Lyon. And we would have definitely won the league if our priority hadn't been Europe or if we'd had a bigger squad. But we didn't – and Lyon celebrated yet another title.

My father called to tell me that he wanted to travel to Gelsenkirchen, a German industrial town in the Ruhr Valley, the venue for our Champions League final against Jose Mourinho's Porto side. My father very rarely came to see me play and I hoped that I could win for him.

The team travelled to Gelsenkirchen five days before the final. That was a mistake because, stuck in a hotel with little to do in the town, we started to feel the pressure. We also had significant media interest in us, which we'd never had before, with journalists and film crews from around the globe.

The song on the bus to the stadium before the match was 'I Will Survive' by Gloria Gaynor. I'd heard that a lot when France won the World Cup, it was a celebration song. The players started singing along to the 'la, la, la, la' bit and banging the windows. We looked like a group of fans, but it was our way of letting the tension out. I knew it would be difficult, though. I saw 'Nando' Morientes on the toilet talking with Lucas Bernardi in Spanish. Nando, an experienced player who'd been a star at Real Madrid, was white with worry. When I saw him I thought: 'We're in trouble.' Giuly got injured early in the game.

We thought he was faking it and were so upset with him – but he was actually injured. He was replaced by Prso.

Porto's Deco was magnificent and Jose Mourinho was a wily coach. They'd won the UEFA Cup a year earlier and they were wiser than us in that final. Carlos Alberto, still a teenager, scored just before half-time and did the greatest celebration, taking off his shirt and holding it like it was weighing him down. We lost 3–0. We were outclassed, but we really tried to attack Porto. Morientes had a chance to equalise after half-time but was offside.

It was a sad moment, but the Monégasque people were waiting for us en masse when we came home. Prince Albert was upset and didn't mince his words: 'You should have done it for my dad [Prince Rainier, who was ill and would die the next year after 56 years on the throne]' – and I thought we should have done it for mine. We were the first team from Ligue 1 to reach the European Cup final since Olympique de Marseille but, despite being named the Young Player of the Year for Ligue 1 – which was very rare for a defender – my greatest season so far ended in disappointment.

That would be the beginning of the end for our Monaco adventure.

Monaco bought and lost good players that summer. Morientes went to Liverpool. He'd only been on loan, but he'd been a success, the top scorer in the Champions League with nine goals. Rothen went to PSG for €11 million. He'd been a PSG fan as a kid and was following his dream. Giuly went to Barcelona to join Rafa Marquez. Giuly was unique. He barely trained in the week because he was lazy yet he was so talented that he'd score and assist in the games that mattered. We'd miss his character, the team joker, the captain who didn't lead by example in training. Prso joined Glasgow Rangers, where his headers made him a hero in Scotland.

The Uruguayan striker Chevanton arrived from Italy. We called him 'Animal' – probably because he'd joke that he'd lost his virginity to a cow in Uruguay. Some of the players believed him. Chevanton was small but wide and strong. Mohamed Kallon, another striker, also came from Italy. He was from Sierra Leone and was the first footballer who I saw could also be a businessman. Kallon was a very talented player who had been at Inter Milan. He said he wanted to build a city named after himself. The city, he promised, would have the best disco in the world with a pool in the middle. He would tell me this as he lay on the massage table and also talk about his plans to be something in politics. He made me laugh a lot. And yet another striker, Javier Saviola, arrived on loan from Barcelona. I've never seen a small guy eat so much food. Another good signing was the Brazilian right back Maicon, a real fighter who was powerful and technically at a high level. He'd later be crucial to the Inter side that dominated Serie A and won the Champions League.

Plenty of characters remained. Emmanuel Adebayor had arrived a year after me. He bought a BMW X5 car – I'm not even sure he'd had driving lessons. He fell asleep and crashed on a long drive across France, nearly killing himself. Adebayor would travel to Togo for international duty and return three days late. Once, an exasperated Deschamps heard Adebayor's explanation for being late and then, after saying he was going to fine him, told him to tell the rest of the team his reason.

'I couldn't travel on the Wednesday because my uncle said Wednesday is not a good day to travel for superstitious reasons,' explained Adebayor. 'On Thursday, I said prayers for all of you and I also walked across fire, but I fell over.' We couldn't contain our laughter. 'On Friday, I missed my flight.' By then we were crying it was so funny. Even Deschamps was laughing, especially when Adebayor added: 'But relax, because we will win the Champions League this season.' Adebayor is one of the most positive guys I've met in football. This is a man who held a party on the day his father died because he said his father would not want to see anyone unhappy.

After one game that we lost, Adebayor came into the dressing room, dancing and laughing. Squillaci and Givet didn't like it and asked him what he was doing. Adebayor replied: 'It's only football. I've just lost my dad. You should be happy that you are still alive.' The more I sat there and thought about what he'd said, the more I thought he was right. It's not good to lose a football game, but as long as you learn from it and don't repeat the mistake, how can anger help?

Zikos, a defensive midfielder, was like the prime minister of Greece. He dressed beautifully and was always calm, like a statesman. Bernardi is now a manager in Argentina. He would kick your ass if you upset him. He complained about everything but he was always willing to fight for the team; underneath it all, he was a good guy with a big heart.

With that team we finished third in the league in 2004-05. At one point in the autumn we drew seven out of nine league games and altogether we drew 18 times. You can't expect to win the league when you draw half your matches. We also reached the last 16 in the Champions League after winning a group that also contained Liverpool, Deportivo and Olympiakos. We made the semi-finals of both domestic cups, too. In a normal season that wouldn't be so bad, but we felt deflated after the previous year. Frustrated that we couldn't compete against the biggest teams, I started to think about joining one of them.

The 2005-06 season didn't start well for Monaco. We were knocked out of the Champions League at the qualification stage by Real Betis. Deschamps came to training one day in September 2005 in his normal clothes rather than his tracksuit and told us that he was leaving. The team had not been doing well and I was upset and several of us went to see him in his office to persuade him to stay. I remained silent at the back of the group of players and didn't talk. I was angry.

'Patrice, why aren't you talking?' he asked me. He explained that he wasn't getting on well with the directors, didn't feel in charge and that he wanted to leave. The players left, but I walked back into his office.

'Can I see you in private?' I asked. 'Can I come to your house?'

'You want to come to my house?!' he replied, a little surprised.

'I need to come to your house.'

I went to his big house in Monaco in my new Mercedes that night. I changed car every four months in Monaco. Silly money for a silly mind; I did it because I could. Deschamps' wife Claude was on the stairs when I went through the door. There was no small talk and his wife stayed to listen.

'You are a coward,' I told him. 'You taught me never to jump ship. You are the captain of our ship and now you are leaving. I'm so disappointed in you. You always said that the team came first. You are a liar!'

His wife began to cry.

'Even one of your players is telling you that you are making a mistake leaving Monaco,' she said to her husband. But Deschamps didn't like conflict; he'd already made up his mind. Perhaps, I thought, I should also decide about my future. Deschamps left and the bad Patrice returned. I have to be hurt first for my personality to change. The Italian Francesco Guidolin took over from Deschamps. He offered his hand to every player on the first day. I refused it. That man hadn't done anything to hurt me, but I refused his hand. I was upset because Deschamps had gone, and I blamed Guidolin who had done nothing wrong. He was right to drop me for some games.

Monaco were unsettled – or maybe I felt that was the case because I wanted to leave. In December 2005, I went to see the club president Michel Pastor and told him that I'd had enough and wanted to go. I'd not had any offers from other clubs, but I wasn't stupid, I knew what people were saying about me and that there would be interest. I told him: 'I want to join a bigger club because I want to improve.'

'No chance,' he replied, 'it doesn't matter what any club offers, you will never leave while I am club president.'

Even though I could see why he wanted to keep me and was only doing what was best for his club, I told him that he wasn't respecting me. He told me to take a holiday for the winter break and to come back fit for the second half of the season. When I told him that I was not coming back, Pastor thought I was joking. I then went to see my teammates, said goodbye and told them that I wouldn't be returning. The players also thought I was joking.

That Christmas, my agent told me of interest from other clubs. We were supposed to return for training on 3 January. I didn't. My phone was full of voice messages. One of them was from Prince Albert.

'Patrice,' he said, 'you need to come back because we have to resolve your situation. Come to meet me, please, and we will find a solution because you are like my son.' I was surprised to get that message and I went back to training. But Guidolin said: 'You can't train with us,' so I drove home. He was right to do that.

Jean-Luc Ettori, a famous former goalkeeper and then the sporting director, called and said: 'We'll find a solution.' Prince Albert also reassured me: 'Don't worry, everything will be fine. Just get back to training.' I went back to training – alone. There was one fitness coach especially for me.

The team was preparing to play in Auxerre but I was not going to play. That night, I went to the palace to see Prince Albert. You have to hand over your passport when you go into the palace, which had the biggest Christmas tree I'd ever seen. The Prince greeted us. He was wearing flip-flops, relaxed at home. I respect him because he's so normal. He asked me what was happening and I told him I wanted to leave the club and that I had interest from three clubs: Inter Milan, Liverpool and Manchester United. When I said Manchester his eyes lit up. 'I'm sad that you want to go, but happy for you to play for a great club. Everything will be resolved.'

Then we had a nice chat for 40 minutes and he was asking about my background. He was from another world to mine, but I felt that he genuinely cared. Everything was sorted with Monaco after that meeting. Publicly, the club went from saying that they had received no bids for me to saying that they had received three.

My agent said to me: 'Manchester need a left back urgently.' Gabriel Heinze, the established left back, was injured. So United were in pole position, but as I didn't know much about them I wasn't so excited, even when my agent mentioned Sir Alex Ferguson. I did know about Eric Cantona and that he'd been at United. I admired Cantona because of his personality. Sometimes I judge personality more than talent. French people said Cantona was arrogant, but to me he was confident and not afraid to speak his mind; different, too. I liked his aura, the way he put his shirt collar up, the goals he scored.

Cantona had been the king in Manchester, I knew that when I was 15. I'd watched his funny interviews; I laughed when he told the journalist that he didn't like him and would piss in his ass, when he called the French national team coach a sack of shit. What he said wasn't nice, but I admired his honesty in saying what he really thought. Cantona was the main reason I wanted to join United; he inspired me because I saw if a player with that personality could fit in then so could I. I only met Cantona once and told him that French players were respected in Manchester because of him. The French flags in Manchester – and I'd wave one – all had his face in the middle. I'd love to spend an afternoon with Cantona.

Once Monaco had said that I could go, a meeting was set up with Manchester United in a room at Paris Charles de Gaulle Airport so that we wouldn't be seen. Ferguson flew from Manchester with Carlos Queiroz, who spoke really good French. Ferguson also spoke a little French, which impressed me. It was clear he wanted me to join. He asked me about my private life, wanting to know if I was married, if I drank alcohol. He asked me if I liked to fight and I told him that I had grown up fighting.

Queiroz explained that he'd been coach of Real Madrid when Monaco had played them. He said I'd played well and I felt that Queiroz knew all about me – and that Ferguson trusted Queiroz. I later found out that Ferguson had sent Mike Phelan, another one of his trusted lieutenants, to watch me in Monaco. United were also watching Gareth Bale for my position, but he was young. Ferguson later said: 'With full backs, it's like searching for a rare bird. When we first saw Evra he was playing as a wing back, but he had the speed and was young enough to fit into our system. We knew plenty of his attacking capabilities. He was quick, had superb technique and a strong personality. Very strong.'

Wing back? I wasn't supposed to be so far forward and Deschamps would always say to me: 'Patrice, you are a defender.' And I would reply: 'The best way to defend is to attack.' What more could he say when we'd done so well?

My price, €6 million, was low because I only had one year left on my contract. We shook hands and left the meeting. My agents were bouncing with excitement and they kept repeating 'Manchester United!' The kid they'd picked up from Monza's reserve team was about to sign for Manchester United.

Me? I gave United my word but I wasn't bowled over with excitement because I didn't really know the legend of Manchester United. I also had to tell my partner, Sandra, that we would be leaving a life in Monaco to live in Manchester.

She knew we'd have to move but the reality struck her when I told her. We'd just become parents to our first child, Lenny. We had a wonderful life in Monaco where everyone spoke French. We lived in a beautiful apartment overlooking the port in the sunshine near the Mediterranean. We had friends there and we had money: I was earning €700,000 a year.

And we were about to give all that up to move to the north of England, albeit for more money, perhaps £1.2 million a year. My partner didn't know Manchester and was upset that we would be leaving our home. Lenny was not sleeping well and waking up every two hours. I'm sure he had an alarm clock inside his body which was set to go off at regular intervals. I was lucky that Monaco trained at 3 pm because I could wake up with Lenny in the night.

Next, it was time for me to say a final goodbye to my team-mates. I went back to Monaco and invited them all to the Sass Café, a trendy place where the players went, and I paid the bill. The club was changing and Adebayor also left for England in the January transfer window. Monaco finished tenth that season, a big drop after previous years. They would finish 9th, 12th, 11th and 8th over the following years before being relegated in 2011.

I was leaving at the right time and was convinced that I was making the right move, but it was still emotional for me. Monaco had been so good to me and I'd had a great time at the club that will always have a special place in my heart.

CHAPTER 5

Nightmare in Manchester

The tiny plane from Paris descended through thick cloud into Manchester Airport. Rain trickled down the windows as it taxied towards the terminal. Wearing a new grey sheepskin jacket that was three sizes too big for me and that I had only bought because my agent told me it was cold in Manchester, I was met by a club official in Arrivals. We drove to the Marriott Hotel in Worsley, a hotel in the middle of a golf course, where I stayed in a room with too much carpet in it. I felt cold, I felt lost. It was still raining.

Not for the last time, I asked myself: 'What have you done, Patrice?' Another new signing, the big Serbian Nemanja Vidic was also staying at the hotel. We met and while neither of us spoke English, we managed to communicate by smiling, pointing and agreeing. In truth, we could have been saying anything to each other and we would have nodded. We were nervous and both needed a friend. We had nobody but each other and would help each other out over the coming months.

On that first day in January 2006, I called my partner and told her an enormous lie. I said Manchester was okay.

Nemanja and I took a taxi to training the next morning. A

photograph in the newspapers the next day showed me dwarfed by both the coat and my companion. That coat cost me €3,000. What was I thinking? The shop assistant, who I knew a little, told me that it was limited edition, the most exclusive in Paris and the top line from Hugo Boss. I had more money than sense. There were no helicopters landing or pianos playing when Nemanja and I signed, just a bad coat.

It was utterly freezing, the cold seeped into my bones. All the big names were there at training on the first day: Ruud van Nistelrooy, Cristiano Ronaldo, Wayne Rooney, Giggsy, Paul Scholes, everyone. Albert the kit man handed me my kit. I'd always trained with short moulded studs. He told me that I couldn't in England in January because I'd slip. I ignored his advice and that annoyed him. He was only trying to help me but, as usual, I thought I knew better.

The players were going fast and hard, and while I slid everywhere as Albert predicted in that first session, I did score one great goal that day. People recognised that, even though I couldn't stay on my feet, I had something.

Rooney was the number-one young player at the club in my mind, more than Ronaldo. Rooney had the power, Ronaldo the tricks. Louis Saha would rave about them both to me in French, but I looked up to Giggs and Scholes, the best two senior players, more. I wanted to reach their levels of consistency. Giggs was so fit because he trained like he'd never won a trophy in his career.

I was taken to Old Trafford for the first time that afternoon. There was a classroom full of kids inside the stadium. When I walked in, they all stood up and said: 'Welcome to Manchester, Patrice Evra.' It was amazing.

I looked around the club museum, with its sections on the Munich air disaster, the youth system and European trophies. I sat in the stand and looked at the pitch. It was big enough for an aeroplane to land on it. The red seats rose up and up and up. I realised at that moment how big Manchester United were. I also began to feel the pressure of joining one of the biggest clubs in the world.

After one week the club gave me a car with the steering wheel on the right side. I would put the car into reverse instead of going forwards, but luckily I didn't crash. I tried to drive to training and used the satellite navigation, but it was taking far longer than the taxi I had used until then. Barry Moorhouse, the player liaison man at United, called me to ask where I was. I told him that the sign said 'Liverpool' on the motorway. I'd taken the wrong exit. That was my first experience of driving in England.

The kick-off was at 12 for my first game, a derby against Manchester City away. I'd not played a game that early since I was a child. I saw Mikaël Silvestre eating pasta at nine in the morning so I joined him. Then I went to my room and vomited for reasons that didn't become clear until I'd left United. I thought I was vomiting because I wasn't used to eating pasta for breakfast. I considered going to see the manager and telling him that I was sick, but then I would not have played and people would have considered me 'soft', as they say in Manchester.

My debut was a disaster. United had a great record against City under Ferguson, but City had grown more confident at home against us.

From the start, Trevor Sinclair kept running past me and leaving me on my ass. He knocked my eye with his elbow after two minutes. I also banged my head and couldn't see properly five minutes into the game. I was in shock, asking myself: 'Patrice, what the hell are you doing here? The football is so quick and so strong.' After all, I was a top player who'd been at Monaco and reached the Champions League final and played for France, and there I was on my backside. Now my head was spinning.

Sinclair scored after half an hour and played a part in a second goal just before half-time. I was being targeted by City because they knew it was my first game. They hit long diagonal balls to Sinclair and he would run aggressively straight at me and get behind the defence.

I was taken off at half-time when United were 2-0 down. Ferguson was shouting at everyone. I barely understood him because I couldn't speak English, but I didn't need to know the language to appreciate how furious he was. He looked at me and bellowed: 'Evra! That's enough! Now you can sit down, watch the game and start to learn to play English football in another game!'

Carlos Queiroz, who spoke several languages, translated Ferguson's words into French, tapping me on the shoulder as he did so. I asked him again what Ferguson meant. 'It means that you don't go back on,' added United's assistant manager. I couldn't believe what was happening to me.

Nemanja stayed on the pitch and we lost 3-1. My agent Luca had travelled to watch the game with his wife. For him, it was supposed to be a proud moment. I was the boy he'd rescued from the Italian third division and now I was playing for Manchester United. Luca came to see me at the hotel. I opened the door and he nearly cried when he saw me. Even his wife looked sad for me. I didn't feel sad, I felt empty, like shit, especially after the way Ferguson had talked to me.

Luca told me that he thought he'd made a huge mistake bringing me to Manchester, that he didn't think I would make it at United, that he thought the jersey, like my coat, was too big for me. It was painful, but he motivated me to prove him wrong.

I know my teammates were concerned about both Nemanja and me when we arrived mid-season in January. They thought I was too easy to brush off the ball in training. Scholes said it looked like they had signed a jockey, not a footballer, because I was small and thin.

I was not prepared properly to play for Manchester. I'd been playing in front of 10,000 at Monaco, now it was seven times that number. The football was so much quicker than in France and you had to be stronger, too.

Things would get worse before they got better in my new home. Ferguson sent us both to play for the reserves in a game at Blackburn. We played 45 minutes when René Meulensteen, the reserve-team manager, took us off, saying: 'Enough.' Nemanja and I showered and asked each other: 'What have we done coming here?'

'I should go back to Moscow,' he announced.

'I should have gone to Milan,' I replied. 'I had interest from there.'

We couldn't believe that we had been taken off while playing for United reserves. The media were asking: 'Who are these two guys? If they can't play for the reserves, how can they play for the first team?' It was a tough, tough time, but we both worked hard, improved and established ourselves. It was a good lesson for us, that start. You have to work hard in life.

Manchester took some getting used to after Monaco's sun and sea, beautiful people and expensive cars and restaurants. Lenny was just three months old when Sandra and he joined me in the coldest month of the year. We lived in the Radisson Hotel in the centre of Manchester, on the site where the crazy Sex Pistols had played a famous concert and Bob Dylan had been booed for changing his musical style. Now they had a crazy Frenchman trying to get breakfast and just ordering it was a nightmare. I'd call the kitchen and say: 'Bonjour, sorry, hello. Eggs. Croissant. Hot chocolate.'

We had no experience of being parents and our own parents were in a different country. We didn't get enough sleep, it was so incredibly difficult.

Gradually, we began to adapt and, for the first time in my career, I saw myself as a proper left back. Even at Monaco, I saw myself as a more attacking player.

The first guy I started to know properly was Gary Neville. He took me to see Ryan Giggs's apartment in Number One Deansgate to show us a different kind of accommodation. My compatriot Mikaël Silvestre was a big help, too.

We moved out of the hotel and I rented the apartment of former United winger David Bellion, himself a Frenchman, in Salford Quays. It was difficult because there were stairs and my wife was scared taking our son down them. She was slow to learn English because she wasn't very happy in England. She was returning constantly to Paris to see family, but you have to stick at it.

Slowly, though, I began to fall in love with Mancunians and Manchester United. Every time I pulled on that red shirt I felt I was pulling on history. I'd spend time reading about the history of the club and watching DVDs. I was very emotional and felt pain when I read all about the Munich air disaster and the Busby Babes, the great young players who died. I read about the crazy fans in the 1970s, the wingers, the promotion of young players from the academy. Cantona, George Best, Denis Law and his legendary teammates like Sir Bobby Charlton who I still saw around the club and whose hand I could shake. The legends like Giggs and Scholes who I played with every single day. And Alex Ferguson. I was living history every day of my life.

Before every game Ferguson would tell us a little story and as my English started to improve, I began to understand. Sometimes he'd tell us about when he'd been Aberdeen manager. Other times, he'd walk around the dressing room and tell us how proud he was to have all these boys assembled from around the world, the sacrifices and obstacles we'd had to overcome to get there. He was so inspiring.

Mancunians made me feel welcome wherever I went. Of course, I know that when you are a Manchester United player you're not like a normal person who moves there anonymously, but even when we lost games people were good to me. They blamed the referee or bad luck. I loved how football was so important to the people, more important than anywhere else that I'd lived. I felt that I was born to play for Manchester United, that the city and the club fitted my personality. I'd had a great time in Monaco in a successful team, but Manchester was closer to my way of thinking. I felt like it was a working city and I was there to work. I wasn't there to have fun, but to win football matches for the legendary Manchester United.

I started to feel like a robot that had been programmed by Ferguson to win, only to win, no excuses. I did one interview where I said living in Manchester was difficult because of the rain and the lack of quality restaurants. It was the truth, but the newspapers killed me for that, and Diana Law, who dealt with the media for United, came to see me.

'You're in trouble for saying this, Patrice,' she said.

Ferguson was angry and demanded: 'What is this you are saying about Manchester?'

I explained that I didn't mean to say it in a bad way, more being honest when I was asked for the difference between Manchester and Monaco. From that moment I realised that I had to be careful with the words I said to the English newspapers because they could twist them. I didn't want to offend the people who paid my wages, the people who had made me feel so welcome in their city.

As my English started to improve, I would try to read and I had a few sessions with Phil Dickinson who speaks French and works for the club. And I would absorb all the sounds around me in the dressing room. I find that I can pick up languages quickly and I'd learned Italian fast.

Ferguson would even try to speak French to me. Well, a little. I should have replied to him in back slang to confuse him! He would only start to be really friendly with me after 18 months when he realised I was a true United player.

After my horror debut, my second game – which was another baptism of fire, my first match against United's greatest rivals Liverpool – went far better. I won a free kick that led to Rio Ferdinand scoring. I also went into a tackle with Steven Gerrard that made people see that I was capable of being tough when needed. We won 1-0 at home and I heard how loud the United crowd could be. It was the first time that I thought: 'I can do this in England. I can play for a Man United team that beats Liverpool.'

I played in two games against Blackburn. We were winning but I was not performing at my best. We lost the league game 4-3 and those three goals led Ferguson to say to me: 'You're playing well, Patrice, but we're conceding goals with you.' He was right. It would take some time for me to adjust my game and to win his full trust.

We played Liverpool again a month later in the FA Cup. Six thousand away fans came to the game, which I'd never seen before, with Liverpool fans above the United fans. When Ferguson told me I was only on the bench I was disappointed, especially as it was an important game that was being televised live in France and I knew my friends and family would be watching, but I understood.

I put my kit on and started warming up with the players. When I went back to the dressing room, Queiroz said: 'Why are you warming up? You are not on the bench, you're in the stand.'

I hadn't understood the manager properly. I felt embarrassed and said to Queiroz: 'Can I please keep the tracksuit on and sit on the bench to pretend that I am a substitute?' I was so ashamed, my ego was bruised. My name would not have even been listed on French television. I told people that I'd picked up a knock in the warm-up and couldn't play. I was allowed to sit on the bench.

Not for the first time, Queiroz was the one who was calm with me, the good cop to Fergie being the bad cop who shouted at me and told me that I had to improve.

I was in and out of the team, which was hard to accept after what I'd done at Monaco, but I was in competition with Silvestre, a beast of a player. The French media was saying that I was going to take his place and I don't think he was happy with that, but that meant he trained harder. He warned me, 'You're my friend but you're not taking my place.'

And that's how it should be. And even though I was in competition with him, he was giving me advice and trying to help me settle in Manchester. He invited me to his house to eat, he showed me around and introduced me to Wings, my favourite restaurant in Manchester. There are plenty of assholes in football, but Silvestre is not one of them. As my career went on I learned from him how to treat players in the same position, like when Alex Sandro joined Juventus. I knew he wanted my place and I hated that, but it made me work my balls off.

I came on for the last seven minutes in the League Cup final victory over Wigan Athletic in Cardiff's Millennium Stadium, my first United trophy. I only got on the pitch because Ruud van Nistelrooy refused to go on. He wasn't happy because Louis Saha was selected and, when United were winning 4-0, Ferguson told van Nistelrooy to warm up.

He said no and told the manager to fuck off. I had to ask for clarification of what I'd just heard and then I thought 'Whoa.' Ruud was a big name and personality in the team, the top scorer and popular with fans. Ferguson's face was red with anger and Queiroz had a go at Ruud.

I knew that the sentence was going to be a severe one for

Ruud, but I just wanted to get on the pitch. Ferguson sent Nemanja and me to warm up instead. The Serb's fortunes were similar to mine – he was starting to settle. I played the last few minutes and said to the boss in the dressing room at the end: 'It's so easy to play for Man United. Three months and I already have a trophy.'

'You fucking French!' he said, laughing. I was so happy and so was the manager, who I was really starting to respect. He later explained that he'd brought Vida and me on because he wanted us to experience what it was like winning with Manchester United.

Ruud? In my very first training session he fouled Ronaldo, and Queiroz who was refereeing awarded a foul. Ruud disputed it. Ronaldo had just lost his father and he was emotional. Ruud said: 'Queiroz is your dad! Go and cry to your dad!' Ronaldo started to cry. Things were misunderstood. Ruud wasn't nasty, he was a good guy, but he wasn't happy either.

I did not make the French squad for the 2006 World Cup finals, which was not a surprise. I would have made the squad had I stayed at Monaco. Silvestre was chosen ahead of me. He was right; he wasn't losing his place to me. I spent that World Cup in the gym working hard and punishing myself, thinking: 'Look what you are missing.' And what I missed was France getting to the World Cup final, when Zinedine Zidane head-butted Marco Materazzi. I felt no emotion when I saw that, I didn't care. I only cared that I wasn't there, as punishing myself was a way to get rid of my frustration. As I worked away in the gymnasium, I was thinking: 'You will see, I will prove you all wrong.'

CHAPTER 6

You're Looking Like a United Player Now

Nelson Mandela was standing in front of me – a legend. As I stretched out my hand to shake his, Albert the kit man's phone went off, slightly undermining the solemnity of that special moment. The ring tone was 'The Great Escape', which maybe would not be the choice of many people. Poor Albert panicked and couldn't turn it off.

United were in South Africa on their pre-season tour in 2006, where my focus was on impressing Alex Ferguson with my desire to make it at the club. Albert was the right man to have around in the dressing room, discreet and reliable at his job but also a man to raise a smile, even if he didn't mean to do that most of the time.

We visited a wildlife park on that trip where there were signs telling us not to touch the electric fences. In front of a reclining rhino, Albert got out his old camera from the 1990s and set his zoom off – into the electric wire. Albert was soon dancing like a popcorn with his hair standing on end. Someone in our party was concerned, shouting a warning that Albert had a heart problem, but even that couldn't calm the laughter.

I liked the British sense of humour in the dressing room, but it was sometimes baffling. I ordered a pair of Nike trainers with my son's name on them. They took months to be made and were delivered to me at Carrington, United's training facility. As I took a shower someone set the trainers on fire and burned them enough to make them unwearable. I was furious at the lack of respect, but all the guys were laughing at me so I couldn't win. The culprit was Gerard Pique, so when he took a shower a few days later I tried to shit in his trainers. But nothing would come out. I pissed in them instead, but not too much. Pique was soon asking why his trainers smelled of piss. Word got back to him that it was me. We both knew what we'd done to each other, but neither of us admitted it. There was a truce between us. Gerard was still a teenager, maybe he could be excused, but I was an adult who just wanted a laugh, as well as revenge. But more than anything I wanted to establish myself as a first-choice player in the United team.

After one game on that pre-season tour, one of the United coaches, Mike Phelan, said: 'You are looking like a United player now, Patrice.' I played in the first league game of the season against Fulham and we won 5-1. I felt amazing, physically stronger, fitter and more confident. Despite playing 36 games in 2006-07, I was still not first choice all the time. Wayne Rooney played more than anyone – 51 games. Gabriel Heinze, by then my main competition for left back, played 32 games, but he was used also as a centre back. Gabby and I got on well but we didn't really work together on the pitch. He attacked the ball like I did, so maybe we were too similar to play in the same team.

Michael Carrick and Ji-Sung Park also joined the club that summer. Carrick would make strong and accurate passes from midfield forward to the striker – a quick transition from defence to midfield then to the forwards. He was very effective and improved our team, but he lost some form after three years and Ferguson wasn't happy. Maybe injury was to blame, but then Carra became very important again and spent more than ten years at the club. He's a United legend.

I'd become good friends with Ji-Sung Park. We spoke in English – Ji spoke it better than me but he was really shy so people often didn't hear him. I'm intrigued by shy people, I wonder if I can get to know them. I see it as a challenge. I became close to Ji especially when he was injured, because I was his nurse. I'd go to his house and we'd switch on the PlayStation after training. His leg was suspended in the air as it had to be elevated. Ji's parents also lived in Manchester and his mum would make soup and rice or a Korean barbecue. Amazing food. I've never seen two people play badminton as fast as Ji's mum and dad. I'd watch them in the garden smashing this little shuttlecock at each other. I played against them and they beat me really easily. I told Ji that I thought his parents were on performance-enhancing drugs for badminton. He told them and they laughed – and still treated me like a son. They were the nicest family.

Gary Neville was my captain. United was the most important thing in his life and he was Ferguson's man to maintain standards among the players. One day, Ravel Morrison, a very talented youth player, took Wayne Rooney's phone off charge and plugged in his own one. Gary went mad at him for coming into the first-team dressing room and charging his phone. He picked up Ravel's phone and threw it on the floor. Wazza hadn't been the slightest bit bothered and I thought Gary's reaction was a bit too strong. But Gary's point was that young players needed to learn what they should and shouldn't do.

I only ever had one argument with Gary. Apart from that,

he was very good to me. He'd shown me around houses when I first arrived in Manchester. When I wanted to see a priest, I expected to be taken to a church. Instead, he brought a priest to Carrington. But in one training session soon after I arrived, Gary tackled me hard. He touched the ball but he hit my legs too. I felt pain, I was on the floor. I looked at him, expecting him to say sorry. He looked straight at me and said: 'Fuck off, I took the ball.'

'Really?' I said, 'Really?'

I got up and carried on in pain. The ball came to Gary, who jumped to chest it. I saw my chance. I did a kung-fu kick to get the ball and hit Gary. I nearly broke his shoulder. The other players were angry and crowded around me. Wayne said: 'Are you crazy, Patrice? You could have broken his neck.'

'Yes, but next time Gary will say sorry,' I replied.

This was all too much for Ferguson and Queiroz. They stopped training and shouted: 'Everyone inside.' They were the teachers telling off the naughty children. I was still in pain and putting ice on my leg inside when Gary came to me and shouted: 'You're fucking crazy, Patrice.'

'Next time you will say sorry,' I repeated. Wayne saw this. I think they were in shock because they'd only seen me be nice and respectful. I regret what I did to Gary. It was not correct. But I felt my status as a United player increased because I stood up for myself, and Gary was impressed that even though I wasn't from Manchester, I loved his club as much as he did. Gary expected players to sacrifice their life for United. He didn't like fakes or guys who weren't team players. In return you could always count on him.

We played Celtic in Glasgow early in that season and I'd never experienced an atmosphere like it. It was so loud that I felt vibrations on the bench where I sat for all but the last few minutes. Louis Saha had a penalty saved and Celtic Park moved some more. Louis is a compatriot, he grew up close to me and he's a friend. His biggest problem was that he didn't realise how good he was. He'd talk with reverence about Ruud or Wayne or Ronaldo, but never about himself. One day I said to him: 'You don't realise how good you are. I didn't realise how strong you were until I marked you in training. Nemanja says the same. You're fast, you're two-footed, you're impossible to mark.' Louis was very unlucky with injuries, but he needed more aggression to make the most of his talent.

The team was clicking into gear as United chased a first Premier League title since 2003 and we were also going well in Europe. We beat Lille 1-0 in France to set up a game against Roma in the last eight of the Champions League, although I didn't play in that one.

Before the game, the boss specifically instructed Paul Scholes not to do anything stupid with his tackling. Scholes was sent off after 34 minutes for a second yellow card for bad tackling, but Fergie said nothing to him. Scholes was the only player I never saw Fergie tell off the whole time I was at United. Instead, he'd tell players to give Scholes the ball because he could control the tempo of the game and he knew when to accelerate the play or slow things down. Scholes was Ferguson's brain on the pitch.

We lost 2-1 in the first leg in Rome, but we managed well with ten men, and Wayne got an away goal. Before the second leg at Old Trafford, Ferguson gave one of his inspiring team talks: 'Make sure that when the Roma players go through the airport tonight, their heads are down because they have been beaten by Man United. I want the airport staff to laugh at them, to feel sorry for them. Don't let them have their heads up. You're better than them. Let's show them what you can do.'

I've never seen the players so determined. We demolished Roma 7-1 at home. I felt like we were 100 per cent in every position. Alan Smith was the best player that night, while I came on as a right back and scored my first European goal. A tough and determined player, Alan. Unlucky with injuries.

Henrik Larsson had joined us on loan from Helsingborg in Sweden for three months. What a man he was, what a player. Fergie's respect for him was immediate; you could see it in his eyes. Henrik was so accurate with his shots, so calm, composed, professional and intelligent. He was already a legend and had that aura, but he listened to everyone in training, listened to every tactical lecture by Carlos Queiroz. One of our kit men was Scottish and a Celtic fan and loved Henrik. The players took the piss because he was always ready to clean Henrik's boots.

Henrik was 35 and only with us for ten weeks, but we felt he'd been there for years. He was very down to earth and easy to talk to. Everyone loved him and was sad when he left. All the players applauded him after his last game. I asked him to stay, but he explained it was a family decision. We all wondered what we were going to do without him because the season still had two months left.

We were still on track in the league. We went to Anfield, were outplayed, but beat Liverpool 1-0 after John O'Shea scored a last-minute goal in front of the Kop. Beating Liverpool away was an even better feeling than doing the same thing at Old Trafford. To play against Liverpool you have to feel the hate of the fans. They're wonderful, these strong feelings. You feel them when you arrive at Anfield on the bus and the Liverpool fans are shouting at you.

We played AC Milan, the best team in world in 2007, in the semi-finals. I had been in and out of the team with a broken rib when Giggsy gave me the address of a Chinese man who practised acupuncture in Manchester. I was in so much pain that it hurt when I laughed. I was also desperate. United's doctors said I was not going to be fit for the Milan game but I didn't tell them I'd been to see the acupuncturist who worked from a really shit place, a dark room in a bad part of the city. When I told him I needed to be back for the Milan game, he asked me the date. I told him it was in four days and he assured me I would play.

It worked. While I could still feel the pain, I insisted that I trained the next day. Then I told the boss that I wanted to play against Milan. He told me the physios said I could not. I ended up playing with protection on my ribs, but I was not 100 per cent.

Kaka killed us at Old Trafford and scored twice, but Wayne also scored twice and we won 3-2. The Milan goalkeeper Dida didn't play well and I remember a Milan director being furious with him outside the dressing room after the game. He wasn't the only one in trouble – Ferguson bawled out me and Gabby after the game because we had made it easy for Kaka. When your boss is right you have to take it.

I was suspended for the second leg, in which Milan battered us 3-0 in the rain. Clarence Seedorf pulled the strings, organising everything. Gennaro Gattuso charged onto the pitch with his fists clenched before kick-off to get the fans going around San Siro. The noise almost lifted the roof off. He'd not played in the first leg at Old Trafford and wanted the fans to be as up for it as he was. They were.

I was annoyed. It seemed like we had a good team, but Milan were a class above us – but then we had a lot of players missing in that second leg. We were out of Europe, but it would be our last elimination for a long time.

United won the Premier League with six points more than Chelsea, who we drew with in the last away game a month later. Chelsea had won the league in both the two previous seasons – the first time they'd been champions of England in 50 years. The money from Roman Abramovich had made them the best team in England and many couldn't see beyond them becoming the dominant force in English football, especially as United had been taken over and were paying off debts. United's players didn't buy into any of that 'Chelsea will reign' bullshit. And to Alex Ferguson, it was merely his latest challenge in his career. He knew he had Rooney, Ronaldo and Rio and that they had the talent to become world-class players. He knew that he had the mainstays, the homegrown boys like Scholes, Giggs, Brown, Fletch, O'Shea and Neville. And, in buying Edwin, Nemanja, Carlito and myself, he bought wisely without needing to match what Chelsea spent. He also had something which money can't buy – a hunger to be the best, to keep moving forward even when you are the best.

Take our final game at home to West Ham, when we lost 1-0 and Carlos Tevez scored. Fergie was furious with us. He said we had been going through the motions and he accused us of ruining the party. We'd won the league and he made us feel as though we'd won nothing. When we went back to the dressing room, Fergie told us to take our shitty trophy out and show it to the fans. It was a strange feeling. West Ham stayed up and Sheffield United went down, which was a big scandal because Fergie was accused of letting his team go easy on West Ham. He did not go easy on his players.

My background came back to haunt me several times that season. Before the 2007 FA Cup final a couple of weeks later, the *Sun* ran a story with quotes from one of my friends about our tough upbringing. They mentioned us selling drugs, the fights, making me out to be a gangster. In the final training session, Ferguson handed out the vests to the starting XI. He came up to me but didn't hand me one.

'I'm sorry, Patrice, but you can't play,' he said. 'I've had a call from the Glazers and they think you have damaged the club's image. They don't want gangsters playing for Man United.'

'But, boss,' I pleaded. 'This was my life as a kid, not as a football player.'

Ferguson started laughing. He was joking. He handed me the vest. I was so happy to play in the FA Cup final, but it turned out to be an illusion. On the morning of the final I ordered breakfast in my room. I was dancing with music on. It was a beautiful day and I was going to play in the FA Cup final. There was a knock at the door. I thought it was my breakfast but, no, Alex Ferguson was standing in front of me.

'Patrice,' he said, as he walked in and sat on a sofa in my luxury hotel room. 'What is this noise? Do you think you have a nightclub here?'

He was nice to me at the beginning, but he hadn't come to talk to me about music. I turned the music off, some R&B. His expression changed.

'Son, I will play Gabby,' he said.

My face dropped. I respected Gabriel Heinze, my rival, and we got on well. He'd helped me when I arrived in Manchester, even though I was direct competition for him. I spoke French with him as he'd played for PSG. We also spoke some Spanish. I don't know how the Spanish language came into my head; it just did when I was at Monaco because we had several Spanish speakers.

So Heinze started the final. Heinze had been angry with Ferguson because they bought me when he was injured. Ferguson told him that he was still first choice – which was probably right because Heinze had been one of United's best players in 2005, the year before I joined. But I had been playing so well that Ferguson had no choice but to start me – except that now, in the Cup final, he was dropping me. And right now, with Ferguson standing in front of me, I was angry.

'I know you are upset and you are right to be upset, but I will tell you why,' he continued. 'The pitch is heavy. It's better suited to him. You are quick, fresh and fast. You are going to come on and win the game for us.'

'Boss, I'm really disappointed,' I said. He left the room, I turned my music off. The one-man Patrice Evra party was over.

I sat on the bench, a substitute. Ferguson told me to warm up very early. I thought he'd realised that he should have started me and wanted me on. I warmed up after 10, 20, 30 and 40 minutes. Still, nothing. I was told to warm up again in the second half . . . 60, 70, 80. It was hot and I was fuming, but he didn't make a single change. Drogba scored in extra time.

I went to collect my loser's medal. I walked down the steps and threw the medal on the pitch. Somebody must have found it and they probably still have it. I had been voted the best left back by the PFA, but I didn't play one minute in the Cup final that we lost in the most disappointing and frustrating manner.

In the dressing room Ferguson tried to shake my hand, but I refused. I wanted to leave the club and told my agent. He told me to calm down but I didn't listen. I couldn't get beyond it being my first time at Wembley, my first big game since joining the club. And the manager didn't start me.

There was a party afterwards in London, even after the team lost. Guests, including other players, were asking me: 'Why didn't you play? Are you injured?' I was still blazing. I again called my agent Luca, who is Italian, and said: 'I don't want to play for Manchester United any more. Get me a club in Italy!'

He told me to calm down, saying that I'd just finished a really good season. He was being sensible.

'No, it's over,' I said. 'I've done everything I can do for this team and it's not good enough. They didn't start me in the Cup final. Then the manager told me that I'd come on and win the game. Then he was asking me to warm up after 20 minutes. He lied to me. Lied!'

I hardly spoke to anyone that night. I never spoke to Ferguson about it again, but I feel that he understood my disappointment. He was friendlier with me after that. He could see that I would do anything for United and how much it meant to me that I didn't play. I also began to feel that what Ferguson had done to me was a test. I realised that this was life at United and that you cannot expect to be in the team all the time with all those great players. In later years I would tell this to young players who were frustrated that they were not getting into the first team.

I didn't leave, and instead I faced the next season with even greater determination.

CHAPTER 7

Midnight in Moscow

When I returned to pre-season training in 2007, Gabriel Heinze told the players that he was going to join Liverpool. He said goodbye to us and we saw him collect his boots. Going to Anfield was not the done thing for any United player. The two clubs hadn't transferred a player to each other since 1964. The case went to a Premier League tribunal, where Liverpool claimed they should be able to buy him and United alleged that he'd been illegally approached by Liverpool. For a month Gabby did nothing, until the ruling was given in favour of United and the next thing we knew Gabby had joined Real Madrid.

Although he would later regret being impulsive and strong-willed for trying to force a move, Gabby was not happy with Ferguson. I think he thought he'd be first choice when he came back from injury, but I had established myself as the left back. It was difficult for Gabby. He'd been Player of the Year before I arrived. But that's football.

We also said goodbye to other players. Striker Giuseppe Rossi had scored a lot with the reserves and looked very sharp and quick when he trained with the first team. Rio Ferdinand was very impressed by him and called him a goal machine. Rossi went to Villarreal, where he did so well that Barcelona tried to sign him, before he got several serious injuries. It seems very unfair that a player can work all his life and use his talents, then have much of his career ruined by injury, but that is a risk we all face.

Gerard Pique went to Barcelona at the end of the 2007-08 season. United's players and coaches kept telling the boss that he had to play Gerard because the kid was good enough. Finally, the boss picked him for a game at Bolton in November 2007. We lost 1-0 to a Nicolas Anelka goal. Kevin Davies and Anelka were too much for Gerard that day and he was taken off after an hour. After that he barely got another chance in the first team. We'd meet again soon enough.

I continued to concentrate on my own career at Old Trafford, but while things were going well on the pitch, it wasn't perfect off it because my family was struggling to adapt to the Mancunian culture. Ask me to this day where I most feel at home from all the places I've lived, and I'll tell you Manchester. Maybe my life was distorted because I was a United player, but you can only relate to your own experiences. Mine included a man coming up to me in a garage after a defeat at Manchester City, saying: 'Patrice, don't fucking worry about them. We are better than them.' You'd be killed at other clubs after losing to your big rivals.

That derby was the third game of the season, which would become one of the greatest in the club's history, but we didn't win either of the opening two games and we lost the third at City. The wins started to come, the first against Spurs at Old Trafford. At least I didn't have to mark Aaron Lennon that day. He was such a tough opponent, one I needed to be 100 per cent against. If I was only at 90 per cent, he'd make my game very difficult. He could change direction quickly, he was fast and could get behind players. People said that I always had a difficult game when I played Lennon, but we usually won.

Eight straight wins followed that derby defeat. I was playing every week and felt that the team was getting stronger than the year before. I was called back up to the French national team too and recall some of the France players asking me if the United players were on drugs because we were doing so much running and so much pressing. I seldom re-watched my own games because I was always looking forwards, but I caught one on television and was surprised by what I saw. When an opposing player had the ball, four United players began pressing him.

We scored four goals in four successive games in October 2007, but something happened that made me realise I had to guard against complacency. I found myself applauding a goal from my own half rather than going to celebrate with my teammates.

The standard of the training was getting better and better. Ronaldo was doing stuff none of us had seen before. Ferguson changed the way Ronaldo thought about football. Before, Ronaldo had been all about numbers, about goals and assists, but Ferguson made him think more about the team. I remember Ferguson telling him in one team meeting to stop the circus tricks. He told him that he had the ability to score in every game if he cut the tricks out. Ferguson made him a killer, made him a man.

I was tackling everything in training, Vida was a rock and Rio was his partner and equal in defence. Giggs was flying around like he had been 15 years earlier, Rooney was a machine and Scholes was just being Scholes. We'd play nine versus nine in training on a Friday and it was more competitive than some of the Premier League games, with the winners hammering the losing players in the dressing room afterwards.

Our bench was full of players who would be first on the teamsheet of any other English team, and United had 23 or 24 international players. I would say to Ferguson: 'We have too many good players and the cars will not fit in the car park. Some of them have to park in the staff car park.' Even the reserve goalkeeper Tomasz Kuszczak was the first choice for Poland. We had new players Anderson, Nani and Owen Hargreaves, a top-quality passer who could take a very good free kick. Owen had come from Bayern Munich and was trusted in the biggest games, but was another who really started to suffer with injuries.

Nani became a close friend and still is. He's a funny guy but someone who could irritate his teammates with his style. Maybe they thought he should cross the ball rather than show some skill, but Nani had to play in the position where one of the hardest skills in football is regularly expected: beating a man. One problem for Nani was Ronaldo. People compared him too much to Ronaldo and so he tried to do things to be better than his compatriot, when he was already an amazing player just being Nani. I saw the pair of them practising free kicks in training, with Nani kicking from a long distance with so much power. He said he was practising so that he could take free kicks because Cristiano wouldn't let him, so he wanted to improve.

We did a Christmas show at Carrington, where the young professional players would do impersonations of the senior players. One did an imitation of Nani being Ronaldo's dog. Nani was not happy about it. He's a sensitive boy, but his life has been a success and he became an important player for United in his seven years at the club. On his day, Nani is an exceptional player who will beat a man.

That wasn't the only thing that went wrong that Christmas. We threw a huge party with many outsiders invited, which ended up at the Great John Street Hotel in Manchester. All the players were there, then things went wrong and Jonny Evans, then only 19, was arrested – and then released without any charge. Ferguson gathered us together in the dressing room when we were next back in training a few days later. He was furious and killed us as he reminded us about our responsibility as United players. I sensed there would be no more Christmas parties like there had been, but it also brought it home to me how life was different for United players in Manchester. It meant we hardly ever went out.

Occasionally, a few of us would go to Panacea, a smart bar in Manchester, but you couldn't be yourself there. I was in a minority in there because I still never drank alcohol and have never been drunk in my life. Some of the players would go to the casino and I went a couple of times with Tevez, but I don't gamble. I don't work hard to lose my money.

When you're a Manchester United player in Manchester, there's no privacy, especially now that everyone is carrying a camera in their pocket. We could go in the back door to avoid any paparazzi, but once you were inside the whole club would stop. Everyone would look at you and, while security would try and give you a private area, men would always come over for a picture or to talk about football. If you say that you'd rather not have a photo taken with them, they'd tell all their friends that you're arrogant. It's a bullshit environment. On one hand, you feel invincible because every man and woman wants you; on the other it's a big trap because if you fall into it you're fucked. The women would offer temptations. They would look at you directly and make it clear that they were available.

It also seemed to me that most people in Manchester were United fans. I went to see Drake and R Kelly in concert in Manchester with some teammates. We showed up on the balcony at the arena and we were getting more attention than the stage. A friend said: 'I can't understand why the people in Manchester have this addiction to football,' but footballers are a big deal in the city.

Anderson was a big deal in his first season at the club. The Brazilian was wild – and I mean that as a compliment. I loved him. My mum is from Cape Verde so I could speak to him in Portuguese, which I was also improving by talking with Ronaldo. Ando was only 18 and he was the type of guy who would say to Ferguson: 'How much do you earn?' The manager had never before been asked that by any player and didn't know what to say. One day before training, the manager asked me: 'Patrice, has Anderson put weight on?' Then he called Ando over, who replied: 'Boss, easy. Give me the ball. *Bam! Bam!* I win all the games for you.'

Fergie adored him too and he let him get away with so much. He also knew that Ando had lost his father when he was 11 years old and that he came from a tough background. Ferguson treated him like a son. Some of the older players were annoyed because Ando wasn't showing a Man United attitude, but Fergie protected him and he was correct to do so.

Ferguson also knew that Ando was a very talented footballer. Ando was one of United's characters, a man with a smile who offered to translate for non-English-speaking new arrivals, even though his English was a version familiar only to himself.

I was starting to feel Mancunian. People around me noticed it. They were worried that I wasn't listening to French hip-hop any more. I was influenced by the music from England and I was speaking good English. I was loving living in Manchester, this city that was so proud of its football and music. But I still had to learn the nuances. One day I put on 'Wonderwall' by Oasis in the dressing room. 'No,' said Paul Scholes when he heard it. 'They're City. Never fucking put Oasis on again.'

Our winning machine always had a few hiccups like that. With 25 men – many of them passionate and strong characters and leaders – not everyone is not going to have the same view, but our team spirit was special.

We went to Lyon away in the Champions League last 16. As I knew only too well, they'd won every Ligue 1 title since their first one in 2002 – a French record – and there were hopes that they could become the first French team to win the European Cup since Marseille in 1993. With a team containing Juninho, Hatem Ben Arfa, Sidney Govou and Jérémy Toulalan, Lyon were strong and Karim Benzema, still only 20, scored. Carlos Tevez equalised with three minutes left, giving us a crucial away goal. Carlos was like a lion.

Carlito could change a game. He would give blood for a team, he was always angry and fired up. He always gave 100 per cent, yet as a professional he didn't train hard. He was lazy, he didn't care, he couldn't even be bothered to tie his boots properly. You didn't want him in your team in training, but he did also train at home alone, and when you saw him on the day of the game he was a completely different person. Some players train well but struggle with the pressures of an actual match. Carlito was the opposite, saving his energy for games where he came alive. He gave more than anyone else and he was a real Man United win-at-all-costs player.

Carlos doesn't let a lot of people get close to him and you could never describe him as friendly if you didn't know him. He's suspicious of outsiders, and remember that he grew up in Argentina, where he was educated about the British and the Falklands War. Every Argentinian thinks that the Falklands belongs to their country. Carlos understood English, but he didn't want to talk it. He went to England for football and I think he was surprised when the United fans sang 'Argentina!' or waved Argentina flags. He grew to have a strong attachment to United and while he'll always say that his team is Boca Juniors, in Europe it's Man United, even though he went to Manchester City.

I became good friends with Carlos and we spoke Spanish together. I felt that he would fight for me if needed and I trusted him deeply. He's generous and funny. People don't think he's intelligent, but if you asked him to learn Mandarin he could learn it. If he wants to do something he does it.

Portsmouth knocked us out of the FA Cup with a 1-0 win at Old Trafford in March 2008. Tomasz Kuszczak, who replaced Edwin van der Sar at half-time, was sent off and Rio Ferdinand took over in goal. I was furious, and not only because I hit the post. I know the lads found Lassana Diarra hard to play against in midfield, but he kicked Ronaldo in the neck and didn't get sent off. We should have never been knocked out of the FA Cup that day. That defeat came a few days after we'd beaten Lyon 1-0 to reach the last eight in Europe.

Ronaldo was having his best season so far and when we travelled to Italy to play Roma, the travelling United fans sang their new song 'Viva Ronaldo!' really loud. Cristiano scored a magnificent header and Rooney made it 2-0. My old Monaco captain Ludovic Giuly came off the bench to try to help his team in vain.

I felt like I was playing for the best team in the world and people were starting to compare us to United's treble winners. Ferguson was not having that and warned us: 'You've won nothing yet.' But I knew he was excited by us, especially when he said: 'You will be the worst team in the world if you don't win this competition.' We beat Roma 1-0 at home, thanks to another goal from Carlito.

Manchester United were so strong all over. Rio and Vida at the back gave us the perfect platform. Rio was like a number 10 who played in defence, Vida was a warrior, and they complemented each other perfectly. Rio would finish the game with no blood on his shirt because he'd read everything so well. Vida would be covered in blood because he put his head in where it hurt. He'd smash a striker, as if to say: 'You can't go into that space.' Ferguson always compared them to Gary Pallister and Steve Bruce, with Vida as Bruce.

Wes Brown, who also featured at centre half, played at right back because Neville was injured, and he was our Mancunian warrior, a local boy. I loved playing with them all. They'd say: 'Go forward – we'll take care of everything behind you.' They were so comfortable and confident even when playing one against one. Ferguson always urged us to stay calm and not be too confident, but he also said: 'If any of you can't take one player, you shouldn't be in this team.' Vidic never asked for support with a striker because a one-against-one was a challenge, a talking point in the dressing room afterwards. If a rival striker got a shot on goal, we'd kill the defenders for letting it happen. We could win 4-0 but if Nemanja or Rio had let one player shoot, we'd destroy them for it rather than talk about winning 4-0.

We stood in the tunnel before a game and knew we were going to win. My France teammate William Gallas told me what it was like for an opposing player. He said they'd look at all these tall United players and admit: 'These guys are something special.' We felt invincible, and our opponents knew it and expected to lose against us.

We were going to win the league again, but the Champions League became a bigger focus. Barcelona were waiting for us in the semi-final, with the first leg at the Camp Nou in front of 91,000. We were not scared of them and felt relaxed as we stayed in our hotel on the outskirts of the city overlooking the tower blocks of the working-class areas. The manager didn't want us to be seduced by the sea and sun and the beauty in the centre of the city. I remember another Pat, the 1960s United midfielder Pat Crerand, in our hotel asking how to use the lifts that climbed up the outside of the building.

Barcelona's Camp Nou is so big that you feel like you are in a spaceship or Rome's Colosseum, so big that it's not noisy or intimidating. I was told that I was to mark Lionel Messi and follow him everywhere. The gaffer said to Cristiano in the dressing room: 'Messi is the best player in the world right now' to motivate him. 'Patrice, I don't care about Messi because you are going to keep him quiet. And if you don't keep him quiet the team will lose this game. If you don't do your job then the team will lose this game. But I know you will do your job.' I was nodding in agreement, but deep inside I was thinking: 'If I fuck this up, I'm going to lose the confidence of my teammates and my manager.'

Cristiano missed a penalty after two minutes, but my focus was Messi. We had about 20 one-against-ones, but he only took advantage once when he passed the ball over my head and the crowd roared. But we drew 0-0 and I had done what was asked of me. Messi and I shook hands at the end. He'd played well, but I was like a pitbull always on his toes and maybe that surprised him.

'Well done, son,' the boss congratulated me back in the dressing room. Marking Messi that day gave me a lot of confidence.

We'd done half the job, but there was always the risk Barcelona could get an away goal. Nil-nil is a risky scoreline in Europe, but a Scholesy strike won the second leg at Old Trafford. It was the loudest I heard the stadium in all my time at United. I wish Old Trafford could be like that more often, but it's not every game you beat Barcelona in the semi-final. I felt the pressure during that match more than any other game. All Barcelona needed to do was equalise and they'd be through, and I kept saying to myself: 'If they score we're fucked.'

I had a knock on the head at the end of the game and felt dizzy but we survived until the whistle when Old Trafford roared so loud you could feel the noise in your chest. I was going to a second Champions League final and this time I was confident that I was playing for the best team in the world.

Our opponents would be Chelsea, the pair of us the best two teams in England – and probably the world – that year. I know it can be different for fans who might have long-standing rivalries with Liverpool or Manchester City, but for the players our main rivals in that period were Chelsea. They were the team who pushed us and we pushed them. We drove each other on and we knew if we didn't win a competition, they would. John Terry, Didier Drogba, Claude Makélélé and Frank Lampard were all top class, as were my friends Nicolas Anelka and Florent Malouda.

We'd beaten Chelsea 2–0 at Old Trafford in September in the league but our away league game against them came in between those two Champions League semi-finals. Even though I didn't play, I made headlines because I got into a fight with the groundstaff afterwards, which I regret.

Ferguson made some changes and rested some of us. He knew we were probably going to win the league, but he wanted to win the Champions League too. Those rested still travelled to Stamford Bridge. Ronaldo was on the bench. Even though we didn't play, we were angry because we lost the game 2–1. Manchester United was not about losing games. Defeats hurt. After the match, we were asked to do stretches on the pitch by Tony Strudwick, the fitness man. Whenever I ran past the lawnmower, one of the young guys on it would rev the machine up to try and put me off.

'If you do that again, I will kill you,' I said to the groundsman. Carlito replied: 'Patrice, you can't say that.' The man stopped the revving, but there was another problem. A member of the groundstaff said to Tony: 'You can't be on the pitch because we have to maintain it.' Tony disagreed and said: 'We have to do our work.' I was far away, but I saw the groundsman push Tony. I ran towards him and demanded: 'Why are you pushing him?'

He replied, 'This is not your business.'

He was holding a big pitchfork. I told him to put it down.

He said: 'I will stick my fork in your ass.'

'Really?' I said, 'Come on, then!' Scholes and Carlito came over and told me to calm down. Ji-Sung Park too.

Carlito is from Fuerte Apache, one of the toughest barrios in Buenos Aires. He'd seen a lot of bad things and he was about to see some more. The groundsman called me a son of a bitch so I ran at him to punch him in the face. He was big and I fell on one of the other stewards as we all pitched in. They had the numbers, but we would have been better fighters than them, except we were dragged apart and escorted to the dressing room.

'Fucking hell, Pat,' said Scholesy. He was laughing and calling me a crazy Frenchman. 'If there is going to be a fight in my pub I will definitely bring you next time.'

I was called in to see Ferguson the next day in Manchester. I walked into his office and the fight was all over the papers. The media were calling it 'The Battle of the Bridge'.

'You're in trouble,' he said. 'They were recording everything. You can't be doing this.'

It went to a hearing. Chelsea had a lawyer. I called him Scarface because he was so strong in his mentality. There was talk of it being a racist incident, of me being the victim, but I heard no racist comment. The implication strained relations between United and Chelsea for some time afterwards, but it didn't cause any personal problems for me with my friends who played for Chelsea, far from it. When I next joined up with the French national team, Nicolas Anelka and Florent Malouda were full of admiration: 'That guy you fought with is massive!'

But I was rightly punished, banned for four games and fined £40,000 for what was called improper conduct, an act of 'violent behaviour'. Ferguson was furious at the ban. He'd had another Frenchman, Eric Cantona, banned from playing before because of an act of violence. Meanwhile, Chelsea were fined £25,000.

I came back after my ban the following season ... against Chelsea. I crossed for Rooney to score and we won 2–1, which was revenge of a sort. But I knew I couldn't go on behaving with the instinct of a kid in Les Ulis as such actions could ruin my career. And we would have plenty more business with Chelsea before then.

When I signed for United, I said that I wasn't coming to play for a team that was merely competing in the Champions League final like Monaco, but one that would win it. I said that in January 2006, when United had finished third in the Premier League the season before and looked a long way from being European champions.

By May 2008, however, we were in the final against Chelsea in Moscow. I'm supposed to write about how great everything was, but my strongest recollections are not of glory.

Ferguson came to me the day before the game. He knew I had become close friends with Ji-Sung Park. Ji and I had such a strong connection and we still have it. He's the best friend that I've ever had in football, a man I have so much respect for that I travelled to South Korea for the funeral of his mother.

Ferguson could not understand our connection. He asked, puzzled: 'Which language are you speaking?' Carlos Tevez was friends with us too. Ferguson would say: 'You're French from Senegal, you're from South Korea and you're from Argentina.

How do you communicate?' But we just did using a hybrid of languages and we had so many laughs. Ferguson called us 'the good, the bad and the ugly'. I think I was the bad. We spoke a little English, a little Spanish. Ji spoke English. He's really clever and speaks better English than me, but he's so shy that he was afraid to speak it to strangers.

In Moscow, Ferguson told me to explain to Ji that he was not going to play in the European Cup final and that he wouldn't even be in the squad. That was difficult, especially as Ji's parents had flown from South Korea to see him play. Ferguson told me that he felt terrible, that it was one of the three most difficult decisions of his career. Ji's parents gave Ferguson a present after the game so that probably made him feel even worse. They wanted to thank him for looking after their son so well. I told Ferguson that he was asking me to do a difficult thing, but he said: 'I know, but I know how close you are to Ji. When I speak to him, he's so respectful that I don't know what his expressions mean.'

I learned a lot from Ji about humility and respect, which is important in Korean culture. I went to see Ji in the hotel after training the day before the game. He said: 'Don't worry, Patrice, just focus on the final and win for United.' But I knew he was hurting, and he told me later that he was hurting a lot and had cried alone in his room. I'd never seen him show his emotions before.

Ji was right to be disappointed, especially as he'd been one of our best players in the semi-final against Barcelona both home and away. Even Xavi Hernandez later said: 'Wow, that Korean never stopped running.' He didn't. Louis Saha also didn't make the team. He cried too, but we had to focus on the game.

Ferguson was inspired in his pre-match talk. He told us that his greatest achievement that season was not any trophy, but bringing 21 of us together from all around the world. He was so proud of that. He picked us out individually, saying: 'Can you imagine what it was like for Patrice fighting for food with his many brothers and sisters? Can you imagine Rooney on the streets of Liverpool having a tough time? Or Carlos in the estates of Buenos Aires? Or Vida when bombs were landing on his home town in the war?' It was emotional and we left the dressing room feeling like we could beat anyone. Fergie had barely spoken about the game, but he'd stressed to us throughout the season that if we wanted to be champions, then we had to do better than Chelsea. And we had only beaten Chelsea to win the league by two points, thanks to Giggs' goal at Wigan Athletic in the final game of the season. There wasn't a lot between us and Chelsea.

In our Moscow hotel, we watched a video about the treble in the run-up to the final – 1999 was in our head and one of our motivations. I was feeling confident before the game, and then more so when Cristiano Ronaldo put us ahead. Then Lampard equalised to make it all square. There were battles all over the pitch. Drogba came close to scoring in extra time and it was clear that one action was going to win the game. In extra time I went through with the ball and crossed to Ryan Giggs. He shot but John Terry blocked it, meaning that the game went to penalties.

I can't understand how anyone can miss a penalty, yet I am talking from a position of trauma. When I'd played for France Under-21s against Portugal, I missed a penalty. I didn't think you could – or should – miss a penalty and vowed never to take one again, and I have been true to my word.

In Moscow, Queiroz asked me out on the pitch as we pre-pared for the shoot-out: 'Patrice, do you want a penalty?' I shook my head. He was surprised because I was an important player who should have taken some responsibility. But I feared missing again. The kids like Anderson had no such fear. Giggs had reminded the manager that Ando was good at penalties, and Ferguson had brought him on as substitute in the last minute of extra time. His first touch of the ball that night would be when he took his penalty.

Edwin van der Sar had no choice but to face the penalties, but there was no better goalkeeper to do that. Ed was our brain at the back. A complete gentleman, he was always calm, even if we didn't protect him enough. He'd always shout encouragement or try and help – 'Patrice, look on your left!' I could hear him in the loudest stadiums. He was like a manager on the pitch. He could also hit a very accurate long ball that could kill the line of strikers or even the midfield line too. Sometimes that ball came to me and I'd play it forwards. We were on the attack in only three passes.

Carlito set United on their way with the first penalty, smashing it home. Chelsea and United matched each other until Ronaldo missed United's third penalty and burst into tears through remorse. Lampard, still not sucking my pussy, scored his to put United behind. Next Nani kept us in it, but if Chelsea scored their next penalty they would win the final. It was a surprise when John Terry stepped up to take that penalty, but he was the captain. Drogba would have taken one, but he had been sent off for fighting with Vidic.

Terry slipped and Edwin jumped as the noise flooded over us. Then Ando had his date with destiny. Giggsy had called it right, because Ando buried the ball in the net. Ryan calmly scored United's next one – and then it was all down to my friend Nicolas Anelka to keep Chelsea alive. He didn't look happy and was even unhappier still when Edwin saved it.

We all ran forwards to celebrate. It was beautiful. I ran to the stand to see my family, my brothers, my friend Tshimen and my agent, and I hugged them. We went crazy on the pitch and danced in front of the fans – around 25,000 of them had flown to Moscow. Some had even taken the train all the way from Manchester, journeys that took three or four days. They created a little Manchester in Moscow, a terrace of red, singing 'Glory, Glory Man United'. I took a Russian hat from one fan, another threw me the French tricolour.

My dream had come true. I felt so happy, so content, that I had done everything I ever wanted to do as a footballer. The trophy was big, beautiful and very heavy. It was very late and raining, but we didn't care. Ferguson's glasses were steaming up and he couldn't see properly. He didn't care either; he just smiled and hugged everyone and everything in front of him. I think he even hugged the Russian soldiers and their horses. Ferguson was not the only one struggling to see. I took Albert the kit man's glasses off him and wore them.

I also saw John Terry's tears on the pitch and I felt genuinely sad for him. Unlike my teammates, I had been a loser in a European final too. That image of Terry stays with me. Chelsea were a great team and we pushed each other so hard that we were the best two teams in the world, but they'd lost the league to us and now they'd lost the Champions League.

After a long celebration in the dressing room, we were taken back to the hotel. All the players were drinking alcohol except me. Finally, the bus took us to the team hotel and it was so late that it was getting light, maybe three in the morning. If you look at the photos I'm the only one not smiling. I regret that, but I think I know why. I was disappointed that we hadn't won the treble, that we'd lost in the FA Cup to Portsmouth at home. As I said before, we should have never lost that.

This was what I told my brother Dominique who was back at the hotel for the party. 'Patrice, you're crazy; you've won the Premier League and the Champions League,' he said. 'You have a problem. You have issues.' But that's how I felt. I didn't really celebrate so much.

Instead, I danced with Ji's father. He was disappointed about his son, but decided the best way to feel happy was to dance. A kung-fu dance! I joined in with him, and he could kick really high. Wonderful.

My family and agent drank champagne. Everyone thought I was miserable because I didn't join in. The players said: 'Get Patrice a hot chocolate or a water because he's boring.' It's true, I should have been happier, but I had the medal around my neck and I was kung-fu dancing with Ji's dad at five in the morning which I think deserves some credit.

Unlike every other player, I felt quite fresh the next day. I decided to play some music on the plane, 'American Boy' by Estelle with Kanye West. Ed Woodward says that song always reminds him of me and that night. United's future CEO was on the plane with his wife, a young man not much older than the players. Our paths would cross again many times. None of the other players wanted to hear my music because they were all hungover. Giggsy moaned: 'Patrice, turn the volume down, we need to sleep.'

'No way,' I said. 'Patrice's party carries on.' I needed Ji's dad to dance with, but his parents were flying back to South Korea.

When we landed in Manchester I expected thousands of fans to meet us. I'd seen the images from 1999 and the treble, when they said half a million people were on the streets of Manchester celebrating. As we landed I looked out of the window. There was only a man with two ping-pong bats to guide the plane. We got on a bus from the plane and left the airport. There were a few hundred people at the airport. I was thinking: 'This can't finish here, this is so disappointing.'

Ferguson took hold of the bus's microphone. 'Well done,' he said. 'Congratulations. But if I don't see you work as hard next year to win it again then I'll tear up your contract. Have a good time with your national teams and see you next season.'

There was no victory parade. The police decided it would be dangerous and a risk to public safety and would cause major disruption to people on a normal working day. Rubbish. They'd had parades before and they've held them since, for United and for City.

I got home and said to my wife: 'If this is winning the Champions League then I don't want to win it again.' I was sad. I had felt content on the pitch, but the celebration was a let-down and I didn't enjoy it.

But Ferguson had spelled things out starkly. I couldn't believe how quickly he focused on the next campaign. Didier Deschamps had said to me: 'Winning is important. When I meet Ferguson, winning is normal.' I realised that Ferguson would never stop thinking about winning and that I was also starting to think like that. I was never happy unless we won everything.

My wife said: 'You are turning into a Man United robot; you are not in the real world. Why can't you enjoy the moment? Winning the league has become normal to you. You should enjoy these moments or you will regret them all your life.'

She thought I was becoming obsessed, but that had already happened. One day, my son announced: 'I hate Manchester.' When I asked him why, he replied: 'Because Manchester take my dad away from me.'

There is a red, white and black flag at United games that reads: 'United. Kids. Wife. In that order.' People laugh at it. I didn't find it funny because, I'm ashamed to say, for me it was true.

That obsession is also the reason why I succeeded at United. I felt the club in my blood, even though I wasn't born into it like Gary Neville. I felt I was born to play for it. I was no longer Patrice Evra. I was part of the United winning machine at the most important period of my life and career. United is a powerful drug. When I came off that drug, in the summer of 2014, I was depressed for a month. I didn't know what was happening to me. But I'd have many, many good times before then.

CHAPTER 8

THE GREATEST TEAM
IN THE WORLD

I don't have my Champions League medal. Can you believe I lost it down the back of a sofa somewhere? If you have it, please tell me. But I told myself I'd be winning more to replace it as I had my sights firmly set on staying at the top.

My next aim was to win Euro 2008 with France, to be a champion of Europe with my country as well as my club. I didn't even take a holiday, going straight to meet up with the French squad at the Clairefontaine national football centre. At France's training camp, the coach Raymond Domenech and all the players were congratulating me for my achievements with United. This was reassuring as I'd made the national team squad as I expected but I wasn't yet an established player for France, despite making my debut in 2004 when I was 23.

Four years on, Mikaël Silvestre and Éric Abidal were still ahead of me, although there had been some progress. I was starting to play more and hoped to feature in France's tough group games against Romania, Holland and Italy. So I was surprised and upset not to start our first game against Romania in Zurich.

France drew 0-0 and it was a poor performance that I watched fuming from the sub's bench.

We played against a local team the following day in a friendly for some exercise and I told my teammate Jean-Alain Boumsong that I was losing my head, that I was a champion of England and Europe, but that today I was going to play a friendly against this team of kids and part-timers. Boumsong told me to calm down, and he had a point. I looked at the sky and said to myself: 'Patrice, some people cannot even walk. They have no food. They have disease. And you are complaining because you are being asked to play a football match. Fucking hell, Patrice!' And it worked – it was almost as if I had an angel on my shoulder telling me to cool it.

We won the practice game 7-1 and I scored twice. My commitment and attitude in the friendly were rewarded by selection for the next game against a Holland side containing Edwin van der Sar and Ruud van Nistelrooy in Bern. The game was a nightmare and we lost 4-1.

The France team was still in transition between the older players who'd been so successful winning the World Cup and the 2000 European championships and the newer, younger players who were taking their place. I was one of the newer group, but instead of helping us and encouraging us, the older players shunned us – experienced legends of French football like Lilian Thuram, Willy Sagnol and Claude Makélélé. Football can be cut-throat and I understand the argument that if you take a man's place in the team then you're taking food off his table, but look at how Silvestre and Heinze had been with me at Old Trafford. They used the competition to push themselves on, while at the same time helping me.

There was little of that warmth in that France camp towards younger guys like me, Samir Nasri and Karim Benzema. Benzema would have been a great signing for United under a strong manager like Ferguson, who would want to buy him in

2009. He can score with the left foot and the right and would go on to be one of the best strikers in the world for a decade.

There were also guys who I considered to be in-between such as Thierry Henry and Nicolas Anelka. They were not quite my generation, but nor did they seem to feel like they were playing with kids and look down on us. I didn't have any personal antagonism, just a feeling of an 'us' and 'them' and a lack of the unity that all great teams have. My United team had balance and a ferocious team spirit driven by the manager. The France team did not.

Domenech made more changes for the third game against Italy in Zurich, saying that he trusted the older players more, though I kept my place in the team. It was another disaster. Before the game Thuram and Sagnol had words with Domenech. It was said that they didn't want to play. Whatever went on, they didn't play and players like me were wondering why. That did nothing for the team spirit.

Éric Abidal, playing as a central defender, was sent off after 24 minutes for a professional foul on Luca Toni. Andrea Pirlo scored the penalty that followed and Daniele di Rossi added a second after the break. I was involved in an argument on the pitch during the game with Makélélé, who accused me and Benzema of passing to each other and not to other teammates. It was a ridiculous claim, but one which showed the strain, frustration and lack of trust among the players. We improved in the second half and had chances, but it was all too late. We were out of the competition, which wasn't acceptable for France.

Our manager's reaction? He asked his long-time girlfriend Estelle Denis, a television presenter, to marry him on television. I laughed when I saw it, because I thought he was a crazy guy. I didn't have any personal issues with Domenech for doing that either, but some of the other players thought he was being unprofessional.

Even though he had a contract until 2010, I thought that Domenech would be killed by the media after France's humiliating exit and lose his job. To my and probably everyone's surprise he kept it. As I left Switzerland for a family holiday, the best season of my life was finally over but I felt like a loser.

It was like the team was still on holiday when United played their first games of 2008-09. We'd been to South Africa pre-season and, unlike when we'd been there in 2006, I didn't have to prove anything to anyone. We won only one of our opening seven games that season and lost the European Super Cup in my old home of Monaco against Zenit Saint Petersburg.

I played really badly in that game. Some old friends had come to see me at the hotel and we sat around laughing and eating, even on the day of the game. There were thousands of Russian fans, one of the rare occasions when United fans were outnumbered.

I would never normally meet friends on the day of a game because match day is for concentrating on what lies ahead, but I wasn't the only player with the wrong attitude because none of us prepared for that game well. Collectively, we treated it like a friendly, we didn't realise how important it was, that it was another trophy. The European Super Cup isn't the Champions League, but it's still a significant trophy around the world, though the British tend not to rate it.

The manager was rightly angry with us at half-time after we'd conceded a goal at the end of the first half. It was 2-0 after 59 minutes and, while we tried to recover, it was too late, although Nemanja got one back and Scholesy was sent off for a handball. After we lost 2-1, the manager scowled as he said to us: 'Watch them being handed the trophy. I want you to suffer.' I regret how we approached that game because it was not the Manchester United way. United is about winning and to be a United player you need to have the motivation to win and never stop winning.

Of course you need the highest technical level, but character and drive to win is so important and, as my wife had suggested after Moscow, I had been taking it too far. Maybe I was addicted to this football club led by this great man. Maybe I'd eased off in the summer and the new relaxed me was still in Monaco in my head. I wanted the old Patrice back and was prepared to do everything necessary to achieve that.

You need to make sacrifices – and not only one like not drinking alcohol. Mentally, you need to put your United family at the same level as your real family, but it comes at a price. I had medical issues, as I'd taken too many anti-inflammatory drugs when I had a persistent groin strain at Monaco. Rather than have an operation that would have kept me out for months, I kept on taking Voltaren, which led to stomach problems. Anti-inflammatories are handed out like sweets in football dressing rooms. They gave me a stomach ulcer that could give me so much pain that I vomited. Eggs, for example, would trigger it. I grew to live with it – and with other injuries. I estimate that I was only ever 100 per cent fit with absolutely no injuries for about 30 games in my entire professional career. To me, that was normal. But it took a long time before my gastric problems were finally sorted out. Perhaps I wasn't as indestructible as I thought I was after all.

Before one match in Manchester in 2008 I was feeling really sick. I was sweating and vomiting. I called the team doctor, who came to the house. He told Ferguson that I had a virus and that I couldn't play. Instead of going to the team hotel, I stayed at home and slept for two hours, waking up at 3 pm. The game was a night match at Old Trafford. By that time, the team were all at their hotel for the pre-match preparations.

I called the manager and told him that I felt better, but he only replied that the doctor had said no. I told him that I was fine but he would not listen. So I hung up, put my Manchester

United tracksuit on and drove to the Lowry Hotel in Salford close to the ground where the team have long stayed before matches. I surprised Ferguson in his room and he asked me what I thought I was doing.

'I want to play,' I said. I think that, deep down, he wanted me to play too. The doctor was called and had another look at me before saying: 'It's a risk for you to play. You have lost a lot of liquid, you have vomited, you have diarrhoea.'

'I don't care, I have to play,' I replied, and I got my wish, putting in an excellent performance. I think Ferguson thought I was crazy, but in a good way. He wanted players to do anything for his team and I would have done anything.

United did become world champions in December 2008 when we won the Club World Cup in Japan. The jet lag was terrible for a lot of the staff and players, but I can deal with it. On that trip, we tried to keep our body clocks closer to British time.

We played local side Gamba Osaka in the semi-finals and their players were running around everywhere, so quick, scoring three goals at the end of the game, although we won 5–3. The final was against Liga de Quito and the manager went with his South American players Tevez, Rafael and Anderson. But, in the cold of Yokohama, it was Wayne Rooney who stood out. When Nemanja was sent off, I saw the real Wayne Rooney. He was everywhere, on the left with me, he was defending more than me. He also scored the only goal. I thanked him for his performance after the match. He did that for the team because he really wanted to be world champion.

Wayne won a car for being man of the match, which he sold to Gary Neville. It was an early electric car and Gary liked the idea because he was into renewable energy. We joked that he could drive for a whole year for £10.

I could play in Japan but I was banned from playing in England because of my incident with the Chelsea groundsman, yet once that was all over, the boss would use what I'd done as a positive and tell the players, 'Look at Patrice, he's only four foot tall and he's not afraid of anyone. He's not giving in to anyone. He's a fighter. Now, what about the rest of you?'

In Europe, we played Inter Milan in the Champions League and drew 0–0 away in the first leg. A week later, we beat Spurs on penalties to win the Carling Cup final. If you count the Community Shield, that was our third trophy of the season – and it was 1 March. The winning machine was coming together just when it mattered.

When we played Inter at home in the second leg, I had big arguments with Zlatan Ibrahimovic, Walter Samuel and Mario Balotelli – all in the same game. Balotelli was on the floor, complaining about a foul, and he looked at me and started saying something. He didn't know he was getting subbed, so I indicated that he should turn around because his bench was calling him. The fans were laughing, Balotelli was not.

We won 2–0 and I walked towards the tunnel, holding my shirt up with my chest pumped out. It was in a nice way, to show my pride at the performance, not in an arrogant way, but that was not how one of my opponents saw it. Zlatan Ibrahimovic came by me and said: 'Hey, breathe.' It was his way of telling me to relax.

'Breathe?' I said. 'You are going to watch the Champions League on your sofa. You are going to watch me play from home.' I said it in Italian, which I knew Zlatan spoke. He looked at me and didn't say anything. During the game when I went for a ball and touched it, Zlatan came across me and I felt how strong he was. Zlatan was like Cantona, proud and arrogant in a self-assured way. I prefer to play against a man like that and even if I argue with them, I can still respect them. And I respected Zlatan.

Walter Samuel, that great Argentinian central defender, did

react to my comments to Zlatan. Maybe he didn't realise I spoke English as well as Italian. He started shouting that he was going to kill me. We started to fight in the tiny passage between the two dressing rooms at Old Trafford. For one of the biggest stadiums in the world, there's not a lot of space around the dressing rooms, which are next to each other.

Ferguson saw everything. Samuel kept on threatening me, I was laughing at him and telling him to enjoy the rest of the Champions League from his sofa. I think the English call this type of confrontation 'handbags'. I can see why he thought I was being arrogant because I was, but after all I had been celebrating in front of my own fans after we'd beaten Inter, the champions of Italy on a run of five successive title wins. Under Jose Mourinho, they were tough, hard to get space against. They had Balotelli, Zlatan, Stankovic, Cambiasso, Zanetti, Maicon and Santon. They would be strong enough to win the Champions League a year later. But in 2009, Manchester United had beaten them with goals from Nemanja and Cristiano and knocked them out. We were now in the quarter-final against Porto.

Arguments between players are normal. I honestly bore no grudges against opponents. Well, apart from James Milner. I hated to play against him. He defended more than me and he wasn't even a defender. He worked harder than any player I'd played against. I couldn't breathe when I got the ball because he was always just about to tackle me. When I didn't have the ball he would run at me. I needed two weeks to recover after playing against Milner, with his big English heart and never-say-die attitude. I used to check which club he was playing for at the start of the season so I'd know when I'd be up against him. When he joined City he became even better because he had better players around him. That meant even less space for me because he followed me everywhere. I even had to check he wasn't in my car when I left the ground after a match.

When Liverpool came to Old Trafford three days after that Inter game, we were flying at the top of the league and had won 11 consecutive league matches, recovering from our poor start to the season. Liverpool won 4-1, they hammered us. But I still think some good came from that defeat because we left the field and instead of booing us, the fans were clapping us and singing for us at the end. I was ashamed, yet so proud. We could still hear the fans inside the dressing room.

'Can you hear them?' asked the manager. Everybody nodded.

'Make sure we win the fucking league for them,' said the boss. The bond between the fans and the players was so strong, we played for them, we gave everything for them, not just ourselves.

That result caused us to wobble, and we lost unexpectedly to Fulham a week later and slipped to second in the table behind Liverpool. We had to win against Aston Villa, despite being under strength. Ronaldo scored a free kick from inside the box but then Villa started to play, to counter-attack us well, and they drew level. After 13 minutes of the second half Villa took the lead. We brought on Federico 'Kiko' Macheda, a 17-year-old. Ronaldo equalised but we needed three points, not one. Then Macheda scored. What a moment for him. That goal made the whole team feel like we were going to win the league.

We were winning again and we never stopped until we won the league, but things didn't work out so well for Kiko. While the goal was important, I don't think it helped him. Expectations shot up and he became a hero to the fans over-night, but if United fans have a fault, it's that they build up a player too much. They would do the same with Adnan Januzaj years later because they were desperate for these young players to be the saviour, especially if they had come through the club's academy.

The senior players get used to the fans singing their names, but the kids can get carried away. If they're not careful, they become surrounded by new friends telling them how great they are, how they are already legends. You need to win four trophies before you have the chance to be called a legend. Young players can think they have made it to the top of the mountain when they are merely at the bottom. I helped Kiko a lot, he's a good kid from a tough background in Rome and I felt that I had to try and protect him, but he didn't have the same hunger in training as he'd had in the short time before he'd got into the first team. He should have pushed himself harder.

But it's not easy for a young player who goes from nowhere to playing in United's first team. They benefit from a lot of goodwill from United fans and even get named man of the match when they're not, but not all their teammates are delighted for them, especially those whose places are threatened. If you're taking someone's place, they're going to tackle you hard in training.

Gabriel Obertan, such a talented player from France, told me that it was easy to play for United after one good game. He wasn't being arrogant, he meant it was easy because you're playing with so many good players, because you can focus on attack and not defence. 'It's easy to play one good game,' I replied, 'but trust me it's the most difficult place to be consistent because you have to win every game and that brings enormous pressure.' Gabriel was dropped after a few games and sold to Newcastle.

Now we were up against Porto in the Champions League last eight. Not a team of stars; nonetheless they were technically excellent and they understood each other and all knew their roles. I marked Hulk in the home leg, which we drew 2-2. He was really strong, but even though I was smaller than him, I annoyed him. I was happy with how I played, if not the result. But Porto's 89th-minute equaliser meant they had two away goals.

The away game was where Ronaldo showed his quality. Again, it was tight. United were the European champions, but Porto were favourites after the result in the first leg. We needed a game changer, we needed Ronaldo. He took a shot after six minutes from so far away that I thought: 'I know we need to score, but why are you shooting from there?' It flew in, a magic moment, one of the best. Ferguson's eyes that night were full of admiration for Ronaldo. I looked at Ferguson that night in the dressing room and saw how he realised that he had the best player in the world in his side. I think Cristiano knew it too and that self-confidence, that self-belief, was an important part of his make-up.

The draw threw up an all-English Champions League semi-final, against Arsenal, but we had huge games every week. We lost to Everton in the FA Cup semi-final on another trip to Wembley – our third of the season – when I came on as a substitute because we played some of the fringe players. I was angry, I wanted to start the game. It was the semi-final of the FA Cup, not a friendly match, but the manager wanted to rest some of us because we were fighting for another league title and to retain the Champions League. We drew 0-0 and lost 2-4 on penalties. It still annoys me that I never won the FA Cup.

The two Arsenal semi-finals still make me smile because Arsenal thought that they played well. We battered them at Old Trafford in the first leg but only won 1-0 when John O'Shea, always reliable, got our goal. Ferguson was relaxed because he knew that if we played the same in the second leg at the Emirates, we would kill them. The players felt the same. Ando would announce: 'We kill Arsenal,' and everyone would laugh. Our mad Brazilian was still learning English and would come out with all kinds of phrases like 'My car no fly.' We loved him and he had some of his best games against Arsenal. The media favoured Arsenal. Had they actually watched the first leg?

Sir Alex was at his best. He said this Arsenal team was not as good as their team from 1999, which was involved in some of the greatest games in United's history. We did kill Arsenal, with two goals in the first 11 minutes. Their stadium was even quieter than usual, but in the corner 3,000 United fans were going crazy. They knew they were going to Rome for a final against Chelsea or Barcelona.

'This is football,' I thought. 'This is beautiful.' The way Ronaldo, Ji and Wayne counter-attacked was wonderful to see. Darren Fletcher was sent off and would miss the final. He was devastated because of that fucking referee. Fletcher had the passion to be a United player. I thought he was a Mancunian, but when I found out he was Scottish, I thought: 'Ah, that's why Fergie likes him so much.' Fletcher would die for the club and always fought his balls off. He never complained. He was living his dream playing for the club. He worked so hard and was hardly ever mentioned, yet he was so important to that team. You might laugh at me if I say Fletch is a legend, but he was.

I passed by Arsenal's Mikaël Silvestre when I left the field. 'Men against babies,' I said. He couldn't disagree. In the mixed zone afterwards, a French journalist said to me: 'It was 3-1 but the score didn't reflect the game.'

'Are you serious?' I replied. Then I spoke my mind, which made headlines.

'It was 11 men against 11 children,' I said. 'We never doubted ourselves. We have much more experience and that's what made the difference. We were always confident. It should have been that score in the first leg anyway. It is a great United team that won.

'Football today is not only about playing well, it's about winning trophies. Everybody talks about the way Arsenal play but, at the end of the day, it's about winning silverware. At United, we play well and we win. Tactically and technically we were

Patrice, aged three.

In my brief drug-dealing days,
showing off my pager.

Our house in Les Ulis.

I pretended this VW Polo was my car, but
it was way out of my league at the time.

On holiday in Tunisia, my first trip abroad, when I was wowed by girls wearing bikinis.

My first days as a professional footballer and a dream come true – I'd never been given a new kit before. Pre-season training in the mountains with Marsala.

The price of staying up was blond hair. The deal was that, if I stayed at Marsala throughout the season and we stayed up, I'd have to have my hair dyed blond like the captain, Nino Barraco.

I'd told my Nice teammates that I planned to play in the Stade Louis II, and, in 2002, I got my chance – but it wasn't always a painless experience. *(PA)*

I loved my time at Monaco. We had such an exciting team, a great manager and I really began to be noticed. *(Getty Images)*

Keeping my eye on the ball, as manager Didier Deschamps had advised when facing Real Madrid's Ronaldo, as we set up a Champions League semi-final tie against Chelsea. *(Getty Images)*

Consoled by Deschamps after losing the 2004 Champions League final to Porto. *(PA)*

With my parents, Tim, and Prince Albert of Monaco.

A year on from our 8-3 win, we meet Deportivo La Coruña again. We were so entertaining to watch and French people loved us, just like I'd once loved Monaco as a child. *(Getty Images)*

Battling it out with Ji-Sung Park of PSV in February 2005. Within a year, both of us would be lining up for Manchester United. *(PA)*

After our defeat to Italy saw us knocked out of Euro 2008, in a tournament filled with divisions, our manager Raymond Domenech (right) proposed to his long-term girlfriend. *(Getty Images)*

Flying over Shay Given during our World Cup play-off match at Croke Park.
(Getty Images)

Sharing a joke with Thierry Henry (another product of Les Ulis) and Nicolas Anelka at our training camp before the World Cup in South Africa. *(Getty Images)*

A proud moment leading out the team for France's first game in the 2010 World Cup finals. Little did I know that a storm was about to break. *(PA)*

Speaking to the squad after we had decided not to train on 20 June, after Nicolas Anelka had been sent home and tensions within the set-up boiled over. *(Getty Images)*

superior. You look at our starting eleven and theirs and you see that we are well above. Lots of people are disappointed because they thought they would beat us like they did in the league. But the Champions League is another level.'

Read that another way and it can sound arrogant, but I didn't mean it to. I didn't choose the 'Arsenal are children' or 'Babies taught a lesson' headlines. Some of the Arsenal players were disappointed in me. Sagna and Adebayor were and even Silvestre said to me: 'Patrice, you shouldn't talk that way.'

I was told later that Arsène Wenger reminded them about what I had said before a game at Old Trafford in 2011 and the players said they were going to show me that they were men. We won 8-2! Many Arsenal fans don't like me because of what I said, but I do respect them as a club and I apologise if they feel insulted. I know they featured so many great French players like my friend Thierry Henry, Patrick Vieira, Robert Pires and Emmanuel Petit. I know they'd had a magnificent side who went a season undefeated too. But I honestly feel that when we played them it was like going to Disneyland. Everything was too easy, too enjoyable with their wonderful pitch. It was a feeling personal to me and maybe it was overconfidence, but I was convinced we would beat them every time, and we usually did. We were already champions by the time we played Arsenal in the last home game of the season. As for killing or even beating Arsenal, we drew 0-0, but we had our minds on bigger things.

We got it badly wrong against Barcelona in the Champions League final because we played the Man United way and we shouldn't have. There was no one more wrong than me. I was so confident that we would win. That wasn't me living in a United bubble, because even when I'd been with the French squad, I could see that the feeling was that United were the best team in Europe.

I also feel that Ferguson was too emotional. He played

Anderson and Ji-Sung Park and I think, unusually for a manager who put his head before his heart, they were emotional
decisions because he didn't want to disappoint either of them.
We knew that they would play three in the middle – Xavi,
Iniesta and Busquets. Anderson is not the player to chase the
ball when there are three of them with Lionel Messi dropping
back to help out. Ji played – I felt – as a reward because he'd
not played in Moscow.

We started really well and Ronaldo, in his last United game,
nearly scored. We played Ronaldo as a central striker because
the coaches felt he would be faster than Pique, especially on the
turn. That worked for the first ten minutes in which we had
three chances with a free kick and then two shots. Barça had
started with my old friend Messi wide on the right, Eto'o in the
middle and Thierry Henry wide left. I found that I could break
away from Messi on the left and get forward. I was delighted
with the start, but Barça quickly changed their shape. Guardiola
said that they'd done it to stop me. Messi moved into the centre,
in the hole. We struggled to deal with him, and when Barça
scored after ten minutes it changed everything. They taught us
a lesson about possession. I felt like they had an extra man, with
Eto'o moved right. I couldn't get near him.

None of us could get the ball. Then they scored the second – a
header! – from Messi of all people who was left unmarked and
jumped higher than I jump to fly towards the ball. Maybe we
should have respected ourselves more and played more possession football ourselves. It was a big slap in our face. I was really
pissed off and couldn't take the defeat in. I wanted to play the
game again the next day in Rome. I've blocked the rest of that
night out, I'm still in denial. I have no idea where my loser's
medal is. I think I threw it on the pitch – again.

We were the reigning world champions, the champions of
England, Carling Cup winners, and Champions League finalists

for the second successive year, yet we felt like failures. What must it be like for the rest who don't come close to success?

Cristiano left that summer, Carlos Tevez too. I knew Ronaldo was leaving. He'd told me that his father had wanted him to play for Real Madrid. Ferguson told me too. He said, 'We're losing the boy, he couldn't refuse.' Ronaldo was the best-paid player at United but he would become the best-paid at Madrid, and United would receive £80 million – easily the biggest transfer in the world at that time. Ronaldo has never felt at home like he did in Manchester, but look at what he achieved in Madrid.

I was more surprised about Tevez, my close friend, and I was really annoyed because he was a great player. There are two sides to every story. United had to keep a huge fee to keep him and give him a big pay rise. Players in the United dressing room were talking about the money they'd heard Carlos was on at City, but I know that Carlos was frustrated whenever he didn't play. He once thought he'd heard Ferguson making a joke about an Argentinian player. Carlos didn't like it and said: 'You know why you speak bad about him. Because you don't like Argentinian people. And that's why you don't play me.' Carlos said it in English. He didn't speak English well, but everyone understood what he'd said. Ferguson didn't reply. I don't think that he has any issue with Argentinian people. He wouldn't have bought players like Juan Veron, Heinze or Tevez if he did, but sometimes I think Carlos thought there was a mistrust of Argentinians because of the Falklands War.

All I know was that I didn't like Carlos joining City and I didn't like it when he was on the banner saying 'Welcome to Manchester' after he signed for City, and I called him.

'Carlito!' I said. 'What are you doing? This shirt isn't you! I have been to your house and you have a picture of yourself wearing a United shirt near your pool table! You are a Red, you know deep in your heart that you are a Red.' We joked a little and we stayed close friends. Ferguson didn't always like that, especially when he saw us pictured outside a restaurant in a newspaper. He didn't want his players associating with those from City, who were becoming a much stronger team, but I am not just a footballer, I am a man who is loyal to his friends, and Carlito was my friend.

Ronaldo and Tevez were replaced with Michael Owen, who was unfortunate with injuries, Gabriel Obertan, Mame Diouf and Antonio Valencia. Obertan and Diouf weren't close to being in Ronaldo's class. Who is? At least Antonio was a big success.

I was named in the UEFA team of the year for 2009 and the FIFA Pro XI too, but individual awards came a distant second.

My 2009-10 season started badly when I conceded a soft penalty in the Community Shield against Chelsea, which they won on penalties after the match ended in a draw. There was great pressure on Wayne Rooney to step up and become the most important United player. He'd been one reason why Ronaldo was so successful, putting the runs in out wide. Ronaldo did a lot for us, but we – and Wayne especially – did a lot for him. But Wayne was a magnificent player in his own right and scored 34 goals that season, yet we lost the Premier League crown we'd worn in 2007, 2008 and 2009.

We'd signed Dimitar Berbatov a year earlier. Seeing Berba on the pitch was like watching a beautiful woman. He was a pretty footballer, elegant with the best first touch. Dimi is shy and quiet, but I really warmed to him. I set myself a challenge to make him laugh, to make him my brother. It worked. He still calls me his 'brother from another mother' and we became great friends. He wanted to be an actor and asked me to get him tickets for the Cannes Film Festival. He's an artist, too. He is a very private person, but also very funny and intelligent. We stay in touch.

In September 2009, we took on Besiktas, in their open stadium on the banks of the Bosporus in Istanbul. Wow. I've never heard a noise like it; their fans were louder than any I've heard before. Even Sir Alex Ferguson applauded them at the end – after we'd won 1-0.

We played Manchester City at home the next week. When I'd joined United, City were not really our rivals. Liverpool was the biggest game, the one fans wanted to win and the one Ferguson told us was the biggest. Chelsea was a game for the players, the victory we needed to win the league. Arsenal was the game where we had fun. City? That dramatic 4–3 win made United kings of Manchester for the day.

We also drew City in the League Cup, the first leg away. City were good and Tevez scored twice in their 2-1 win. Then disaster struck before the second leg, when another City, Hull City came to Old Trafford. I was in the team hotel before the Hull game when my phone started ringing. My wife's father had died.

I went to Ferguson and told him what had happened and that I had to go to my wife immediately. I drove quickly to get home. We stayed awake all night. My wife was crying, which was understandable as she'd just lost her dad. But I was also crazy. I slept for maybe one hour and woke up at 7 am. Ferguson called me and I explained the situation. He said: 'Okay, you don't play today.'

'No,' I said, 'I play.' And I did. I played well and we won 4-0. Nothing can stop me when I want to play football.

I felt that my relationship with Fergie was exceptionally strong and I adored him. I looked on him as the most powerful man in football and I believed that he controlled everything at United, everything that made United so successful, but I never told him that to his face. Instead, I'd joke with him and ask him about some of his signings who'd not been too great.

'Boss, did you sign William Prunier?' I'd ask in front of my teammates. Prunier was a good defender in France, but didn't

work out at United. Fergie tried to ignore me, but everyone heard it.

'We had him on trial once,' he replied.

'On trial? For how long?'

'Two games.'

'A two-game trial?'

The boss wanted to kill me, but it was just me pulling his
leg. And maybe he'd wanted to send me back to France after
one United game.

We played City at home. I went up to Tevez on the pitch
before kick-off and said: 'Listen, Carlito, we are friends but
don't try and be nice with me. Don't shake my hand and think
that everything will be fine between us.' He was laughing and
replied that City were going to knock United out, but deep
down I think he still had a great affection for United. He once
told me that he would always respect United fans. I know he
was becoming a great player for City, I know he was a great
signing for them, but he'd won league titles and the Champions
League with United, he'd played in the best team in the world.
He couldn't just forget all that.

We beat them 3-1 in the second leg, with Wayne's header in
injury time sending us through to the final 4-3 on aggregate.
The atmosphere was amazing. I found Tevez again as we left
the pitch.

'Look, there had to be a winner,' I said. 'Make it hard for us
to win the league.'

City had become a really strong team with discipline. They
had lots of foreign players but they looked like a team. I liked
the competition they gave us because I like competition. It
makes you better.

That year was an important one for me. I was captain of
United and France. It was a World Cup year too so I wanted
to prepare well.

We played Aston Villa in the League Cup final and won 2-1. Ferguson said to me: 'Come on, son, you deserve it. Go take your team up those steps and lift the trophy.' It was more important to hear that from Ferguson than to lift the trophy. It was as if Ferguson had full faith in me as a player and as a captain. What a turnaround from that 2007 FA Cup final.

I climbed the steps at Wembley, and when I lifted the trophy I thought: 'The only other Frenchman to do this for United as captain at Wembley was Cantona.' I took the role of captain very seriously and felt that the players supported me. Sometimes there can be jealousy towards a captain, but I felt respect from the players, that they were happy for me. They knew that I would die for them on the pitch, that I wasn't about individual credit, that I wanted the best for them as well as for me. I would give a talk before games, and players would tell me 'you really motivated us.' I spoke at Wembley and explained that it was a chance for us to win another trophy for this great club, one which we had to work hard to reach the final of by beating Spurs and City. We wanted to carry on and win a fourth successive Premier League and the Champions League, but it wasn't to be. We weren't the side we'd been.

I also had off-the-field issues. Karen, who deals with the media at Manchester United, told me there was going to be a story in the *Sun* about me being unfaithful. I was in the United team hotel and Ferguson came in my room and asked: 'Do you know there's a story about you coming out tomorrow?'

'Yes, boss.'

'Do you want to play tomorrow?'

'I want to play. I'd rather play.' I played well, but that was the least of my worries.

In short, I'd been having an affair. My wife had been in France a lot. I was lonely. I started seeing someone else. I caused a lot of hurt and I'm not proud of myself. I damaged my wife's trust. I wasn't a guy chasing every woman. When you play for United and you are not ugly – and I'm not saying I'm beautiful, but I'm not ugly – there are always amazing temptations.

When you're on the front page, people talk about you. I went to training and could feel it. People were also sorry for me. I think Ferguson removed all the newspapers from the canteen, but everybody knew.

We beat AC Milan and played Bayern Munich managed by Louis van Gaal in the Champions League quarter-finals. We lost 2-1 in Munich and as we left the pitch Franck Ribéry said to me: '2-1, Patrice,' as if the job was done. 'Trust me,' I replied. 'You will see that Old Trafford will be a different story, a different atmosphere with more pressure for you. I know you can handle pressure but it will be completely different at Old Trafford.'

Sandwiched between the two games was Chelsea, the team pushing us hardest to take our title, at Old Trafford. This was one of those occasions that the manager called a squeaky-bum time.

'Beat Chelsea and you'll win the title,' he said. We lost 2-1 against a team that had similar personalities and character to our United team. We respected them as men. Didier Drogba scored a goal that was clearly offside.

We didn't have long to think about the defeat as we were preparing to come back from behind to beat Bayern Munich. We started that game so well at Old Trafford. We played fast, everyone was on top of their game and we scored three first-half goals, two from Nani and one from Darron Gibson – the first two inside seven minutes and Nani's second after 41. Then we conceded a shit goal just before the end of the first half. We tried to keep our heads up at half-time and we were still leading 4-3 in the tie, but when they scored that goal I knew it would have given them hope. Then I saw Ribéry's eyes in the tunnel and I could tell he was in awe of Old Trafford.

We had chances to make it 4-1 on the night but Rafael was sent off after a second yellow card. The manager was so angry with Rafa; we needed to stay as 11, but even with ten men we had chances. Robben's volley near the end changed everything. It was so painful, like someone had put a knife into my heart. I was playing in pain, I knew deep down we were going out and would miss out on a third successive Champions League final. I'd been convinced that we would win it, but now we were out on away goals, with the tie at 4-4.

Ribéry came up to me at the end. Frank and I get on well and he didn't glory in the victory. 'Wow,' he said again. 'The atmosphere was electric. And you deserved to win.'

'I told you,' I said, knowing that United were interesting in signing him. 'You should come here and you can be like Cantona.' He had the mentality to play for United. But Franck was happy in Munich, while his wife liked the idea of Real Madrid. He stayed in Munich where he did well, but not before United had tried to sign him. I kept telling the boss how good Franck was. He has a lot of energy and that can annoy people, but he's my type of man. He loved doing tricks and once put a bucket of water above a door so that it would fall on the head of Oliver Kahn after training.

The Bayern defeat killed us. People said we missed Cristiano – any team would miss Cristiano – but we went out to a very good Bayern side that reached the final. In the league we kept on winning, but it was enough for us to drop points against Blackburn so that Chelsea kept the advantage and beat us to the title by one point.

That was a bad way to end the season, but things were about to get much, much worse.

CHAPTER 9

Chaos in South Africa

Being made captain of the French national team a couple of months before the 2010 World Cup finals came as a complete surprise. I expected to play because I was now the established left back, but Thierry Henry had been their captain for a couple of years and William Gallas was vice-captain and considered Henry's natural replacement.

Henry and Domenech had had a chat about his future in the team. When I saw that he was not starting in the friendly games leading up to the World Cup, I thought that something was wrong and was a little concerned because Henry is like a brother to me. He's a private guy who doesn't open himself up too much to people, but I know him well, like him and trust him.

We're from the same part of Les Ulis and we shared a room when we played for the national team. I didn't know him in Les Ulis because he lived a kilometre away and that was like another continent in my little world, but I met him in a Milan restaurant when I played for Monza. Henry was with Edgar Davids, and I — a nobody starting out in football — approached those two big stars. Both were friendly and Thierry was pleased to learn that I was from Les Ulis and had made it as a professional player. They were two good examples for me to follow. Thierry has never lost touch with his roots and he paid for an artificial football pitch close to where he grew up in Les Ulis so that future generations of footballers can practice on a far better surface than I did.

When I joined the French squad in 2004, Thierry introduced me to the rest of the players as 'the new left back of the national team'. It was meant to be a light-hearted comment, but Bixente Lizarazu, the existing left back, was not impressed. He turned and asked, without smiling: 'Didn't someone tell you that I've already returned?'

Not once did Lizarazu shake my hand or speak to me in all my time with the national team. I didn't make the squad that travelled to Euro 2004 and then coach Jacques Santini explained to me: 'I can say nothing bad about you, but I prefer to take Lizarazu and Desailly because they are more experienced than you.' I accepted that.

But by 2010 I was a mainstay. I'd played in the two play-off games against the Republic of Ireland to reach the finals. Those games were so tense; we felt a lot of pressure despite drawing away in the first leg. There was a negative atmosphere in Paris for the second leg and the travelling Irish fans were much louder than the rest of the stadium. With the score 0-0 at half-time, I spoke to the players in the dressing room and announced: 'Guys, we are just shitting ourselves. If we don't show our balls then we're not going to the World Cup.'

We went through after that controversial goal, when Henry controlled the ball with his hand in extra time. I was angry with the French people and the way they treated Henry after that. They said he was a cheat, that he should never play again. He didn't even score from the handball, it was William Gallas who got the goal that knocked Ireland out. I understood why the Irish people criticised him because they were so disappointed at not going to the World Cup, but not people in France. Henry felt isolated and down, and I supported him publicly, saying we should put up a statue of him for what he'd done in football.

When I'd returned to United after that game, journalists asked me if I thought it should be replayed. I joked that it should be replayed on a PlayStation, and received a lot of criticism in Ireland for this, but again I was joking.

I think Domenech remembered my speech against Ireland at half-time. Why else would he have wanted me to be captain? What else was he thinking when he approached me before we played a game against Tunisia in May 2010 and said: 'Patrice, you are captain.'

I was stunned but my first reaction was to think about my friend William Gallas. I walked into the dressing room and picked up the armband with 'CAPITAINE' written on the French tricolour. I looked at Gallas and saw his face change. That's the shit I didn't want. Even close friends asked me why I was captain and not Gallas. We played the game and drew 1-1. At least Gallas scored the goal, but he was grumpy in training and I can understand why – the manager had not explained to him that he wasn't going to be captain. I went to speak to my friend.

'William,' I said, 'I want to make sure that you know I knew nothing about being captain.' Gallas told me that he had no problem with me but that the manager should have respected him. He was right, but how could I refuse to be captain of France? Imagine the reaction if I'd said no.

Ten days later, Gallas and I were fine. He's a good man and was a soldier on the field, someone who could see things on a pitch before they happened, that anticipation only a few of the top players have. He had high standards and always wanted everything to be perfect so that he could be at his best. Some could misread that as him being bad-tempered, but he was

merely being ultra-professional. I wasn't prepared for our friend-
ship to be destroyed just because I'd been given the armband.

I was very proud to be captain of my country and determined
to do my best, but I took the role too much to heart and got
far too emotionally involved. I wanted to be like Napoleon, a
heroic French leader. The initial media reaction to me being
given the captaincy was positive, and with the great players we
had there was some optimism ahead of the World Cup finals,
but there were big issues which people outside our camp were
unaware of.

We had too many players who were main men at their clubs
and used to getting their own way. It was impossible for them
all to go on doing that and play exactly where they wanted for
France. With so many egos, we needed a very strong boss, a
Ferguson type to control everything, because while we didn't
openly clash with each other, there wasn't enough unity on
the pitch.

Our families were with us in Tunisia for that trip – a chance
for us to spend some time together before the World Cup – but
now I had the armband officially for the first time, it was far
from relaxing. Nicolas Anelka, probably my best friend in the
team along with Abidal, Gallas and Henry, came to see me and
told me: 'Pat, I'm going home. I feel something's wrong, that
something bad will happen. I don't like the way we play with a
lone striker. I don't want to go to the World Cup.'

'Nico, come on,' I said. Then I persuaded him to stay and
thought that I had sorted things out. With hindsight, knowing
what happened later, maybe I should have let him do what he
wanted and leave the squad.

I had plenty of other issues to deal with as captain. Yoann
Gourcuff was a big problem for me. He had a perfect image
as the pretty French boy and the cultured footballer. He'd just
been named the best player in Ligue 1, the new Zidane. In the

France squad, he cut quite a lonely, shy figure and would eat alone rather than with the group. One time when he did sit with us, Henry said to him: 'Man City want you. You should come to the Premier League, it's tough but you could do well there.'

In a really soft voice he replied: 'I am fine in France. I have to keep working hard. I don't think I have the level yet to play for City.' We couldn't understand that. He was lacking confidence, and Ribéry, Henry and I laughed at him and thought he was too soft. That leaked out to the media as a story that we were bullying him, the black street gangsters ganging up on the perfect, white, middle-class French boy, the son of a football manager. I refute that absolutely.

Many players had issues with Gourcuff – not because of his personality but because they wanted him to perform better. You could see that Gourcuff didn't want the ball in training, and some players asked me to speak to him about it. I don't blame Gourcuff for feeling like that because it was an unforgiving environment for everyone. Miss a pass in training and players would scream at you, the same as it was at Man United. It's tough at the top and you have to take it, but Gourcuff retreated into his shell.

Our next pre-World Cup friendly was against China on the French Indian Ocean island of Réunion, which was en route to South Africa. The locals were delighted that we were going to play there, but the stop-off was a disaster.

We stayed in a beautiful hotel with a view of the sea and began to relax and feel like we were on holiday. Then we trained, for two hours in the rain, too much for a session before the game. We suspected we would be fucked for the next day, and we were as we lost 1-0.

I tried to be positive when I spoke to the media afterwards, to say that it was only a friendly. Then I went into the dressing room, changed my tone completely and announced: 'Come on, guys. That was shit.' Some answered me back and said – rightly – 'Don't you remember how hard we trained yesterday?'

A few started to say: 'We are in shit,' and a defeatist attitude began to develop. Players blamed the manager for not having a real structure of play or tactics, for the wrong training schedule, but I wasn't that worried as we flew to our hotel for the finals by the ocean on the Garden Route in Knysna, South Africa. I thought that this was just normal player grousing and that it would be sorted out as the squad began to gel.

The hotel was amazing, local people danced and sang for us when we arrived, but we felt disconnected from the rest of South Africa, like we were in a bunker away from the real country. It was like being in a reality show away from the rest of the world. I wanted to have some contact with French fans, who'd tell us how far they'd travelled and how much they'd spent getting there. I didn't want fans in our hotel all the time, but some contact can be positive and provide motivation.

As we hung around together, watching TV and joking, the mood had become largely positive again. The players had at least some unity from living side by side in the hotel, but less so on the training pitch. As captain I was listening to problems every single day, with players coming to me every hour with their grievances and fears. Nobody told me that you have to become a social worker when you become the captain of France.

One teammate said we should be training more, another that we should be training less, one that we should play this formation, another that we should play that formation. One player complained that everyone shouted at him when he passed the ball, another that nobody passed to him. One player was annoyed about what another had said in an interview, another that teammates were ignoring him. And I'd – maybe naively – thought we were doing okay!

I had a big capacity for dealing with problems, but being

captain could be a real pain and I had little time to think about my own game and preparation. I was being fed too much negativity from hearing people's worries every day and was struggling to transfer that into positive energy. On more than one occasion, my teammates said to me: 'Patrice, you look like shit.' Nobody had ever said that to me before.

Thierry Henry told me to think about my own football and reminded me that I was not the team's babysitter, that some of the players were adults and family men. He was right, of course, but in my mind I was still thinking: 'I will die for this team, I will take the first bullet for them, I am the captain.' I think I was a popular captain, but the griping continued. One player wanted to know why Gourcuff didn't speak out and say that he wasn't being bullied, which was still a big issue in the French media. Fresh accusations were being made, this time against Franck Ribéry. I went to Yoann and said: 'Can you please say that it's not true what the media is saying about you being bullied by Franck?'

He replied: 'There's no problem, but I never speak to the media.'

The suspicion was that someone was advising him to say nothing so that he could play the victim if anything went wrong. The result was that many players were really angry with Gourcuff for not setting things straight. I wasn't, that was his right.

There was a far more significant problem before our first game, against Uruguay in Cape Town. Florent Malouda was moaning in training when Djibril Cissé, who was playing for the other team, got the ball off him. Malouda tackled Cissé badly to win it back and Cissé went to the ground and screamed. We thought it was serious and so did the manager, who shouted at Malouda and told him to leave training. Malouda was really angry and watched the rest from the side. An hour before the team line-up was given out in our first game, Domenech called me and Thierry Henry in to see him and declared that we should tell Malouda that he wouldn't start against Uruguay.

'He could have broken Cissé's leg,' he explained. 'I won't accept that.'

'But boss, it's not for us to tell him,' I said. 'You are the manager and I think that's up to you.'

'You think I should tell him?' snapped Domenech. Henry and I looked at each other, surprised. I asked the boss if he was sure he was making the right decision because Malouda had been playing in the run-up to the World Cup and was an important, talented player. I also told him that I didn't think we should do it and we refused, and the result was that no one spoke to Malouda.

Before the team was announced, I asked Diaby, who was 24 and inexperienced at international level, 'Are you ready?'

'Yes, I'm always ready,' he replied. I didn't tell him that he was starting, but I wanted to put the thought into his mind.

The team was unveiled on a board at a team meeting at our hotel, and Malouda was furious when he didn't see his name. He stared ahead, not speaking to anyone. I could understand how he felt, we were all very surprised, but also determined to play well in Cape Town, a spectacular stadium in a spectacular setting between Table Mountain and the ocean.

It was the second game of the whole competition and there was a lot of focus on us. We drew 0-0 against a talented Uruguay team with Diego Forlan, the player of the tournament, and Luis Suarez, who I would later come across when he moved to Liverpool. Uruguay were strong enough to reach the semi-finals. Not that we played badly. We were the better team and we had chances to win. It wasn't the ideal start, but neither was it a disaster and things seemed pretty normal after we flew back to the team hotel at Knysna.

We would have six days until our next game, against Mexico in Polokwane in the north-east. Despite the arguments, there was nothing noticeably wrong. Okay, players were continually complaining about tactics, and Anelka was again asking to play with another striker, such as Henry. He asked me and he also asked Domenech, who said: 'It's my decision, Henry won't play.'

Gourcuff was still a problem. One player specifically came up to me and said: 'Patrice, you have to go to the manager and say that Gourcuff should not play.'

I'd had enough of this particular topic. 'Stop killing me,' I replied. 'I am the captain, but I will never fucking go to the manager and say that one of my teammates shouldn't play. Are you crazy, asking me to do this?'

It didn't stop there. He discussed it with other players and soon three or four of them were on my back. 'Why are you protecting Gourcuff when you know he's a pussy?' they demanded.

'Guys, don't say this to me,' was my reply.

But I did think that I had to speak to Domenech about Anelka, who I knew was deeply unhappy at playing up front alone. I went to see Anelka before the game and told him I would put his concerns to the manager. Before I had even opened my mouth to speak to Domenech, he snapped: 'I know what you want! You want me to cut the head off the lamb. Gourcuff is not playing tomorrow.'

'No, boss, I didn't come to see you about this. I came to speak to you about Anelka who needs support in his position. I think if you play Henry, Gignac or Cissé, it will help.'

'No,' he replied firmly. 'I am the boss, I will decide. But I know Gourcuff is the main problem and you will see that he's not playing.'

I suspected that another player had told the manager what the feeling about Gourcuff was. In our next training session, the manager passed a starting bib to another player, which Gourcuff took to mean that he wouldn't start. Without that pressure, he suddenly played like Zidane. Gourcuff was laughing with Gignac on the bus back from training.

'Yoann,' I said, 'you seem happy that you are not playing. You were brilliant in training when you found out you were not playing.'

'There's too much pressure,' he replied softly. 'It's better this way.' I had to admire his honesty, but as captain I wanted soldiers, fighters. I couldn't understand why he appeared happier not to have been selected.

We played against Mexico, with Malouda in for Gourcuff. We weren't playing well, but had gone in at half-time with the game at 0-0. Domenech came into the dressing room and said nothing. For ten minutes there was silence. Nobody spoke.

'Fucking hell, Nico!' shouted Domenech suddenly. 'What did I tell you? Don't come to the ball and just go into the channel!' There was silence and Anelka looked stunned.

'Okay,' he replied in a very quiet voice. 'Get to fuck with your team. I won't play for your team.' It was very rude, but let's get this straight: he didn't tell him to fuck off. Domenech couldn't have heard what Anelka was saying correctly because he was talking so quietly, I'm sure of that.

'You won't come on,' continued Domenech to Anelka, who then started taking his boots off.

I stood up and shouted. 'Guys! Are we joking? It's 0-0. We can still get through. Nobody has beaten us yet; nobody has even scored against us. I can't believe we're throwing this away. Why are we fucking arguing? Shame on us! Everyone is counting on us and we're doing this at half-time. Nico, you have to keep playing.' Domenech, who was angry, stayed silent when I said this. I felt he was agreeing with me, but that was only my interpretation.

Amid the shambles and chaos, Anelka started to put his

boots back on, but as the players started to leave to go back onto the pitch, one of the other coaches said to Anelka: 'No, he [Domenech] has already sent Gignac to warm up.' Nico was visibly upset.

We fell apart in the second half. Mexico scored twice, the first from a man who was about to be my new United teammate, the substitute Javier Hernandez. We were fucked and we were probably out of the World Cup – such a shame given the talent in our squad.

As the players returned to the dressing room, there was silence, like someone had died. I didn't say anything. There was huge tension, a really bad atmosphere. You knew that if someone spoke then everyone would fight each other, because we were all pissed off, pumped full of adrenalin and anger. I was deeply frustrated. We had so many top players and, while Mexico were a good side, we had enough to beat them.

I spoke to some journalists, as was my duty as captain, and talked about taking the responsibility as captain for what had happened. What else could I say? We'd done the damage to ourselves on and off the pitch.

We flew from Cape Town back to Knysna in near-silence for the hour-long flight. The team spirit had been smashed and I was really down. I felt for Anelka, for Domenech, for all the players and for France, yet the storm was only beginning. The argument at half-time should have stayed within the dressing room and been sorted out. It was bad, but I'd often heard players in the heat of the moment say far worse things that they'd regret.

Instead, I woke up the following morning with my team-mates asking me if I'd seen the front page of *L'Equipe*. A phone with a photo of the cover was thrust in front of me, showing Anelka with the quote: 'Go and fuck your mother, son of a bitch.' Wow! There were no asterisks. That was what they reported Anelka had said at half-time. Except it wasn't, because Anelka didn't say that.

Jean-Pierre Escalettes, the president of the French Football Federation, called me, as did Domenech. They both explained that Anelka was to go back to France, that they didn't want him in South Africa any more. I asked why and they said it was because of the incident in the dressing room. They also told me that people above them had made the decision.

'You can't send Anelka home, it won't be good for the team,' I replied. 'I'm scared how the team will react.' I begged Domenech to stop it and said that I would get Anelka to apologise for his attitude. He appeared to accept that on condition that Anelka made a public apology to him in front of the TV cameras. He told me to go and speak to Anelka, so I went to Anelka's room.

'Nico,' I said, 'I know you are a proud man but please do what the manager asked you to do, for the benefit of the team, just say sorry to Domenech on TV. If you respect me as a captain then you should do it.'

Nico shook his head and said: 'No chance. I would consider doing it privately, but not on television.'

I called Henry and Abidal, asking them to come and help me. We sat talking to Nico in his room and repeated the request for him to apologise, telling him that when a manager speaks you should not question his authority. A player has to shut his mouth, yet Anelka had not said what was being reported.

'Okay, Patrice, I will,' he finally replied. 'Call the manager.' We asked the head of security to find Domenech and explain that Nico wanted to apologise. He went to find the manager and we waited . . . and waited. We heard nothing after ten minutes, 30 minutes, an hour.

'You see, Patrice, they just want to blame me,' said Anelka. Mohamed 'Momo' Sanhadji, the head of security, wasn't answering his phone and so I went to find the manager myself. Eventually, I found him upstairs having a drink with Escalettes. He looked exhausted.

'Patrice, it's too late,' Domenech said before I had a chance to speak. 'People above me have made the decision to send him home.'

My face dropped.

'I know,' said Domenech.

'It's a big mistake,' I replied.

'I can do nothing. It has been decided by people above me and above the French Football Federation.'

'But the people above them are the government,' I said. 'Who wants Nico to go home? The president of the French Republic?' He didn't reply. 'The government want him gone,' I said. I was convinced that the deeply offensive front page had spooked the government, that France wanted a scapegoat for us going out of the World Cup.

I returned to Nico's room. Five minutes later, Momo came in and told Nico that his flight ticket was booked and that he had a few minutes to pack his bags. Nico was being treated like a piece of shit. I told Momo that we would like a meeting to say goodbye to Nico. It was becoming a World Cup of meetings. Word quickly went around the players and we met in our team room in the hotel.

'Listen, guys,' I said as I stood up. 'I have to tell you the news that Nico is being sent home. The French Federation has decided this.'

The response was instant. 'No way!' 'Fuck off!' 'We don't play!' 'We don't play the last game against South Africa!'

'We can't do that, guys,' I said.

One young player said: 'We shouldn't train tomorrow. That will show that we are behind Anelka, who is being punished for something he did not say.' The idea won approval.

Anelka wasn't a bad boy, he was a brother to us, he was prepared to say sorry to all of us and the manager. Trust me, it's not easy to get Nico, a very proud man, to do this. But he was a straight man, he was not a snake who would go behind your back.

There was a problem with cancelling training the next day as local kids had been invited to see us train. We had seen some local people on the trip and visited a township, but even that didn't go to plan. Instead of giving the kids real presents that could improve their lives, we gave them pencils. I was embarrassed and spoke to Momo about it. We gave him some money to buy some food, which was appreciated.

We agreed that we would go to training, sign autographs and have photographs taken with the kids, but not train. I asked the guys in the team three times if they were happy with the plan. Everyone said yes, nobody said they were not. We then said goodbye to Nico. I was sad to see him go, to see his face as he got in the car to travel to the airport for the long journey home. I feared for him going back to France and being abused for France's failure in the World Cup. I also feared for his family, who might also bear the brunt.

But we had to carry on. The atmosphere in the team was sad but defiant, united and revolutionary. I held a press conference with Escalettes, with whom I had a positive relationship. I was still angry that someone would leak such a damaging lie from the dressing room and did a crazy interview where I said we had to find who had set Nico up.

'The problem is not Anelka, it's the traitor among us who told the press what was said,' I said. 'There's somebody in our group that wants to harm the France team.'

We didn't know who had done this. We heard that *L'Equipe* called the manager at 3 am and told him about what was going to be on the front page. Domenech was still awake reading and we understood his reply was: 'I don't care.' He must have felt the damage had already been done.

Everyone there will have their version of the truth. This is mine and the players respected me for sticking up for them.

While events in Knysna were dominating the media, our World Cup was not yet over. We still had a small chance of qualifying for the knockout stage if we beat South Africa, a team much weaker than us, though they had the advantage of playing at home and the advantage that the country was behind them after they'd started the competition well. Winning wasn't impossible, but a lot more would happen before that final group game in Bloemfontein.

After Nico's departure, the tension was still there the next day when we met for lunch and, rather than sitting as one group, the manager and his staff sat separately from all the players and waited for us to finish before eating. After the manager had eaten, he called over me and another player, who said to him, face to face: 'You are disgusting, you kill my joy in playing football. I will never play for you again.'

'Don't say that,' I said to him, feeling that he was being too strong.

Domenech, who actually liked the player, said: 'I think you are making a mistake. Imagine how the French people will react.'

I warned my teammate: 'You should consider this because you will get hammered.' But I couldn't shift him, and Domenech accepted his decision. That player did not feature against South Africa. When he left the room, Domenech turned to me. 'What's happening with the team? I see that something is happening. What is the atmosphere like?'

'It's a disaster,' I replied. 'Shit.'

'So what have you decided to do?' he questioned me, suspecting we were planning some kind of protest.

'I will never cheat on my teammates and tell you what we are going to do, but something will happen.'

'I don't know what you have prepared, but don't be stupid,' replied Domenech. 'Remember that there are cameras outside.'

I went to join my teammates who were waiting on the team bus. None of us were wearing boots as we should have been for a training session, but normal trainers. I was handed a note of neatly typed paper in perfect French that the players wanted me to read in front of the cameras. I felt like they were saying: 'Come on, Patrice, you walk into the fire and if you die then you'll still be a hero.'

On the paper were the words 'We are not going to train', together with a list of reasons why. When the bus came to a stop and with the players still on board, Domenech took the paper from me and I explained that we wouldn't train because of the situation with Nico.

'Patrice, you are crazy,' he told me.

'I know, boss, but this is the team's decision. As the captain, I have to respect it.'

Domenech handed the paper to the fitness coach, Robert Duverne, saying, 'Look what these crazy guys want to do.'

The players left the bus and went to sign autographs for the kids. Duverne, a good guy, walked with me behind the other players. He was furious and shouted as he said: 'I closed my practice so that I could come to this World Cup and I have lost money.' He threw his accreditation badge on the floor. I told him to calm down and explained that all the cameras were watching.

'I don't care!' he said. He was furious.

'Calm down,' I replied. Journalists watched on, aware that there was a problem as the players eventually walked onto the training pitch and stood in a circle.

'Are you sure you want to do this?' I asked them. 'Sure you don't want to do some running as a token show of training?'

They were sure and so we walked back to the bus and got on. The driver had already turned on the engine, when the head of the security took the keys off the bus and gave them to Domenech. After a minute or so, the players became agitated because the bus wasn't moving. I got off and asked Momo if we could leave to go back to the hotel.

'The manager says that nobody is leaving,' he replied.

It was as if we had been hijacked and held hostage, especially when the players started to close the curtains so that we couldn't be filmed. Representatives from the players' federation, the LFP, came onto the bus and begged us: 'Please, you don't know what you're doing. Please go to training.'

I stood firm. 'We respect you, but it's a team decision.'

Domenech came onto the bus with the paper in his hands.

'Okay, guys. Are you sure you don't want to get off the bus?' Everyone said yes.

'I'll give you five minutes to think about your decision,' he continued.

'You don't need to give us five minutes,' I said. 'We want to go back to the hotel.'

'Okay,' he said. 'You think you are men, but now I will take the paper and read it to the cameras.'

It was then that differences of opinion started to emerge among the players.

'You read it, Patrice,' shouted one player. 'Don't let him because he won't read what is on the paper.'

Like a stupid man, I said I would read it, but I didn't because Domenech had already left the bus and was reading it out to the media. I asked the players again if they were all in support of not training.

'If someone wants to get off the bus – just one person – then we all get off the bus.'

Nobody did.

I said it again. Nobody did.

I said it a third time, and Gourcuff said in his soft voice, 'But guys, are we going to be okay if we don't train?' He was feeling the pressure, but I was prepared to follow him off the bus if he wasn't comfortable.

'Don't be a pussy,' shouted a voice – in a gentle rather than bullying way. Players were relaxed and laughing. There were no threats.

This is the statement that Domenech read out:

'All players in the France squad without exception want to declare their opposition to the decision taken by the French Football Federation to exclude Nicolas Anelka from the squad.

'If we regret the incident which occurred at half-time of the match between France and Mexico, we regret even more the leak of an event which should have remained within the group and which is quite common in a high-level team.

'At the request of the squad the player in question attempted to have dialogue but his approach was ignored. For its part the French Football Federation has at no time tried to protect the squad. It has made a decision [to send Anelka home] without consulting all the players, on the basis of the facts reported by the press.

'Accordingly, and to mark the opposition to those at the highest level of French football, all the players decided not to train today. Out of respect for the public who came to attend training, we decided to go to meet the fans who, by their presence, showed their full support. For our part we are aware of our responsibilities as those wearing the colours of our country; also for those we have towards our fans and countless children who keep Les Bleus as role models.

'We forget none of our duties. We will do everything

individually and also in a collective spirit to ensure that France regains its honour with a positive performance on Tuesday.'

I'm glad I didn't get to read it out and I don't think it did Domenech any good that he did either – it was as if he was endorsing the strike when he hadn't. At the very least, it was not what the French Federation would have wanted. I'm sure that got him the sack.

I don't think any of us realised the impact those pictures of us on the bus refusing to train would have. We were in a bubble and were laughing and joking as we got back to the hotel. We all agreed not to speak to the media – apart from me as captain. Matters actually felt quite normal. We believed that we'd made our point about Anelka being sent home and that we could carry on.

I turned my two mobile phones off, my French and English one. That was a mistake because events would now move rapidly ahead without me knowing, but I wanted to focus on the final game, which I thought we could win well enough to still go through to the knockout stage. And I didn't want to have the same conversation with countless people in France who wanted to know what was happening.

When I woke up the next day, I switched on my phone to find all hell had broken loose. Firstly, the national team director Jean-Louis Valentin had resigned and, when asked why, said: 'Ask the players, they do not want to involve themselves any more. It's unacceptable. They don't want to train. It's a scandal for the French, it's a scandal for the Federation and the French team. It is a shame. As for me, it's over. I'm leaving the Federation. I'm sickened and disgusted. Under these conditions I've decided to return to Paris and to resign.'

I left my room to see Gallas laughing at me with gallows

humour. Then Henry asked if I was okay. I said that I was – I think. I saw some of the other players at breakfast and gauged the mood. I could see that some were worried about what had gone on, and so I proposed a meeting. Franck Ribéry didn't turn up to the meeting and so I asked where he was. Players started laughing. 'He's doing an interview for [the TV channel] TF1,' came a reply.

I was stunned. We'd agreed that no players would do any media apart from me. Franck returned to the meeting. He was emotional and said: 'Sorry, guys. Sorry, Pat. It's too much on my chest. I know what we agreed but people are killing me in France. I've spoken to my family and they said that people are saying that I was threatening Gourcuff and stuff like that. It's not true, it's too much.'

Franck was under serious pressure. In 2009 he and Karim Benzema had been involved in a scandal where they were alleged to have paid an underage prostitute for sex. They always denied that charge, but it took until 2014 for French courts to drop the case because the prosecutors believed there was no case to answer. The investigation had started by the time of the World Cup finals and Benzema didn't even make the France squad, with Domenech saying it was because of his Real Madrid form as he'd only scored nine goals in his first season, but every-one suspected the scandal had played a part in the decision.

'Okay, Franck,' I said, 'but when we decide something as a group, you must at least tell me.' The other players told me that he'd apologised to TF1 for the players not training, and they were upset with Franck for doing that because, rather than justifying our actions, it was an admission that we were in the wrong.

We trained the day before the South Africa game, when Domenech tried to be positive: 'What has happened was in the past; we must focus on the South Africa game. Some players have told me that they don't want to play in this game, so I won't play them. And some of you won't play.'

Domenech then read out the list of names. I was not on it.

'Are you serious, boss?' I asked.

'Yes,' he replied.

'I will play. I want to play. I'm not a player who says he does not want to play,' I said. I thought he had changed his mind because when we trained, I was given a bib with the starting players. But I was not starting and nor were five other players who'd started the previous game. I was stunned, then I had to do a press conference when we landed in Bloemfontein ... alongside the manager.

The mood had started to turn among the players. On the flight, players including Toulalan and Govou and several others asked me to apologise for our protest. They had the impression that there was a revolution back in France. I asked the other players if they thought I should apologise. The consensus was that I should.

Normally, a car would be waiting to take the manager and myself straight to the press conference. This time, I looked for the manager and the car, only to be told that they had gone without me. I called the guys from the communications team. Nobody answered my calls. The head of communications texted back and said that the manager wanted to do the press conference on his own.

We got to the hotel, when Franck Ribéry and Thierry Henry came to my room to say that they'd had a message from home to say that Patrice Evra was going to be suspended for not attending the press conference, where Domenech had called us players 'imbeciles'.

I was furious, absolutely raging at the deceit and picked the television up off the wall, threw it and smashed it against the floor. The TV shattered. The devil was in my body and I went to get my bags to leave, but Franck and Thierry grabbed me and asked where I was going.

'I'm going home,' I said. 'I'm getting a taxi now. I wanted to apologise and to be at that press conference. It's not my fault I wasn't there.'

I was going mad, but Franck and Thierry stopped me going anywhere. They were right to do that. Imagine the impact of the news that I'd voluntarily left the France camp in a taxi. I gave my own interview to TF1, and said: 'Tonight it's time for a big apology toward the French people, because I share the pain of all these French people. What hurts even more is that this apology should have been made yesterday, but my coach stopped me doing it as captain.'

There was a knock at door. Still furious, I answered it. It was the bodyguard of Roselyne Bachelot, a very important politician, the French Minister for Health and Sports in Nicolas Sarközy's government.

'Mrs Bachelot wants to see you,' he said. I had no idea that she was in South Africa.

I was taken with Domenech and Escalettes, the three of us like naughty schoolboys, to meet Mrs Bachelot in a room in the hotel. This was not the time to confront Domenech with my feelings about the press conference. We sat on three chairs, with Mrs Bachelot in front of us, flanked by two bodyguards. She took a paper out with notes on it and put it on the desk.

'What the fuck is going on?' she asked calmly. 'What the hell are you doing for the image of our country? From now, you won't get any salary from the national team.'

'I'm sorry, what are you talking about, a salary?' I asked. The minister understood that we got paid every month by the Football Federation.

'We don't get paid a salary, we just get a bonus,' I explained.

'Who put this on my paper?' she asked as she'd been given

the wrong information. 'And, Patrice, why didn't you go to the press conference?'

Before I could answer, Domenech put his hand up and said: 'Because of me.'

I explained that I was going to apologise on behalf of my teammates at the press conference.

'What! Really?' she replied.

'Yes.'

'And you didn't allow him to go to the conference?' she asked Domenech. He nodded.

'You stopped your captain from apologising?' she said, shaking her head. 'From now you won't be the coach of the national team after this World Cup, and you, Escalettes, won't be the president of the French Football Federation any more.' They'd both been sacked before my eyes.

'Mrs Bachelot, they took away my liberty,' I said, at my most polite. She nodded.

I thought that meeting with Mrs Bachelot was constructive, and she asked Domenech and Escalettes to leave the room and for the players to join me. After the players sat down, she explained that I'd said I wanted to apologise and that she was happy about that. Then she started to talk like a manager, explaining that it was important that we did our best in our final game against South Africa, that we should do it for ourselves and for France. Some of the players applauded, including myself. They felt more motivated by Mrs Bachelot than Domenech, yet I'd misread the mood of my meeting with her because she killed us in the French parliament when she returned, claiming that we were all gangsters traumatising some poor little French boys. I shook my head, wondering if all politicians were so two-faced because I was very disappointed in Mrs Bachelot.

I was not in the team the next day. I left my hotel room door open so that I was available for any player and I put on my pre-match suit, knowing I would be on the bench. Alou Diarra was named as captain in my place and I was vice-captain. I felt very alone and saddened.

We lost again – 1-2 – and Gourcuff received a red card. We were out of the World Cup and set to fly back to France the next day on a chartered Air France plane. I passed Escalettes in the hotel lobby and he was playing the pinball machine, completely engaged by it. You remember the surreal images like that.

Henry called a meeting of the players and he was very emotional as he announced that he was retiring from international football. Thierry had played 123 times for France and won the World Cup and the European championships. He was France's second most-capped player after Lilian Thuram – and we'll return to him. When Henry flew back to France he had a private meeting with President Sarközy.

The rest of us flew back to Paris, and the players were worried about the reaction back home. I tried to tell them not to worry, that they should go on holiday and be with their families, but it was probably easier said than done as the plane headed north over Africa.

Hundreds of fans were waiting for us at the airport in Paris. I wasn't sure what the reaction would be, but fans clapped me as I came through Arrivals into a scrum of fans and media. I heard the comments and, far from being critical, people were praising me for having balls, for being a real captain. I was very surprised by the reaction, although not so surprised that fans were happy that Domenech was to be sacked.

Drivers had been sent to pick up the players who lived in Paris. I got into my car and quickly realised that I was being followed by six or seven paparazzi motorbikes. The chase was even broadcast live on one TV channel. My driver realised what was happening and put his foot down as the bikes followed. As I got close to our house in the centre of Paris, I called my wife to explain that I didn't want them to know where we lived. As we spoke, she looked out of the balcony and saw the commotion on the street below. We sped on and tried to lose them in a car park, but the bikes followed us. Thinking of what to do next, I said to the driver: 'If they want to chase us then they can follow us to Les Ulis.'

It was time to see what they were made of and we drove across Paris to where I grew up, where I'd be on home turf and comfortable. One bike went past us and waved goodbye – indicating that they'd run out of petrol. I laughed and waved goodbye. By the time we got near Les Ulis, there were only two left. I decided to go to my sister's house and when I arrived only one paparazzi remained, taking pictures from a distance. The rest had either given up, run out of petrol or not wanted to follow me into the estates that they wouldn't know.

I stayed with my sister for three hours and talked to her about everything that had gone on, then I took a regular taxi back home. The taxi driver knew me and said he was glad that I'd stuck up for my teammates. Nine hours after landing, I saw my wife. My son was already asleep. I slept surprisingly well that night, and the following morning I suggested that we go for lunch in the centre of Paris.

'Are you crazy?' friends asked. 'Have you seen what the press are saying about you? That you're a gangster, a bad boy, that you should never have been made captain of France because you're from the street!'

We went for lunch by the Champs-Élysées. When we arrived at the restaurant, some of the other diners started to applaud me before we were taken to a private room. 'I swear the media are killing you,' a friend said.

'But this is not the reality,' I replied. 'It's only in the media. People don't live their lives by what they read in newspapers or TV. They can make their own judgements.'

What happened to me when I met real people wasn't untypical. Anelka told me that he had the same treatment. I don't think that the whole country loved us, but my own experience of meeting people in real life was almost always a positive one. I think people appreciated me being real, for standing up for my teammates. They also wanted to see the back of Domenech.

Friends weren't completely wrong, though. There were critics in the media, including Lilian Thuram, who said that I should never play for France again. I was surprised by this, though Thuram had never been a friend. I'd played with him but we'd never had a positive connection. We would shake hands and I never had a problem with him, I respected him as a player and a man too. He was strong and would give everything for France, but we were never going to be friends and we'd barely communicate. That seemed to suit us both.

When I broke through into the national team, I found out that Thuram called the younger players 'young boy' on the pitch. It was disrespectful, but he never said that to me, probably because he knew that I was hot-headed and would have punched him. I was certainly angry at his comments that I should never play for France again, and I called Thierry to ask for Thuram's phone number.

'Why?' he said. He knew why. 'Don't do something stupid.'

'I ask you as a friend, as a brother. Just give me the number.'

I called Thuram and it went straight to answerphone.

'Can you please call me back, Thuram?' I said, calling him by his second name. 'I respect you so much as a player and for what you have done for the French national team, but I can't believe what you have said. I am the captain and I take responsibility, but you are going too far. If you call me at least I can tell you exactly what happened.'

Thuram didn't call me. Ten minutes later I called back and left another message.

'I swear if I see you I will hurt you, you son of a bitch. Call me back. I just want to hurt you now. Fuck off with the respect.'

He never called me back. Fuck him. He thinks he's Malcolm X because he wears glasses and reads books.

A couple of years later I was training with the national team at Clairefontaine. Someone said that Lilian Thuram was there. That was my moment. Momo, who I have a lot of respect for, grabbed me.

'Look at my eyes,' he said. He could feel my anger. 'Please, listen to me. Don't do anything, please,' he said.

I made a wild threat.

Unsurprisingly, I was never allowed near Thuram and was asked to leave. I've not seen him since. I was wrong to react like this, but that's how angry I was at the time. What would I do if I saw him now? I don't think I would be at all angry. It's the past, I forget quickly. But I would like to ask him why he was so negative about me, why he didn't speak to me in person.

On 6 August 2010, five France players including me were summoned to a disciplinary committee. Abidal, Anelka, Ribéry and Toulalan – an honest, principled guy – were there with me. As was Domenech. Once again, I found myself facing politicians who weren't really familiar with how football works. I told them my version and I was asked if it was normal that a football manager was allowed to shout at players.

'Which planet are you on?!' I laughed. 'In Manchester Ferguson threw boots at his players and told them to fuck off!'

'Really?' they asked, stunned.

I was pushed again and again over whether I had led the strike. And again I said: 'I am the captain. Ban me, that's fine, I'm not here to cry. But I'm not going to admit to things I didn't do. I was the captain of the team and I did what the team wanted to do. I did not cause the strike.'

They were so nice with me, but it was suggested that I should not be captain any more and that it should be Toulalan. He spoke up and said: 'Patrice is a good captain and I was the one who wrote the letter.'

Nobody outside the team knew that he'd written it. By admitting that, he cost himself the captaincy of France. He's got balls of steel, Jérémy Toulalan. The committee killed him and I think they were surprised. They thought he was only a nice, white, intelligent French boy and not a black gangster kid like me.

I was always aware of how some sections of French people perceived us. Win a game and we were the united French, Arab and black. Lose and some of us were bad-boy immigrants. I felt sad for Jérémy, but my respect for him was absolute. We were never the type of friends who went to a restaurant together, but I hope there was a mutual respect. There was certainly respect from me: he could have said nothing.

I was suspended for seven international matches, hardly the lifetime ban Thuram was looking for. France's Sports Minister, Chantal Jouanno, said: 'I have nothing against Evra but, as a France player and especially captain, he did not defend the values of sport which are shared by the Republic. I am sure there exist other talents who have not sullied France and are waiting for the chance to write new history.'

What a dreadful mess the 2010 World Cup finals were, but I have given you my side of the story honestly and tried to show you how events seemed to spiral out of everyone's control.

CHAPTER 10

Manchester – not Madrid

After the chaos of South Africa and the intensity of life back in France, I wanted a break with my family somewhere where I could walk down the street unrecognised. I'd been playing football non-stop for 11 months and Alex Ferguson gave the players who'd been at the World Cup an extra few weeks' holiday.

That hadn't been the only complication in my life. I was told that Real Madrid wanted to sign me, where I would play for Jose Mourinho. They knew that my United contract was coming towards its end and so they contacted my agent. They were also offering more money than United and, with all that swirling in my mind, I rented a villa in Los Angeles and flew west with my family. I didn't speak directly with Madrid and my heart was saying that I would never leave United.

Meanwhile, my wife was telling me: 'We have to leave Manchester.' She wasn't happy about life there, chiefly because of my affair and what she considered to be my addiction to Manchester United that prevented me giving my full focus to our family. I don't like it when people are critical of footballers' wives for being rich and having an easy life where they don't have to look at the price of the clothes they buy. It's not fair.

Of course they're not going to say out loud that they have a shit life because it's not true and they are privileged, but my wife described it as 'a golden jail'. When she used to complain about it when I was younger, my attitude was: 'Shut up, you are lucky.' As I grew up I began to see it wasn't the right way to talk.

My conscience was clear over what had happened in South Africa and I was not going to become down about it. I don't get depressed, I just turn the page and look forwards, but I didn't just have myself to think about. My wife was from Paris – that's where her friends and family were. Secondly, she had lost her husband to Man United. That meant a lot of time away.

In the summer of 2010 I called Ferguson from Los Angeles and told him that I needed to talk to him face to face, that it was really important. I didn't tell him that I was considering leaving United, but he must have guessed something.

'If you want to talk with me, come to Chicago,' he said. He was already there with United on a pre-season tour because it was where some of the club's sponsors were based.

Before the call ended, I admitted that I was considering leaving United as I wanted him to be prepared for what I was going to say. I expected him to be shocked, but he repeated: 'If it's so important and you want to talk with me, come to Chicago.'

There was no emotion in his voice. He was a hard bastard with 40 years of football management experience who was used to dealing with problems every day. My problem was a huge deal to me, but it was not going to take him away from his focus: winning trophies with United. His loyalty was to the club and no player was bigger than the club.

I still don't think he expected me to go to Chicago, but I was determined to see him face to face and so I booked a private plane from Los Angeles. It cost $45,000 for a nine-hour return flight, a lot of money to me, but I did it because I didn't like the way Ferguson had taken my announcement. Could you blame him, though? His left back had just told him out of the blue on the eve of a new season.

I didn't even look at flying with a normal airline because I wanted to see him as soon as possible and I also didn't want to see other people that summer after events in South Africa. Although I didn't realise it, the events there had worn me down mentally. I flew from LAX on an eight-seater plane. After I landed at O'Hare I took a taxi to the Four Seasons, a classic old Chicago hotel in the middle of all the skyscrapers. I went to Ferguson's room and we got straight to the point – or rather, Sir Alex did.

'Patrice, I know you have a lot of things going through your mind, son,' he said, 'but I need you. By the time you come back to Manchester, I will try and find a solution. Come and see me on the day when you get back to Carrington, but you have to give me time to try and find another left back.'

I nodded, then the boss asked me where I'd come from.

'Los Angeles,' I said.

'And you flew here to see me?'

'Yes.'

He shook his head. I think I'd surprised even him.

I flew back to California and finished our holiday, my head spinning about what was going to happen next. The wheels were in motion for me to leave Manchester and when I eventually got to Manchester after the holiday, I texted the boss and told him that I'd come and see him the following day at Carrington as arranged.

When I showed up at the gaffer's office, he wasn't there so I called him on his phone, but he didn't answer. I was starting to get worried, even angry. The boss was always at Carrington, why wasn't he there today? I was told that he was expected in the following day. When the club needs to close ranks, they stand behind their manager.

I had to wait another 24 hours, trying to second-guess why he had not been there. The next day, I got up prepared to finally see the manager. It was a beautiful morning where I lived in the Cheshire village of Alderley Edge. I would miss England on days like this. The problem was there were too few, especially in winter when it gets dark at 4 pm. I was sad inside, but had mentally begun to prepare to leave for Spain and join back up with Cristiano, plus my French teammate Benzema.

At Carrington, I knocked on the manager's door.

'Ah, Patrice, lovely to see you,' he welcomed me in, all smiles. 'Please sit down. How are you doing?' The tone was the opposite of when I'd called him in Chicago.

'Boss, I'm not good,' I started. 'I have been looking for you for 24 hours. I needed to talk to you. As I said in Chicago, I need to leave United for personal reasons.'

I sat down and Mr Ferguson started to talk.

'You know, my son,' he began, 'I've looked all over the world since I met you in America. Everywhere. I've been trying to find a left back just like you, but you know what? I can't find one.'

'Of course you can't,' I replied, brightening up, 'I'm unique.' I wasn't being arrogant; I thought then and still do now that I am unique. 'So find someone who is not me and who is good enough to play for Manchester United.'

'No, no, no,' he said. 'I will get you a new contract. I want you to stay another one or two years and then I will help you leave Manchester United.' Then he stood up and shook my hand and smiled, like he was congratulating me.

'You deserve a new contract. Well done, son.'

I was really happy inside, but puzzled too. I'd said nothing about Real Madrid and it was never mentioned, but I think he knew – and not just because he knows everything. Why? Just before I met him, I saw the important football agent Jorge Mendes at Carrington.

'Whatever Mr Ferguson tells you, you should respect his choice,' Mendes said to me.

When I came out of the office into the canteen, I saw Mendes again.

'You made a good choice,' he said.

I'd not made any choice! I'd not even spoken. I was also in trouble because I needed to go back home and tell my wife that we were not going to move to a new life in the sun – not that I'd even spoken to Madrid. She was waiting for me when I got home.

'What?' she said before I'd said anything. 'I can see it in your face again. You're weak! Ferguson is the devil! You can't say no to that man! What is wrong with you? Speak!'

'Ferguson says that I cannot leave,' I said, pushing all the blame onto my manager.

'That man is your god!' she said. 'You do everything that he says! He sends me flowers for my birthday and for Christmas but he should not do it again because if he really cares for me, then he should let you leave Manchester.'

I was happy inside and started to laugh. Ferguson, the gentleman, was now being accused of being bad for sending my wife beautiful bouquets from him and his wife Cathy, but she was just upset because she was unhappy in Manchester at that time. Even now, the Fergusons send Christmas cards. They don't need to do that, but it shows how they are as people.

Once my wife calmed down, she accepted that we'd be in Manchester for another year. I returned to Old Trafford and was glad to get back into the rhythm of club football, where I was hungry to win trophies. I spoke to Ferguson about what had gone on in South Africa and I suspect that he'd felt Domenech wasn't the right man to lead France after he proposed to his girlfriend on television in 2008. He didn't think the manager of a leading football nation should do that when things were going badly.

I felt no guilt. My only frustration was that we'd had all those top players and failed to do ourselves justice on the pitch in South Africa. There was still hostile media interest in me from France. I bought a new car and that was turned into a negative – how dare I be rewarded with a new car? It was clear to me that I was still a target for them but I had no interest in courting the media. I was never going to be their golden boy. I came from a different world to the journalists. My formal education had stopped before theirs. Maybe they didn't like the way I spoke when I was interviewed, but I was always true to myself and I think a lot of normal French people could identify with that. I was not full of clichéd bullshit like some footballers who are scared to say anything.

There was no time to brood because our whole focus was on preparing to win the league back from Chelsea. There had been several new signings and some of them joined up with us: Bebé, Chris Smalling, Javier Hernandez and Anders Lindegaard. Bebé turned up looking like Bob Marley with his big dreadlocks, and the players were like: 'Wow, who is this player?' None of us had heard of him. The dreadlocks were soon gone – the very next morning, in fact. He went from Bob Marley to Danny Welbeck overnight. We understood that Ferguson had had a quiet word.

When Bebé started to train, the players began to ask more questions about where he had come from. We heard that he'd been a star in the homeless World Cup, and some players started laughing, but not me. I admired that he'd gone from that to Manchester United, but the problem was that the standard was so high at United that players were sceptical that a footballer could come from nowhere and play with us.

Bebé was actually very good in some training sessions. He would shoot harder than Cristiano Ronaldo and Nani, surprising the squad. He was fast, strong and he was a humble person, too. I sat next to him in the canteen one day and he said: 'Patrice, it is a dream to sit here eating with players like you.' Bebé told me there had been times in his childhood when obtaining food was difficult after being abandoned by his mother and his father.

I was impressed by him as a man and I told him to give his best for the club, that God had given him this chance to be an inspiration to others. Bebé was raw and needed to work on his technique, but he was still young and had time to do that. It was still an odd signing, but while he wasn't good enough to play for United, he had talent and has had a career playing in La Liga, one of the best leagues in the world. He would have accepted that when he was living in a hostel and starving.

Ferguson was fair with him, but when Bebé had his chance at Old Trafford, I felt that he suffered from the pressure. If you're a player who feels pressure, then it's like carrying another ten kilos on your back in a game. You have to overcome it and some players can never do that. Some players can do everything in training but nothing in front of 75,000. Bebé never showed anything like the quality to be a United player, but he should never be ridiculed as he had achieved something very few manage.

I played with Dong Fangzhuo at United, and wondered why he had ever been brought to train with the first team. Dong couldn't speak English and I felt sorry for him, but could you blame him for accepting a chance to join Manchester United? I wanted to help Dong, but it would never have been enough; he wasn't close to United quality and there was a suspicion among the players that he'd been bought because United were popular in China.

One player who did shine immediately was Javier 'Chicharito' Hernandez. I'd played against him when France played Mexico in the World Cup finals, and I knew that he was sharp and that he had killer movement as he looked around the box for goals. His movement behind the defenders made him hard to mark in training where he was crazy for goals.

Chicha was well educated, always smiling and delighted to be at United, even if he was with the reserve team. He was immediately respected by players who were usually so tough to please. New arrivals were judged not only by the way they played but also the way they acted. Personality was important and anyone thinking that they were the star would have been kicked in training and mocked. Judgements could be harsh: if you wore a cap back to front or if your car was too flash, then the players would bring you down a peg or two by taking the piss. The older players told a story about Liverpool players turning up to the 1996 FA Cup final wearing white suits. The boss seized on that and the players felt they had an advantage before the game had started.

Chicha's behaviour was fine and when he got chances with the first team, he took them, scoring 20 times in his first season, which he ended by starting in the Champions League final against Barcelona. Little wonder the Mexican was smiling all the time.

Chris Smalling came from Fulham. He had potential, but how could anyone follow Vidic and Ferdinand?

Ravel Morrison played his first United game that season. Ferguson treated him like his child, just as he did Anderson. He knew he had come from a challenging background and wanted to help like a good father. Ravel was such a talented player. We watched him for the reserves, then, when he trained with the first team, Paul Scholes used to smash him every day to show him that he needed to be a man, that being a talented street footballer wasn't enough. Ravel was tough and wasn't afraid of the challenges on the pitch, but his influences off it were a problem. United felt that they did everything they could to support him, but he should have had a bed in Carrington and not been allowed to leave. What a waste of an amazing talent who was good enough to be a star for United.

That season, 2010–11, was a good one for us. In December Sir Alex Ferguson became the longest-serving United manager, and we equalled the club-record unbeaten run of 29 matches until we lost a game at Wolves in February. We were very strong at home all season and that home form helped the club win a 19th Premier League title – one more than Liverpool – but the boss remained very hard to please.

I was playing every week and the manager liked my consistency. He knew he could depend on me as a senior player but was hard on me when I made mistakes. In one game, I played really well but I gave one ball away. 'Patrice, you shouldn't give the ball away,' said Ferguson.

'But boss, one ball . . .'

'A player like you shouldn't give one ball away.'

He was hard on me but never as hard as I was on myself. Ferguson would compliment me too, though. 'Patrice, what a man!' he'd say. 'Even when things are happening in your personal life, you still play well.'

The compliments continued as he was keen for me to sign a contract extension for three years, which I did in February 2011. I was happy to sign and stay at United. I felt my family was okay in Manchester again, too. The negotiations took a few weeks because my agent pushed to get the possible best deal for me and that frustrated the club, but that's entirely normal. Still, the boss approached me as I took to the training field one day and asked why I hadn't signed the contract offered.

'Boss, I'm not dealing with that side of things, it's for my agent,' I replied truthfully. 'I'm concentrating on my football.'

'But you decide, not your agent,' he replied.

'Don't worry, boss, you know how much I love Manchester United.' But given what I'd told him at the start of the season, I could understand why he might be worried.

I signed the contract, but there was a sting in the tail. The following season, the boss told me that he would give the cap-taincy to Nemanja Vidic because I had previously asked to leave United. 'You should never have asked to,' he said. He played the situation with me perfectly and exerted his authority.

With my biggest-ever contract, I bought a large house in Manchester. I'd never owned a house before, one with my own garden. In Les Ulis, everything was communal. At all my other clubs I'd lived in apartments. I wanted to own some land, some earth, and I became fixated with a big tree in the garden. I couldn't believe that I now owned that tree.

I'd realise that I didn't really own the tree because that tree will be alive after I have died.

As well as winning the league, we did well in Europe once again. When I spoke to my France teammates, they would say they thought the final would be United and Barcelona again. We were the best two teams in Europe, and they were right as we reached the final of the Champions League for the third time in four years.

We also played Manchester City in the FA Cup semi-final and we lost at Wembley, but none of us were thinking that City were suddenly a major power. As I said before, I continued to socialise with Carlos Tevez until the boss told me that he didn't like us being seen out in public together. From then on I'd have to go round to Carlito's house.

Carlos found it funny. At the end of one game against City when United fans had booed him all match, he put his arm around me. 'I'm doing this on purpose so the fans will kill you,' he said.

'Don't worry, you could kiss me and the United fans would know that I'd never join City like you!' I replied. Then I threw some water over him.

We finished top of our Champions League group, which contained Valencia, Rangers and Bursaspor, and were unbeaten. Then we knocked out Marseille where I was booed by some of the crowd. Maybe the booing was because of what happened in South Africa, but I've long felt that French players get booed when they return to France with a foreign team. You get called Judas or a traitor, and I've heard suggestions that we play abroad because we don't want to pay the high levels of French tax, but I moved to Manchester United and England because I felt the Premier League was a higher standard than Ligue 1 and that I would win the Champions League with them. I think I made the right decision, but Marseille fans were hardly going to welcome someone like me to Marseille when they were desperate for their team to win.

We beat Chelsea home and away in the last eight and did the same to Schalke 04 in the semi-final. The final against Barcelona was to be played at Wembley, the fourth of five European Cup finals in my career. It was also my worst performance. I felt heavy, too warm, and I couldn't get into the game. I was very disappointed with myself and I was rightly criticised for not following my man which led to Pedro's opening goal. I could criticise us more, but that Barcelona side was the best I've ever played against in my career.

Although it had ended with the disappointment of defeat at Wembley, and I still couldn't shake off my persistent problem with vomiting, it had been another successful season for United. Sandra would not get her move abroad for a while yet.

CHAPTER 11

Getting the Blues

Sir Alex Ferguson came into the dressing room at half-time, looked at Rio Ferdinand and calmly asked: 'Rio, why are you shitting yourself today?'

'I'm not shitting myself,' replied Rio.

'You're shitting yourself,' replied the boss.

Rio denied it.

'That's enough for you and Vidic, I'm taking you both off,' he said. 'You are too deep, too slow. It's time for the kids.'

It was the Community Shield between the league and FA Cup winners. United against City for the second time in four months. They'd beaten us and we wanted revenge, but things didn't go to plan. We did beat City in a top game, but it was the first time I thought the regular centre-back partnership of Rio Ferdinand and Nemanja Vidic could be in jeopardy.

City had quickly gone 2-0 up and our new goalkeeper, David de Gea, struggled with long shots because, we were told, he had a problem with his eyes. Edin Dzeko had scored from a long shot and Joleon Lescott had headed in the second, for which I was criticised by the media.

After the half-time showdown, the boss brought on young

Jonny Evans and new signing Phil Jones in defence. It was a major change in a big game but it really paid off. We pressed them high. Smalling, playing at right back, scored and Nani got two. Nani was amazing that day. We battered City in that second half to win 3-2. But when we went back to the dressing room, instead of celebrating our comeback, the talk was of how Nemanja and Rio might be replaced by Jones and Evans, who'd performed superbly. When I say 'the talk', I mean the vibe that you get in the dressing room. It comes from players, from physios, from people close to the manager who pick up things. There's no shortage of opinions in a football dressing room.

It was a jolt to all of us that we couldn't relax, and from that day the boss felt he could trust young players like Evans, Jones, Smalling and Tom Cleverley, who'd also done well. We needed them as John O'Shea had left for Sunderland. John was the solution to many of United's problems and I used to joke with him that he could play everywhere except goalkeeper . . . then he ended up as a stand-in keeper against Tottenham! He was a significant loss for United, and the club shouldn't have let him go, but I understood why he went. John wanted to play more – footballers do. But I can't remember John ever letting United down. He wasn't the biggest star but teams need players like him.

There was a new breed coming through like Tom, who I'm convinced is a black man in a white man's body because of the music he's into. Clev got some stick off United fans who didn't think he was good enough to play for the team, yet he's the type of player who can perform really well with top players around him. Clev's passing was sharp, quick on the transition and he could finish.

Clev started to feature that season, as did Ashley Young, who United had signed from Aston Villa that summer. I know some fans wanted bigger star names, but we knew him from playing against him. We felt he was good enough to play with us, and he could play in different positions too. Despite many ups and downs, Ash had a good career at United, was recalled to the England team after a long absence, and, like me, went from the wing to left back.

David de Gea, our new goalkeeper, also found it very tough. He had to replace Ed van der Sar, who'd been ultra-consistent for six years. It wasn't only the fans who were surprised when a slight Spaniard just out of his teens took over from him, and the surprise grew as he struggled to settle. Fans judge you before you play. They judge the way you walk onto that pitch. Do you look confident or nervous? David certainly didn't look confident. I'd seen the boss welcome David pre-season with a handshake and then turn to me and joke: 'I thought he was taller than that, Patrice.'

I laughed along with him, but no man would have as much influence on David as Ferguson. David was really bad at the start. He was weak, and teams could smell that weakness. They knew they could be effective at set pieces by launching the ball at the skinny goalkeeper. We, his teammates, knew that David was being targeted right from the first game of the 2011-12 league season, at West Brom.

I felt for David and wanted to help him, not only because I'd been made team captain because Nemanja would be out for the rest of the season through injury and neither Giggsy nor Rio was considered fit enough to be regular starters. He was young and living in a new country where he didn't speak the language – just as I'd struggled myself when I arrived at United. The boss was very protective of De Gea, but he also started to rotate goalkeepers, with Ben Amos playing League Cup games and Anders Lindegaard playing some Champions League games. Anders was the man with too much class off the pitch. He was like a posh gentleman and nobody laughed at his jokes because he was on a higher intellectual plane. He was a good lad, but he knew he wasn't going to be first choice.

After years of being able to absolutely depend on having Edwin behind us every week, the defenders did not like the change. We conceded three goals at home to Basel to draw 3-3 and David was rooted to his goal line for one of them, though he wasn't to blame entirely for the defence shambles. Then David started to play more – but not always well.

In the dressing room after one game against bottom side Blackburn where David failed to clear for their winner, the boss seemed to lose patience. He wasn't happy with David and told him in front of us all that as manager he kept getting criticism from the fans and journalists for continuing to pick David when he was making mistakes. The manager's solution?

'I'm going to play you every game because you have to learn to deal with this pressure,' Ferguson explained. 'You have to deal with this shit because we thought you were going to be the best goalkeeper in the world when you signed and we still do.'

David could see that his boss was angry, yet from that day on he changed. He worked harder in the gym and built himself up. His diet improved and he ate food at Mancunian hours not Madrid's where the main meal is at 10 in the evening. He needed to adapt to his new life and I tried to help him, speaking to him in Spanish, but Rio, Vida and myself really pushed him to speak in English.

On the pitch we needed David to be more vocal. He was too quiet, whereas van der Sar always shouted at us to help with our positions or warn us of danger, even if he didn't scream at us. If a goalkeeper doesn't shout for a ball, then how are the defenders to know that he wants it?

Soon, David was bellowing 'My ball!' in training. And if

anyone had a problem, they told him to his face. I loved that trait at United – that feeling that you shouldn't say things behind the backs of others. If someone had a bad game in training, then they were told about it immediately. We gave an award to the worst player in training, the 'black cat' award – I assume because black cats are considered unlucky. Not that it was an actual trophy. David didn't win it much in training where we could see his sharp reflexes every day, but he would have won it in a few games at the start of that season.

David was determined to improve. He was not going to give up after six months in Manchester. He played one game at Chelsea on a freezing day in February 2012 where he was poor in the first half but spectacular in the second. We drew 3–3 and it was a turning point for him.

Despite David's teething problems, we hit the ground running in the league, winning our first five league games – including an 8–2 drubbing of Arsenal. That was probably our best performance. Arsenal's Brazilian player Denilson said before the game that the babies – which you may remember I'd called them in an interview – had become men and were ready for United. I was told after the game that Arsène Wenger had put my 'babies' interview in their dressing room to motivate them. That worked, didn't it?

That Arsenal game was on a beautiful day and I felt strong and proud as a red Mancunian. I knew by Arsenal's faces in the tunnel that we were going to destroy them. Sometimes you get days like that, when you can see the fear of the opposing players before the game. I respect Arsenal, they're a big club, but United is a bigger club and we were far better that day.

When we played Liverpool away on 15 October 2011, we were expecting our usual hard game at a ground where United had struggled to get results. The small pitch didn't suit our style. I was getting plenty of time and space to get forward and, though the score was 0–0, I felt that we could get something from the match. Then, after 58 minutes, Luis Suarez kicked me on the knee and United were awarded a foul.

A few minutes later, Liverpool were awarded a corner and Suarez came close to me in the United area. 'Fucking hell, why did you kick me?' I asked him in Spanish.

'Because you're black,' replied Suarez in Spanish.

I couldn't believe what he had said.

'Say that to me again and I'll kick you.'

'I don't speak to blacks.'

I was angry. 'Okay, I think now I'm going to punch you,' I told him.

'Okay, negro, negro, negro,' he kept repeating. As he spoke, he pinched my left forearm. The referee, Andre Marriner, stopped play and Suarez called me a negro again.

A lot of things went through my mind. My first thought was: 'If I punch him, then kids around the world will see me, and I know I'm a role model.' The referee came up to me and asked what had happened. When I told him that Suarez was racially abusing me, he said: 'We'll deal with this later.' I got close to Suarez and I was still thinking: 'Punch him or not?' but I restrained myself.

Suarez put his hand on the back of my head and I pushed it away. The referee came between us again and I said that I didn't want Suarez to touch me again. Suarez said: 'Why, negrito?'

If he intended to make me lose focus then it worked. I stopped bombing forward as much to support the attack and the game ended 1–1. I was also booked for shoving Dirk Kuyt in the chest, and Ryan Giggs told me to calm down. Then I told Ryan that Suarez had racially abused me. The Liverpool fans were booing me at the end, maybe because of what had happened or maybe because I kissed the Man United badge in front of them.

I sat down in the dressing room, visibly upset. My teammates

Nani, Antonio Valencia, Javier Hernandez and Anderson all said that they'd heard Suarez say he wouldn't speak to me because I was black. Valencia and Anderson told me to tell the manager, but Ferguson could see I was really down and he asked me why.

'I heard Suarez call me a negro,' I said.

'Really?' said Ferguson.

'Yes, I'm sure.'

'Then we have to see the referee so that he can include it in his report.'

We went to Marriner in the referee's room and Ferguson said: 'Evra has been called a nigger by one of the Liverpool players.' I then gave my account and Ferguson said he wanted to make a formal complaint. Marriner asked Phil Dowd, the fourth official, to make notes of the conversation. He said he would include it in his official report to the Football Association.

While we were with the referee, Ray Haughan, an administrator for the Liverpool team, overheard everything. He told Damien Comolli, who was Director of Football Strategy at Liverpool, and Kenny Dalglish, the Liverpool manager, that Ferguson had alleged that Suarez had called me a nigger five times.

Comolli speaks Spanish and went to get Suarez's version. Suarez admitted using the word 'negro', saying that I'd said: 'Don't touch me, South American.' Dowd then asked Dalglish and Suarez to come to the referee's room. Dowd asked Comolli to spell 'Tu es negro' – 'You are black'. Comolli explained there had been a mistranslation and Suarez hadn't used the South American equivalent of 'nigger'.

I was then asked to give an interview for Canal+, the French TV channel. I'd gone from being desperate to be seen on French TV when I first played at Anfield for United and was so ashamed that I'd been dropped that I begged to sit on the bench, to being the player French TV wanted to speak to. The journalist could see I was upset and I told him that I had been abused with a certain word 'at least ten times'.

The next day, the storm broke, with Suarez called a racist. I honestly never thought it would be such a big story, which was probably very naive as everything connected with Manchester United, and Liverpool as well, is a big story. In the face of a media storm, the Football Association said they would hold an inquiry into the matter.

I started to receive hate mail from Liverpool fans, handwritten letters sent to United. They were opened by Barry Moorhouse, then the player liaison officer and long-time United servant. Barry was based at Carrington and saw the players every day. 'Pat, this is a really serious case,' he said as he showed me some of the letters. One was from a man in prison who said that the first thing he was going to do when he got out was kill me.

The police came and told me they had to take it seriously. For two months, I had 24-hour security in front of my house. Given my background, I wasn't scared, but my family were.

One day, I was driving my car and I could see someone following me. When I stopped, the car stopped and did a U-turn. The police had already been tracking the car. Nothing came of it, or if it did I wasn't told. It was bad period for me. The day after the game, a Liverpool spokesman said Suarez 'categorically denied' the allegation. Suarez said on social media that he was upset about being accused of racially abusing me. He wrote on Twitter: 'I can only say that I have always respected and respect everybody. We are all the same. I go to the field with the maximum illusion of a little child who enjoys what he does, not to create conflicts.'

I was accused of being a liar, but Sky TV had pictures which showed that Suarez had said the word 'negro'. He then said that in Uruguay it could be used in a non-offensive way. That may be true, but the name given to me by my mother was 'Patrice' and not 'negro'. I would never call someone 'white' or 'yellow', but I know some players do.

The Football Association held a disciplinary hearing in December 2011. I received support from many people, but I did not want to be seen as a figure for black power, despite groups trying to get me to push this angle. I spoke to the commission from my heart. The theme of my words was: 'I don't think Suarez is racist, but I don't know him well enough to know if he's racist or not. The only thing I want you to do is punish him.'

Suarez argued that he used the word 'negrito' and that he used it all the time as a term of affection to his black friends in Uruguay. A language specialist commented: 'Yes, you can call a friend negrito, but you can't use it to a stranger. In doing that, in an argument, it becomes racist.' However, the commission was very influenced by the fact that Damien Comolli had spelled out for Phil Dowd that Suarez had said 'negro' – his aim had been to make sure that Suarez had not said 'nigger', but it was taken as reliable evidence that the stronger term 'negro' had in fact been said.

After seven days, Suarez was found guilty, but not before Liverpool's lawyers had described me as being 'not credible' on account of the fight I'd had with the Chelsea groundstaff three years earlier. A perception grew that I like to play the race card, when it wasn't true. I never cited racism in the Chelsea case; it was Mike Phelan, United's assistant manager, who said he'd heard something racist.

The Football Association handed Suarez an eight-match ban and a £40,000 fine for racially abusing me. They produced a report of 115 pages that said I was a credible witness. The conclusion of the report said: 'Suarez's use of the term [negro] was not intended as an attempt at conciliation or to establish rapport; neither was it meant in a conciliatory and friendly way.' He was warned that two similar offences in the future could lead to a permanent suspension from football in the UK.

Liverpool's reaction surprised me. Despite Suarez being found guilty, they got behind their best player. Dalglish and his players wore a shirt with Suarez's face and name on it before their game at Wigan. Liverpool released a statement saying: 'We totally support Luis and we want the world to know that. We know he is not racist.'

When I saw them with the Suarez shirts, I thought: 'Really? He's been found guilty and you're still supporting him.'

Liverpool were critical of the three-man independent commission and issued a statement with the full support of their owners, saying that the case was 'highly subjective' and that it was based on 'an accusation that was ultimately unsubstantiated'. I felt they were trying to say that it's okay for one of their players to call another a negro.

Liverpool got it badly wrong, but I actually respect Suarez. I saw him in the 2015 Champions League final against Juventus in Berlin and shook his hand in the tunnel. I don't know him and we haven't spoken but I think he's a good guy. He played with my France teammate Mamadou Sakho, who speaks very highly of him. I feel that I could speak to him if I saw him now. I even voted for him to be PFA Player of the Year in 2013–14, even when people were telling me not to. If I picked a team of the best XI players in the world between 2013 and 2018 then Suarez would be a striker.

But my problem with Suarez took a long time to calm down.

A week after, we played Manchester City at home. David, one of my brothers, died two days before the game. I went to the team hotel and Sir Alex Ferguson came to my room. 'I've heard that you've lost your brother,' he said with great compassion. 'I realise you can't play.'

'I want to play, I want to play to forget.'

My brother did not die in a brutal manner. He'd had a haemorrhage two years previously and lay in his apartment for two days. Nobody could contact him. The police had to break into his house. He stayed in a coma for three days and when he woke up he was badly impaired. But he fought hard to improve his physical and mental condition. He taught himself to walk again, even though his left side was paralysed. Then he decided to go to Senegal without telling people.

People have blamed me because they think I bought his plane ticket, but I didn't. I didn't know he'd gone back to see my dad. My dad went to the kitchen to get him some water. When he returned my brother gave him some coins. My dad was very confused. My brother said: 'I don't need the money any more.' Then he passed away.

I don't think Mr Ferguson knew what to do, but I insisted that I wanted to play and he agreed. I wanted to black out the pain of hearing my father crying down the phone to me, not something I'd heard before.

When we conceded the first of six goals against City I was not in pain. It was like I was not on the pitch at all. I realise now I was in shock. When I drove home after the game I met a Man United fan at the petrol station. 'Patrice. We are the best team. Never mind that we lost against them, we're Man United. Never forget that.' I did not forget. If that had been in another country they would have chased me out of the petrol station after losing 1–6 to their derby rivals. What he said meant a lot to me at a difficult time.

That City defeat, humiliating though it was, proved to be a blip. We didn't lose in the league until that Blackburn game at the end of December 2011, which I've already mentioned. Europe was different. We'd reached three finals in four years, but then United failed to qualify from a Champions League group for the first time since 2005. We couldn't even qualify from a group of Basel, Benfica and Otelul Galati, and I was critical after we finished third in the group, saying that the players needed to look in the mirror, that we hadn't been professional and needed a reality check.

We were too sure of our past in Europe and became complacent, and we looked as though it was our first appearance in European competition. I was as bad as anyone, and everyone was blaming everyone else after we were 3-0 up against Basel but then drew 3-3. Wazza told me not to worry, that we hadn't won because he hadn't played. He said he would take care of the return in Basel, but we lost the game 1-2 and also lost Vidic to a bad injury. It was a horrible night and meant we'd play in the Europa League.

The Premier League would now become our focus. The boss told us that the Europa League was the only competition the club had not won and that we had to win it, but I didn't feel that conviction among the players and it wasn't the priority. Instead, I was ashamed that Manchester United were in the Europa League, with the Thursday games that the players hated because there was less time for recovery ahead of the weekend fixture. More than once, players said it would be better if we were out of Europe altogether so that we could focus on winning the league.

In the FA Cup, we were drawn against holders Manchester City in the third round. Away. It was a chance for us to get revenge for the semi-final defeat the previous season and the 1-6, and a chance to show that, while we'd struggled in Europe, we were still the best team in England.

We had a little surprise for City: Paul Scholes. He'd retired at the end of the previous season, but we kept seeing him around at Carrington. He would do a little bit of coaching with the younger teams, train with the reserves and sometimes with the first team. He was as good as ever and I told him that he should come back, but he would reply that it wasn't fair on his family for him to keep playing, that he was happy with life. He was one player who didn't enjoy the commercial demands that were put on players, but Ferguson would always tell us: 'Stop moaning, this pays your wages.'

But when I saw Scholes on the team bus on the way to the game against City, I asked him what he was doing. 'I'm coming to watch the game,' he replied.

'So why are you on the team bus and not the stand?'

Paul smiled.

We went into the dressing room and saw a shirt hung up with '18' and 'Scholes' on it. It was like winning the league for us, it gave us such a big lift and, even though he didn't come on until the second half, we'd already run into a 3-0 lead at half-time. City mounted a fightback after the break, but we hung on to win 3-2, a familiar scoreline in Manchester derbies at City.

Bringing Scholes back in was the right decision, but it meant less space for younger players like Paul Pogba, who is also from the Paris region like me. Paul was quiet with me when he joined United; young players are often timid around the senior professionals. I knew little about him other than that Rio Ferdinand had told me he was a good player. I didn't even know that Paul was from France until we spoke.

I told him that I would always be happy to help a young Frenchman, and I took an interest as Paul started to train with us. He had an excellent touch, but Scholesy – always Scholesy – and Giggsy used to smash him in every training session. Paul would be challenged so hard that he'd be on the floor. When he moaned at me that training was tough because they were kicking him so hard, I told him that if he kept crying, then they would kick him more. Scholes, I said, used to kick me every day when I arrived, and when I'd asked him why he kept kicking me, he just looked at me and said: 'Why not?'

Scholes and Giggs wanted me to be a United player, to be a man. Paul Pogba started to understand the message, to kick them back. He really improved in training and when the boss asked me: 'Are you happy to have another French boy, Pat?' I nodded.

'The boy is good, with potential,' he went on, 'but he's got to learn. There's too much show at the moment.'

I became friends with Paul; he trusted me. One day in early 2012, he came to see me. 'I have something to say to you, Uncle Pat. I'm going to leave United.'

'You are making a big mistake, Paul. I respect your decision and it's your life, but you have worked hard to get the respect of the senior United players. I'm not talking about the fans or the manager, but to win that from the players means you're special.'

Paul was frustrated that he wasn't playing, that he wasn't even getting a chance.

'Hey, calm down, you're playing with guys who've reached three Champions League finals in four years. They're among the best players in the world.'

But still, I could appreciate where Paul was coming from – and I would soon see where the manager was coming from when he told me: 'I have some trouble with Paul Pogba. I want him to sign, but his agent is asking me for crazy money. I can't do that, I have to respect the club.'

The manager asked me to speak to Pogba and I did so every day. Paul's agent Walid, the man who looked after him before Mino Raiola, told Paul not to speak to me any more because I was changing his mind. When Paul told me that, I was not happy and said I was looking forward to seeing his agent in person. It wasn't like I was making any money out of Paul, I genuinely thought he would be better staying at United and that he just had to be patient.

I saw Walid a few weeks later and he was friendly with me,

but I asked him why he was telling Paul not to speak to me. He claimed that I wanted what was best for United and that wasn't necessarily what was best for Paul.

When Paul switched to the agent Mino Raiola things went from bad to worse with Ferguson. They had a meeting and it was a disaster. Ferguson told me that Raiola asked for too much and didn't even know if Pogba was left- or right-footed, yet Raiola had simply replied: 'I know his value.' It was clear their relationship was over before it had started.

I adore Sir Alex Ferguson, but Raiola is liked by players because he does what's best for them. He's honest, too. If the players are motivated by money then he talks numbers to them. Some of his players are, but Paul just wanted to play first-team football. The boss really wanted to keep Paul and I think he even went to his house to speak to his family, but it didn't have the desired effect. The boss then asked me to go and see Paul at his home in Sale, and I was there for three hours as I explained to his mother how Paul could be to Manchester United what Patrick Vieira was to Arsenal.

I told Paul's family that I would protect him, that he had every quality to be a Man United player, that United was the best place for his development. They were listening, but Paul said nothing, merely looking lost. Paul's brothers stepped up and said: 'Ferguson doesn't respect my brother; even when there were injuries he played Rafael in midfield against Blackburn.'

I agreed that Paul should have played in that game, but I also saw the manager's perspective. Rafael had some good games in midfield for United, and Michael Carrick alongside him was an experienced player. 'I'm not working for the club,' I pointed out. 'I should be at home with my wife instead of spending the night here, but I think he's better off at United.' Paul still said nothing.

The next day, I told the manager where I'd been. He thanked

me but said he was convinced that Paul had already made his mind up. He was right.

Paul came up to me at training. 'What's wrong with you? You look like a zombie, like you've been hit by a truck,' I said.

'I didn't sleep, Uncle,' Paul replied. 'I listened to everything that you said, but I'm sorry, I'm going to Juventus.' He was clearly very emotional.

'Don't be upset,' I said. 'It's your life, your decision. You should feel blessed that you have two fantastic football clubs wanting you. I wish you well and will support you, watch you on TV. And I'm sure that you'll make it.'

Other players had told Paul not to go to Italy, that the fans were racist, but I'd played in Italy and knew it was still a great football country. 'It will be hard,' I said to him, 'but you can do it. Show me what you've got and if I can help you then I'm always there for you.'

When Paul left I felt like I'd lost a brother, that's how close I'd become to him over a year or so, but when he started to do well in Italy I was happy for him.

As 2012 began, City were now our main domestic rivals as far as title contenders went. They were mounting a serious challenge for the title, the first one of my whole lifetime. United fans would joke with the City fans that they never won anything. Now they had the FA Cup and they wanted a league title. They'd certainly spent enough. While City beat Liverpool 3-0, we lost our second league game in succession, conceding three goals at Newcastle on a windy January afternoon where nothing seemed to go right, putting City three points ahead of us.

The next time United and Liverpool met was when they knocked us out of the FA Cup at the end of January. Then, barely two weeks later in February just after Suarez's eight-match ban finished, we met them in the league at Anfield. It was

I flew in to Manchester from Monaco in January 2006 to find it freezing cold and raining – but there was a warm welcome from Sir Alex Ferguson. *(Getty Images)*

My debut was a disaster, as Trevor Sinclair kept bombing past me, and I was taken off at half-time. *(Getty Images)*

Celebrating my first trophy with United with Mikaël Silvestre and Louis Saha: the 2006 Carling Cup. Silvestre (centre) did more to help me settle in than most. *(Getty Images)*

Training with Gary Neville. Our only argument came during a practice match, but he showed me what it meant to be a United player. *(Getty Images)*

In the 2008 Champions League semi-final, I was given the job of marking Lionel Messi and kept him quiet. *(Getty Images)*

I hadn't even played in the game at Stamford Bridge, but still ended up getting caught up in a post-match scuffle with the groundstaff there. *(Getty Images)*

Going past Claude Makélélé during the 2008 Champions League final against Chelsea. *(Getty Images)*

I have the honour of lifting the trophy as United secure the 2010 Carling Cup.
(Getty Images)

Tussling for the ball with Luis Suarez of Liverpool during the match in October 2011
when he abused me. *(Getty Images)*

Celebrating against Liverpool with Robin van Persie, who made such an impact in 2012-13, as we closed in on our 20th title. *(Getty Images)*

In discussion with new manager David Moyes during our pre-season tour of the Far East. In Sir Alex, he had an impossible act to follow. *(Getty Images)*

'Uncle Pat' with Paul Pogba at Juventus ahead of our Champions League semi-final game against Real Madrid in May 2015. We'd both made the journey from United to Italy. *(Getty Images)*

Action from the France friendly against Germany in November 2015. Although I heard a dull bang during the match, we didn't realise that a horrific terrorist attack was taking place. *(PA)*

When someone in the crowd threatened my family, I took matters into my own hands. *(PA)*

Celebrating with Chicharito after his equaliser against Chelsea in April 2018. I didn't play as much as I would have hoped at West Ham. *(Getty Images)*

With my lifelong friend Tshimen.

With Margaux and Lilas.

Suarez's first start back after the ban. I knew the world would be watching to see if I shook his hand.

I stayed awake the night before, thinking it over. There was a lot of talk and tension around this game. I spoke to my mum and asked her opinion. She was convinced that I ought not to shake his hand, as were my friends, who said that he did not deserve my handshake. In the United dressing room, opinions were divided. Ferguson got us together a few days before the game and said: 'You need to be big.' His inference was that we didn't have to be nice to them, but we had to be bigger than them.

He was right, but Rio Ferdinand said that I shouldn't shake his hand and that the other players would support me. I was thinking about what I would do more than the game itself, whether to shake his hand or hit him hard in a tackle.

In the end, I said: 'As a Catholic, sometimes you have to forgive.' I went onto that pitch ready to shake Suarez's hand. I saw him coming towards me out of the corner of my eye. He seemed to get quicker. I hesitated as I went to shake his hand. He refused to shake mine. He moved on. I threw my arms up as he went down along the line to shake hands with other United players. Rio refused to shake his hand.

Suarez had made a great mistake because now, through his own actions, he was the villain. I wanted to pay him back on the pitch by hitting him with some hard tackles. I went to crash into him but tangled with Rio Ferdinand instead. We beat Liverpool 2-1 with two goals from Rooney and I celebrated crazily that day. Sir Alex Ferguson called Suarez a 'disgrace to Liverpool' and said they should get rid of him. Kenny Dalglish claimed live on television that he didn't know that Suarez had refused to shake my hand.

The world started to criticise Liverpool. Suarez apologised for not shaking my hand – not to me but in a statement. Liverpool's managing director also criticised Suarez. Dalglish then said sorry for what he'd said on television, while United accepted Liverpool's apology. I think both clubs wanted to draw a line under events, and I understand why, but I was still angry.

I also saw Suarez one day in Selfridges in Manchester city centre. I was with my brother; he was with his wife and daughter. My brother said: 'Look, he's there, let's go and have it out with him.'

'We can't,' I said. 'He's with his wife and child.' But if he hadn't been, I don't know what I would have done that day as I was still so frustrated and angry.

That Liverpool win started a league run of eight straight victories, which ended with a 1-0 defeat at Wigan – the game that, with hindsight, changed everything. Wigan's tactics caused us problems. They played three at the back, five in the middle and they played the game of their life. We found it difficult, we didn't know where to press, they had more men in the middle of the pitch. They deserved their win. The defeat stunned us and in the heat of the moment the manager said that it had just cost us the league even though we were still five points clear of City.

Rather it was a home game against Everton on 22 April that cost us the league. We were winning 4-2 with seven minutes to go when I hit the post. Everton went up the other end and scored. 4-3. Then they scored an equaliser. City, our rivals, won at Wolves. The gaffer was furious afterwards, telling me I should have scored. He shouted at us that it was over, that we would watch City celebrating with our trophy 'because you've given the fucking trophy away'. I watched him and he was really hurting. He kept calling us stupid, which we were.

Yet we were still top of the league, three points clear of City, but they had a better goal difference than us, partly because of the six goals we'd shipped against them the previous October.

Our second league game against them – as April came to a close – was billed, quite rightly, as the biggest-ever Manchester derby. We needed to avoid defeat to keep our three-point lead with two games to play, but psychologically we'd gone. You need to live in the present to get out of such a state, but we were still in the past and thinking of those defeats. We had great players and a great manager, but we'd gone, that Everton game had killed us.

In the old days, the solution would have probably been a big team night out, where we'd drink, air our grievances and some good could come from it. In 2012 we hardly went out as a team. We'd go out on special occasions, but even the Christmas parties brought too much negative attention on the club, which Ferguson hated. It got so bad that he said that if he saw another story in the newspapers of a married player with a girl, then he would cut their contract up. It was said half jokingly, but he was serious.

In Manchester, we tried to get up for the big derby match, but we should never have put ourselves in that position by losing to Wigan and drawing against Everton. The momentum was with City, and Vincent Kompany scored the only goal of the game. City were good, but not as good as they would become under Pep Guardiola.

City had some top players and I love Sergio Aguero. He's like a little bull, so strong and yet so sharp and clever. He never goes to the floor, which is something I respect in a striker. I would tell him if he played well against me, and I feel that the respect was mutual, but I wasn't feeling like I wanted to praise City after they beat us. They were now level on points with us with two games to go, still with that superior goal difference.

We both won our penultimate matches, and then we went to Sunderland for the final game while City were at home to QPR. I'd kept the captain's armband all season, and did my best to motivate the players, telling them that anything can happen in football, that City were under massive pressure that their players hadn't experienced before.

We needed to get a better result than City and we played well, even though Sunderland were flying in with the tackles and their goalkeeper Mignolet was superb. At the end of the game, the gaffer told us to go and thank the away fans and he also told me that City were losing. United were going to be champions, yet by the time we'd reached the United fans, a big roar went up from the Sunderland fans. We didn't know what was going on.

'We're champions if it stays like this,' said the manager. We were champions for 30 seconds because by the time we walked back to the tunnel there was another roar. City had scored twice in two minutes. The manager told us to get in the dressing room and we walked in past Sunderland fans laughing at us and dancing around because a team they don't support had won a game of football.

The United players were devastated. Several of them were sitting slumped on the floor, silent, like their life had stopped. Their heads were in their hands. Our manager knew what to do. He congratulated City, told us that we were to walk out of the stadium with our heads held high, that we had nothing to be ashamed of. He said that we were not to show any weakness when we spoke to the media. As captain, I said that we would come back stronger, and I believed we would.

I was disappointed in my captaincy. We'd picked up 89 points, then the highest-ever total for a runner-up, but there was nothing to show for it. We'd gone out of the Europa League to Athletic Bilbao, who outplayed us, and that may have given us some reward, even though, as I said, we tended to regard it as a booby prize. I don't like to lose any time, but if we were to lose one game in order to let us concentrate on the league, then I would have chosen one in the Europa League.

I knew that I wasn't everyone's first choice to wear the armband, that other players had ambitions to wear it too. Louis Saha, who was at Everton, had told me that Phil Neville told him I shouldn't be captain. There were doubts about me, but two years later Neville, who came back to United, apologised to me and said he'd been wrong. Phil wasn't the only one who doubted me. Bryan Robson, a United legend who works at the club as an ambassador, believed that Wayne Rooney should have been chosen.

I think the United players saw me as a serious captain because I was. They seldom saw the lighter side of me, which people have seen since. In the gloom of that Sunderland away dressing room, the manager told us that we would not want to feel this way again, that we had to come back stronger and win the league the following season.

I became very angry when I later saw the television pictures of the end of City's title-winning game. I felt that QPR stopped playing once they had got the message that they were safe from relegation, and I was sickened when I saw Djibril Cissé smiling with Samir Nasri at the end of the game. Naturally, QPR players should have been happy, but I didn't like the images of them celebrating with City's players. They actually did me a big favour because I was highly motivated not only by the reaction of Sunderland's fans, but also by what I saw on the pitch at the Etihad.

The boss had actually asked me to speak to Nasri at the start of the season because United wanted to sign him. I told Samir that it was a once-in-a-lifetime opportunity. He'd agreed with me and told me that he was going to sign for United and that he'd see me pre-season ... then he joined City. I was sorry, as was the boss and David Gill, but Gill then said: 'Patrice, if a player like him doesn't want to join United then he doesn't deserve to play for United.' To this day, I think Nasri made the wrong decision, even though he won the league in his first season at City.

But you know what he said to me on the pitch when we

played against each other in that crucial derby in April? That he should have joined United. Even though City were the champions of England, I knew that their camp wasn't the happiest. We'd have to take advantage of that, as well as our hurt, in the following season.

CHAPTER 12

Twenty Times

Robin van Persie walked into the gym at Carrington. I could see him coming towards me while I pedalled on the bike that players warmed up on before training, but I pretended not to until he was right in front of me.

'Welcome to a real man's club,' I said to Robin in front of everyone, prompting several grins.

'You bastard!' he replied, laughing.

'Don't forget you were the captain of the Arsenal team in the 8-2 game. You're with the men now, you're a good player and you're a United player.' Robin shook his head and at the same time laughed again. Then the Dutch striker got to work, starting training and making as big an impact as I've seen any footballer make at any club. Robin was magnificent; his control and turns in the box were so impressive. You could shoot the ball at him and he'd stop it with his first touch. In games, he could also hold the ball up. He hardly ever lost the ball and this allowed the team to breathe and catch up with the play.

I'd heard the criticism about Robin – that he was too old, too injury prone, yet he was about to turn 29 when he arrived at Old Trafford and hardly a grandfather. If anything, his sustained experience of not winning the league at Arsenal had made him more determined. Robin would be magnificent for us and full of a positive determination to win the league after eight barren years.

A few weeks in, Robin turned to me and said: 'I can't believe the amount of hard work here. I've been at clubs where players finish training, get in the shower and go home. Here, I see you, Ryan Giggs, Paul Scholes, Rio . . . Nemanja. You've won so many titles yet you're so motivated. I see the way you all work hard with extra practice. I don't have any choice but to do the same.'

Robin had several points to prove: firstly to himself that he'd made the right decision to leave Arsenal, where he'd been very popular; then to Arsenal fans who wanted to see him fail when he left and abused him when they saw him in a United shirt; and finally, to everyone at United who wondered just how good he was going to be.

Robin joined us after Euro 2012, which we'd both played in. France had decided to bring me back into the squad after my five-match ban for what happened in South Africa – albeit slowly. Laurent Blanc had replaced Domenech as France coach and he came to Manchester to see me, accompanied by Fabien Barthez, both of them former Man Utd players. Blanc told me that he wanted to see me face to face and we had a productive chat.

'You're a good guy,' he said to me, 'so why do they say such bad things about you?'

'They' must have meant journalists, because he then asked me if I could be nice to the journalists when I returned to the France set-up. Blanc, who wanted to play me, was close to several French journalists and I thought he was scared of them. I also think he was scared of playing me, the perceived bad boy of French football, in France.

My impression seemed to be confirmed because when I first played for France again, it was away in Luxembourg in a qualifier for Euro 2012, then I was on the bench for the next two games. I played away in two friendly games against Poland and Ukraine, the countries who would jointly stage Euro 2012, then I was not in the squad for a home friendly against Chile. I was used in the next two away qualifiers, in Albania and Romania. I didn't feature in a match on French soil in front of a home crowd until nine games after my suspension, when I was given 45 minutes against Albania. However, as we didn't lose one of those nine games, the critical opinions about me gradually improved, but I think Blanc was scared of what the reaction to playing me would be if France lost.

The French people were fine with me when I played at home, just as they'd always been. Honestly, I didn't hear a single boo. Maybe people react differently when they see you face to face in real life to what they say when they comment on the internet or ring a radio station, but I can only say what I saw.

We reached the finals of Euro 2012, but Blanc called me one day and told me that I needed to fix my problem with Franck Ribéry. That was a surprise to me because I wasn't aware that I had one. I went for a drink with Franck at Clairefontaine and he told me that he had said that because I didn't call him any more.

'It's nothing, Franck, I have no problem with you whatsoever,' I replied. And that was the truth.

I think Blanc had had a meeting with several players including Franck, where he told them what he expected from them in the competition. My strong personality was mentioned and this is where Franck had aired his mistaken impression.

Blanc wanted to use my knowledge. 'You're Manchester United captain and we're in a group with England. You have to tell me about England.'

I told him what I thought would be useful, such as about the speed of Theo Walcott. I also started against England in France's opening game of Euro 2012 in Donetsk. We drew 1-1 and that was about the highlight of the competition for France.

Before that game, I told the players about my trip to see our teammate Éric Abidal in Barcelona. Éric was very poorly with cancer and in May 2012 I'd tried to go and see him. He didn't respond to my texts, which wasn't a surprise since he'd just undergone a liver transplant. Éric's wife, Hayet, replied saying that Éric didn't want to see anybody because he was so sick.

I couldn't accept that and pushed again to go and see him. Éric finally said that I could come so I flew to Barcelona, where he was in hospital. He was so happy to see me, but I was shocked when I saw him. His eyes were sunken, he'd lost a lot of weight and looked like a skeleton.

'Have you been doing Ramadan every day?' I asked him, trying to bring some humour to a dark situation.

'You don't change, you bastard,' he replied, and I was pleased to see the spark was still there.

Abi's cousin had been the liver donor, but the operation had complications and he'd needed further surgery. It was a painful moment and I felt even luckier to be healthy. I explained that to the players in Ukraine, that if they saw Abidal like I had, they would never moan about the small things in life like training again. I said that we had to win for him. At no point did I ever think Abidal would walk again, let alone return to football and play in the Champions League.

We couldn't beat England, but a draw was not a bad result. Despite my good performance, Blanc told me that he was resting me for the second game against Ukraine because he wanted to keep me fresh. Gaël Clichy started and France won 2-0. Clichy did okay, but the media made out that he'd played like Zidane at his best. I felt there was a push for Clichy, a happiness that I would no longer be the left back for France. That was the battle I was facing, especially as the manager was influenced so much by what the media said.

I sat on the sidelines as Sweden thrashed us with Zlatan Ibrahimovic monstering central defender Philippe Mexès and scoring a great goal in a 2-0 win in Kiev. That defeat meant we finished second in the group and would play the holders Spain in the quarter-finals rather than an easier opponent if we'd won the group.

Even though I'd not played, I wasn't the only angry France player in the dressing room after the match. Hatem Ben Arfa, a funny guy who I like, was quickly on the phone, telling whoever it was at the other end that the team had lost. Laurent Blanc asked him if he could wait to make the call. Hatem replied: 'What, so we lost 2-0 because I'm on the phone?' He added: 'Anyway, I don't need you. I feel no love here, I feel love in Newcastle where I play. And you only play the players who have the same agent as you.'

Wow! Blanc shook his head. Suddenly he didn't look quite the presidential figure, the hero of France that he was portrayed as by the French media.

Alou Diarra, the captain, came into the dressing room and he was furious, calling us all 'bitches' for losing to Sweden. Samir Nasri objected to his words and – not for the first time – it was getting heated. Blanc started shouting at Diarra, saying that if he had a problem in his private life, he shouldn't bring it into the dressing room. A furious Diarra, the captain, stepped up to face Blanc, then I stood up and said: 'Boss, what are you doing?'

Then I looked at the other players and shouted: 'Are you crazy, guys? Remember what happened with this team in 2008 and 2010? We're in the quarter-finals and we shouldn't be arguing like this.' I was one of the few players who'd been an international in those days and I didn't want the team coming apart again, especially as we'd actually qualified.

I politely asked Blanc to leave the dressing room and told him the players would sort out the issue among ourselves. The manager left. He shouldn't have said that the player had a private issue in front of his teammates and I later told him that, but maybe he was caught up in the emotion like the rest of us.

We returned to the team hotel where our families were also staying. It was getting late, but Blanc called a team meeting in the early hours. Hatem's words about picking players because he had the same agent had clearly struck a nerve because our coach began denying the accusation. Hatem didn't back down, demanding: 'These are just words. I want facts!'

'Hatem, calm down,' I said because I felt he was going too far. He's a good kid with a good heart, but he sometimes said whatever he was thinking without caring about the consequences. Blanc came to me the following day, full of renewed determination.

'Patrice,' he said, clenching his fists, 'we're going to do it, we're going to beat Spain!'

I took that as a sign that I'd be playing against Spain. The players were given a night off and several went out, but I stayed at the team hotel to prepare. In training, I was given the bib of a starting player, right up to the last training session. The team went for a walk on the morning of the Spain game in Donetsk – it wasn't yet a war zone. The manager stopped us mid-walk and told us that, while he wouldn't normally name the team like this, he was going to do it now because he wanted to talk tactics. He started with the goalkeeper, named the whole team and then said: 'Left back,' and then, after a pause, 'Clichy.'

What! There were some words about wanting to stop Andres Iniesta, but I was furious. Malouda, who knew me, told me not to be stupid. Momo Sanhadji, the head of security, also told me not to do anything stupid. I was thinking of doing something very stupid because I wanted to slap Blanc in front of everyone.

Instead, I went to my room and started flinging things about. Ribéry and Diarra followed me and tried to calm me down, but I felt so cheated. I started to pray to calm myself down, asking God not to allow me to do anything silly. While I paced around my room, the other players were eating but I did not want to eat. I felt humiliated, angry, rejected and embarrassed, but I calmed myself down enough after 15 minutes to go down to the dining room.

I walked into the room and everyone stopped and looked up at me. There was near-silence as people put their forks down. I looked at Laurent Blanc, had a moment of hesitation, and then, just before I sat down, I said: 'It's just football! Anyway, guys, are we playing cards after the meal?' Everybody breathed more easily and the smiles returned, but I was masking my anger. That anger made me the player that I am on the pitch, but off it I was learning to control it.

We played Spain, lost 2-0 and went out of the competition to the eventual winners, while in the dressing room Malouda repeated Hatem's accusation, saying that he was sick of the manager selecting players he shared an agent with. None of those players took the bait.

I was still fuming that we were out and that I hadn't been on the pitch to try to prevent our exit. I punched the fridge onto the floor and shouted: 'I'm waiting for our coach!' Another coach shook the hands of the rest of the players, but I refused to shake his hand. He knew I was still fuming and that it wasn't the moment to deal with me. For the first time in all my career, the manager didn't come into the dressing room. Such was the mood among the players, he probably did the right thing.

We left to return to France the following morning. Before we went, I told Momo Sanhadji – who, as before, was the conduit between the coach and the players – that I wanted to speak to Blanc and that I was in my room, and Momo said he would tell him. I waited and waited. I called Momo after a while and he said: 'Mr Blanc said he will speak to you on the plane.'

Blanc was deep in conversation when I got on the plane so I didn't interrupt, but he didn't come to find me either. I intended to speak to him when we landed but couldn't see him. I assumed that he was avoiding me. A few hours after landing, Sanhadji called me to ask when I was going to speak to the manager, but I was already in Cannes for a family holiday. I asked Momo for Blanc's number, which he passed on.

I called Blanc straight away. He didn't answer so I left the following message: 'Hello, coach, it's Patrice. I want to say thanks that you brought me back to the France team, but I'm really frustrated because you didn't play me and you barely gave me any reason why. If I have done something wrong, call me. If you didn't play me because of pressure from the media, that's fine, just tell me. I need an answer, please. I just want you to be honest.'

Like Thuram, he never called me back.

A few days later, I was watching TV and saw that Blanc was not going to continue as France coach. The French Football Federation had announced that they were not going to renew his contract. I called Blanc's number and it went to voice-mail again.

'Hello, coach, it's Patrice again. Thank you again for bringing me back to the national team. I'm sad for you that you are no longer our coach. Please call me back.'

Again, I heard nothing and I've never seen or heard from Blanc since. I would have preferred it if he had been honest with me.

That summer of 2012 I decided to stop playing for France, but I didn't say anything publicly. I'd had enough of the national team and was looking forward to being away from the politics, but there would be another twist. Blanc's replacement was the great Deschamps – King Didier! My former Monaco manager soon called me.

'Congratulations on getting the job, boss, but I'm finished with France,' I told him. 'I'm sick of the injustice, the stress, the unhappiness. I'm a positive person, I'm full of happiness, but I don't feel any of that when I'm with France.'

'No chance,' Deschamps replied, 'I need you.'

A meeting was arranged and the first thing he asked me was if I'd like to read the report from South Africa, to see what the other players said about me when they were questioned by the commission.

'No, boss. Why would I want to see that?' I replied.

'Patrice, some of your teammates say bad things about you. I have it here. Look.'

'I don't want to read it.'

'Some of the players close to you said bad things about you, the ones who call you brother,' he waved it at me. Deschamps wanted to know everything about every player, to leave no stone unturned.

'I'll leave those players in the hands of God,' I replied. I never did read the report.

Deschamps shared his plans for France with me. 'People want to cut my head off for playing you, but I need your experience,' he continued. 'I've even lost a friend because I've called you up. The journalists don't want you to play for France, what happened in South Africa will never go away, but I am the manager and I want you to play. I know the person you are, I know what you can do for me and I also know, Patrice, that you love the French national team. If you play badly I won't play you. If you play well then I will.'

I admired Deschamps' honesty. I wanted to play for him and I watched as he brought pride back into the French national team.

He needed soldiers in his dressing room and I was delighted to fight for that little man from Bayonne.

After Euro 2012 and what followed, I was keen to get back to Manchester and win back the league with United. Back at Carrington, Robin van Persie wasn't the only new arrival. Nick Powell also joined us that summer, a very talented midfielder but not one with the personality to play for United. He didn't integrate, wasn't part of the group and you had no idea what he was thinking as he looked through you. He was only a young lad, but you're not too young to be judged at United.

Shinji Kagawa, United's first Japanese player – who did look like he had the personality – also arrived. Shinji had a bit of the showman about him and we had high hopes for him after he'd done well at Borussia Dortmund as a goalscoring attacking midfielder. He was intelligent on and off the field, a cool man who understood some English even if he didn't speak it, but injuries and the manager moving on would disrupt his career.

Shinji became close friends with Alex Buttner, another left back who joined from Holland. Alex was very self-confident – you need to be to play for Man United. He had a good left foot and I started to hear people saying that he would replace me in the future. The manager needed cover at left back after Fabio, the young Brazilian who played in my position, moved to QPR. With Paul Pogba gone and Ji-Sung Park also moving to QPR because he wanted to play more, the lads joked that I was now on my own. All my other closest friends, Cristiano and Carlos, had gone too. That's football and you get used to it. I still speak to them all.

Fabio was a very good player – his biggest problem was me. I was playing close to 50 games each season and was determined not to lose my place. I would play 379 times for Manchester United; only 36 players have played more games than me in the history of the club. I didn't want to give up my place for anyone, and Fabio and his twin Rafael would joke: 'Come on, Patrice, can't you ever be injured?' The manager wanted a back-up, obviously, but Fabio was better than that and he was right to take his chance elsewhere.

Buttner's arrival made me sharpen up because I knew that he was competition for my place. I lived in my own little Man United bubble. I didn't read any newspapers and tried to steer clear of what the media were saying about us. It can play with your head because they'll build you up and then knock you down. Friends would send me articles that people had written about me – I threatened to block their numbers if they carried on doing it.

When I was young I was happy to see my name in the paper, but journalists would over-praise you if you played well and overcriticise if you played badly. It could affect your mentality, and your head is better off without that noise. I have enough love in my life without searching for compliments. I don't need anyone to tell me how I have performed in a match.

I didn't grow up in a world where I was taught how to deal with the media. You get that training at the French academy in Clairefontaine, but I was not at the academy. When I gave interviews, I wanted to be the real me, not another player with boring and safe answers. The problem is that the real me gets in trouble. So when I said the weather in Manchester is shit – which it is – I got in trouble with the club. But that doesn't mean that I didn't love to live in Manchester. Even Paris is hardly St Tropez.

I was never friends with journalists like some players. I couldn't understand players shaking the hands of the journalists when they played for France. Why make them feel so important? When I turned out for France, the journalists would ask me to stop to talk in the mixed zone and I would say 'Bonjour! Have a nice day!' as I walked past them.

If I had to do my media commitments then I would do them and enjoy them. I had to do them when I was a captain, but I felt like I didn't need the media to build me up, that my success had been down to my hard work, although I do appreciate that the journalists have a job to do.

As I said, we started the 2012-13 season hurting and determined to win the league back. The only change to my game was that I asked the boss if I could be more forward at corner kicks. I always jumped really high – I think it's because my calves are small but explosive – and could be a threat. Even as a kid, we'd have jumping competitions and I'd win. In athletics at school, I was one of the best jumpers. The manager agreed with me, and it worked because I scored three goals in only 13 games from corners – I hadn't scored any goals in the previous season.

In the league Robin van Persie started scoring immediately and got us off to a good start – even though we lost our opening match to Everton at Goodison, which we had never done all the time I was at United. I was happy to set up Robin's first goal in a 3-2 win in our second match of the season against Fulham.

We beat Chelsea in October and Manchester City in December 3-2 away. Robin scored a 92nd-minute winner after Pablo Zabaleta's 86th-minute equaliser for City. There's a picture of me in a red shirt, celebrating Robin's goal in front of the United fans. That moment made me so proud to be a United player, with Robin wearing the number 20 shirt and the players feeling confident that we could win a 20th league title.

City could not spoil that moment, even when a fan threw a 2p coin at Rio Ferdinand that cut his head. Another fan wearing the type of blue hat you put on a baby also ran onto the pitch to confront Rio. City's goalkeeper, Joe Hart, held the fan back and Carlos Tevez held Rio back. What on earth did the scruffy little fan with a stupid hat think he was going to do to Rio?

In just a few months, Robin had become a really important

player for us. Not only was he scoring great goals, his hold-up play was faultless. The boss handled him brilliantly. He'd told the whole team when Robin arrived that he wouldn't be training with us all the time because he had injuries that meant he'd be better training by himself. Fergie was upfront with everyone, there could be no complaints when we saw Robin training on the adjacent pitch with the physios at the start of the week and joining us later on in the week.

Robin's rise wasn't good for Wayne Rooney. Robin became the main man, the leading striker. Wayne's relationship with the manager deteriorated, more so after he didn't start in some key games. We weren't stupid, we could see that the chemistry between them wasn't the same, but there are times in a career when you don't see eye to eye with your manager. It's how you come through that, to continue being a successful player at a club like United, that matters.

People asked me what it took to play for a successful United team. I think the manager liked me for several reasons. Firstly, he felt that I was a warrior who would die for the club and die for him. He also knew that I would do that without being his lapdog, that I could think for myself and that I had a strong personality, but also a personality that can bring something to the dressing room – just not Oasis songs.

Occasionally, Ferguson shouted at me. I did not answer him back, especially if it was a criticism of my performance after a match. He shouted at me after the 2013 Manchester derby when we lost 2-1 at home to champions City. We'd also lost against Chelsea, after a replay, which knocked us out of the FA Cup, and to Real Madrid in the last 16 of the Champions League, a game that stung more than any that season. The boss told me that it was one of the three most painful moments of his entire Man United career, along with City winning the league in the last seconds and Ji-Sung Park's parents offering him that present in Moscow when they knew their son wouldn't play in the 2008 Champions League final.

In that last 16 Champions League game in the Bernabeu, we successfully withstood their white storm of attacking football in the first half before becoming the far better side. Danny Welbeck scored and we had lots of other chances. Cristiano scored for Madrid and the boss blamed me for the goal after the game. I did slip, but the boss apologised to me the next day, saying that Ronaldo had jumped so high that he nearly touched the sky. Ronaldo came to sit with us in the dressing room afterwards. We all missed him and maybe I wasn't alone in thinking how good we'd be if we'd managed to keep him at Old Trafford.

The second-leg game was a killer because I was convinced we had a side strong enough to win the Champions League again. We were on fire and played so well, so fast, against Madrid at Old Trafford, where we took the lead after a Sergio Ramos own goal. The game had a huge sense of occasion, where it felt like it was the only game in football that mattered.

David de Gea had almost nothing to do, but the Turkish referee Cuneyt Cakir ruined the game by sending Nani off for an innocuous challenge on Alvaro Arbeloa in the 56th minute. The United players were furious – and this is where the emotional side of football is important. Instead of carrying on playing with concentration, we were more focused on our anger and sense of injustice at the referee's mistake. The boss was furious and I saw him gesticulating to the referee several times that he had killed the game.

Madrid, meanwhile, kept their cool, worked out where to hit us now we were a man down, and brought on Luka Modric, who scored. Cristiano then finished us off – though he didn't celebrate the goal – and while we had a lot of attacks in the final ten minutes, it was a shocking night for us. The referee needed a police escort into the tunnel after the game, where I heard Ferguson shouting: 'You should arrest him, he's a gangster for what he has done tonight.' I've never seen my manager so angry, and the referee was shitting himself. The manager then made the decision not to speak to the media, which, given the state he was in, was probably very wise.

Mourinho came to our dressing room afterwards, shook the hands of all our players and told us that we were the real winners. Benzema also told me that he'd said the same thing to the Madrid players in their dressing room, telling his teammates that they should be ashamed to have gone through.

It would turn out to be one of Ferguson's last games in charge, but United set up for the next game against Stoke City without me in the starting XI. Alex Buttner was in all the preparation games. I began to realise that I was being dropped. René Meulensteen, United's Dutch assistant coach, asked me in training why I was so angry. 'I am angry because I'm not playing against Stoke,' I replied.

'How do you know you're not playing? Who told you that?'

'I just know,' I said. 'I'm not stupid. I know the team and you do too. You know how he prepares for matches.'

Ferguson wasn't looking at me either. He was angry with how I'd played against City. The atmosphere was not positive between us and so I went to see him. I knocked on his door, like a small boy going to see the headmaster. He told me to come in and, when he saw me, said: 'What do you want, Patrice?'

'Why aren't I playing?'

'I've not made my mind up,' he replied.

'Be honest with me.'

'Buttner will play because against City I saw that you were a little bit tired,' he replied. 'I'm giving you some rest.'

'This is bullshit, boss. I will play against Stoke.'

'Pat, you can't. I've already told the kid he will play.'

'Boss, I respect you, but you know that nobody jumps higher than me. We're playing Stoke. They're playing the long ball, the high balls. I can win those balls. I can play against Peter Crouch. I will play.'

'No, Patrice.'

'Boss. I. Will. Play.' Then I left his room.

We were in the team hotel a day later when Ferguson named his team with me in it. I remember Buttner's face. I felt sad for him because I felt selfish. I was selfish, but I did the job I said I would and we won 2-0 away, gaining an important three points. René Meulensteen complimented me on my performance. I knew that René was pushing for his fellow Dutchman Buttner to be selected. I think Ferguson agreed with René initially, but then he saw my focus.

There were a couple of rumours that the boss was going to step down, so I asked him outright one day in his office. He laughed it off, told me that it was all rumours and said that he was going to carry on managing United. He also told me that he was 99 per cent certain that Cristiano Ronaldo was coming back to Manchester United in the summer of 2013. He also said that he was trying to sign Gareth Bale from Tottenham. I was buzzing when he told me that and vowed to train even harder because I wanted to play with Cristiano again.

We also had van Persie, who finished the season as well as he'd started it. His best goal was part of a hat-trick in a 3-0 win against Aston Villa in April 2013. City were 11 points behind us and we won the league back – my fifth league title with United – with ease. The fans and the players sang '20 times, Man United' for the number of titles that we'd won and we finally did have a really great title celebration through the city, where fans were hanging off five tiers of scaffolding on a building in Deansgate. I was worried for them, but proud of their efforts too. A comparison was made with the pictures when City had won the league a season earlier when two men and a dog celebrated with the team. Manchester was United, yet the end of that season is remembered for one thing more than any other: the departure of Sir Alex Ferguson.

I was stunned when he told us but, unlike the rest of the players who left after training that day, I stayed behind. I was doing my professional coaching badges with a view to becoming a manager in the future. That afternoon, as the world was digesting the thought of Manchester United without Sir Alex Ferguson, I walked into the canteen at Carrington, where I saw David Moyes and the boss talking.

'This is my little soldier,' said the boss to Moyes, as he introduced us. Moyes looked very happy to be there.

'David will be the next United manager,' said the boss. 'Do well for him.' I said I would.

I thought Moyes was a tough manager when he was at Everton, but he needed to be exceptionally strong for United and I would never have wanted to be the man who followed Sir Alex, the greatest manager ever. We still had two league games to play that season, but all the talk among the players was that the boss was going and what Moyes would be like as his replacement.

CHAPTER 13

More Nightmares in Manchester

The problems with David Moyes started soon after he'd taken over in pre-season 2013. David was really nice with everyone as he tried to settle into the job as Manchester United manager, but it was almost an impossible task. Everything he did was compared to how things had been under Ferguson. It was natural that he'd want to do things his own way, but even the slightest change would start players griping about how this wasn't what the old boss would have had us doing.

We flew to Asia for a long warm-up tour in Thailand, Australia, Japan and Hong Kong. In Sydney on the second stage, David suggested that we should do some stretching on the famous Bondi Beach near the hotel. He wanted the players to relax, to get out of the prison that hotels can become when you're a United player. United's own security, who travelled everywhere with the team, suggested that it wasn't the best idea because we'd instantly be recognised. David just replied that he'd been to the beach with Everton and that there were no problems.

'Yes, but you're at Man United,' one of the security team pointed out.

So we went to Bondi, even though there were already fans gathering outside the team hotel. We got off our bus and started to stretch on the beach. Within five minutes, around 50 people started running towards us as word spread. Security, who were furious as the situation began to spiral out of control, tried to stop fans who were barging right into the session, but they had no chance – Man United were training right in front of people in a public place. Mounted police arrived within a few minutes to restore some order. It was a shambles and we had to leave for everyone's safety. From that moment, before we'd kicked a ball in a competitive match, some members of the dressing room began to mutter that David Moyes wasn't the right man for the job. They would find any excuse; it was almost as if they didn't want him to succeed.

I continued as captain, but I don't think David knew how to deal with me initially. It was well publicised that he was trying to sign Everton's Leighton Baines for my position and he knew I knew that. He must have thought I had a negative opinion of him, but no transfer deal was done for Baines. After three or four league games that showed I had not lost any of my form, David walked up to me in the car park at Carrington.

'Patrice, we haven't had a proper chat since I arrived but I want to be clear with you that, while I wanted Leighton Baines, I don't need him any more,' he said. 'You've really impressed me with your performances and your attitude.'

'Boss, you don't need to apologise for anything. If you think there's a better left back for Man United then please sign him. The most important thing to me is that United keep winning.'

From that moment, David started to trust me. I knew what he was saying about Baines was true because Louis Saha had told me what was happening at the Everton end as he knew a lot of the players there. Everton had rejected a bid for Baines, but even after that United wanted him. Yet after Moyes spoke to me, United had stopped calling Baines's agent. That didn't stop them looking elsewhere for a left back. There was talk that David and his staff didn't think I'd be good for 50 games in a season and they were interested in Real Madrid's Fabio Coentrao. But Coentrao didn't sign, nor did anyone else, apart from Marouane Fellaini.

United had also tried to sign Cesc Fabregas, Ander Herrera and Toni Kroos that summer. Fellaini arrived at the last minute on transfer deadline day, someone we knew as an awkward player to mark who'd caused us problems for Everton, especially in the match that lost us the league last season. There was every reason to be optimistic for the new season despite the change of management, with one trophy in the Community Shield and a comfortable 4-1 win at Swansea in the league opener. Wayne Rooney came on as a substitute that afternoon, following a summer where he was linked with a move to Chelsea. I'd asked Wayne outright if he was leaving and if he'd asked to leave. He assured me he hadn't and I had to take his word for it.

A draw against Chelsea in the first home league game was nothing unusual either. But then things started to go wrong. Nobody associated with United wants to lose at Anfield and, when Daniel Sturridge scored the only goal after three minutes, we couldn't find an equaliser. When we lost our next away game 1-4 at Manchester City on 22 September, players really started to pin the blame squarely on the manager.

We'd faced Liverpool, Chelsea and City, got one point from nine and scored one goal. Suddenly, for the first time in my stay at United, we were sixth and seventh in the league table. The fear other teams had of us disappeared in a few short months. Old Trafford had simply stopped being a fortress. You only had to look at David's face to see the pressure he was under. But the way he dealt with it and us was, in my opinion, a big mistake. In the dressing room before one game, he said: 'Guys, you've won everything here, you have to show me the way to win. I have never won the league, you have to show me how to do it.' I could see what David was trying to do by making the players feel responsible, but Ferguson would never have asked his players how to win a game. He would have told us how to do it. Some players used that against him because they thought they were now in charge. Players who'd accepted being on the bench under Ferguson would complain if they were on the bench under Moyes. That made a very hard job even harder.

I remember one time when Alex Buttner had a massive plate of chips in the hotel before a game, which the manager objected to and banned. Chips aren't the best food for a professional athlete so I can understand that, and David had a point, but the story appeared in a newspaper two days later. David was slaughtered in the media for making changes like that and he reacted by letting players eat chips again. The players knew they were in charge, and there was some sort of incident every single day, always an unhappy player. Players became cruel and joked that Bebé had won more medals than Moyes.

'Guys, we have to take some responsibility,' I said in training after weeks of this negativity. 'We have to give the guy a chance.'

'How can you kiss his arse when he tried to sign someone in your position?' one came back at me. 'He's tried to sign every fucking left back in the world!'

'He can sign who he wants but he won't get me out of the team,' I replied, as I have always been ready to fight for my place and was completely confident in my own abilities.

I'd also gone to talk to David after our drubbing at City, where Sergio Aguero had run riot. I gave it to him straight: 'There's something wrong here, boss. The dressing room is not happy and I've not seen that in my time here before. This dressing room was always alive, now it's full of people complaining.'

David admitted that he wasn't the best communicator with the players, but told me that I should focus on my own game as I was playing well. What was a big issue in my mind didn't seem to worry the manager. But as the situation deteriorated I decided to text Ferguson to see if I could go and talk to him at his home. I did this not to undermine David, but because it was killing me to see what was happening to United. I remembered when I'd gone to see Deschamps when he said he was leaving Monaco and his wife stood on the stairs, crying. Cathy Ferguson made me a nice cup of tea.

'Boss, you have to help David,' I told Ferguson.

'Patrice, I appreciate your concern and I'll try and speak to him, but I've given him the biggest chance of his life and I think it's fair that I keep a distance and let him do his job.'

I could see his perspective, and appreciated that he could easily be seen as interfering.

We lost at home to West Brom at the end of September, a humiliating result for a team who had won the league five months earlier. I wasn't alone in thinking David had made a mistake by getting rid of Ferguson's three main coaches, Mick Phelan – a real football coach who held enjoyable training sessions – René Meulensteen and Eric Steele. Ferguson had advised him to keep them, but David had a loyalty to his previous staff and that's not unusual in football. Managerial teams tend to move around in groups, and David had made some United-friendly allowances by bringing in former United player Phil Neville as a coach. But it would prove almost impossible for David's other coaches Jimmy Lumsden, Steve Round and Chris Woods. They'd done well at Everton, but Everton didn't win trophies. What were they going to teach players who'd won the European Cup?

Adnan Januzaj's rise to becoming a player in the starting XI really pissed players off, too. They felt that Adnan was really disrespectful in training, that he was too individual, not passing the ball, and too mouthy off the field in the canteen. A young United player was not supposed to have his attitude – he even had an argument with the chef, who was an ordinary guy doing his job very capably. Adnan scored two goals on his debut at Sunderland away at the beginning of October, a game we really needed to win. Adnan has got talent and I actually liked him, but I kept trying to calm him down, to keep his feet on the ground. I told him to be more respectful to the established players, not to take the piss out of them in training.

'But I did that because they're not that good,' was his answer.

'If you try and humiliate me with your skill then I'll kick your arse!' I warned him.

He just smiled but I think he got the message. I would have said the same thing at his age and that's perhaps why I wasn't selected to play in Italy or my first season at Nice. Adnan started to feel that he was not popular, but he had the wrong explanation.

'They're just jealous of me,' he told me.

'No, Adnan, they just want more respect from you. And don't forget, when you play you're eating the food of the players whose place you are taking. Don't expect them to be delighted for you when they have wives and kids.'

Adnan started laughing again. His arrogance wasn't nasty, he just didn't understand how he was being perceived, from what he did in training to the way he wore his cap back to front. He has a really good heart and he's a nice boy, but even Wayne Rooney, who was very popular in the dressing room and who was the best player for most of the time Moyes was there, snapped and threatened to punch him once.

I started to protect Adnan. He did deserve to be brought down a peg, but at the same time the other players were too harsh on him. I'd been that young player with the cap on back to front, the player who thought he knew everything when he didn't. Though they wouldn't know it, United fans didn't help the situation with Adnan because they began to hero-worship him after only a few games and they had a song for him. Some of United's greatest-ever players didn't even have songs. That made him even more confident that he was right and his team-mates were wrong. He was an excitable young lad who had become a star overnight; it was bound to have an effect on him, although you can hardly blame the fans for encouraging an exciting new talent in what had become a poor season.

Although I was concerned and upset by what was happening, United still had great players and at times we showed it, like when we went to Bayer Leverkusen away and won 5-0 on a freezing night in Germany. We saved our best performances for Europe, as if we didn't want to be embarrassed and had to save face in front of the rest of the world, but we were just terrible in the league and lost all our consistency.

We lost at home to Everton and Newcastle within four days at the beginning of December. But then we got a run together of six straight wins – before losing consecutive home games to Swansea, which knocked us out of the FA Cup, and Spurs. We reached the semi-final of the League Cup and played Sunderland over two legs. We lost on penalties.

A month later we lost 2-0 at Olympiakos in the Champions League in February 2014. Our performance was utterly dreadful and as captain I felt responsibility for it. As I got back onto the team plane, I walked past David Moyes' father sitting at the front. I really felt for him, he should have been proud to see his son managing Manchester United in a big European game, but the defeat overtook everything.

I expected the players to be distraught on that plane; instead they were laughing around and playing video games, which admittedly was the normal thing to do on the way back home, but I didn't feel it was the right thing to do after a humiliating defeat in Greece. The players had decided that the manager, not them, was the problem. Again, I went to see David and told him that I was going to call a players' meeting because the season was turning into a disaster.

'I'm telling you because I don't want you thinking that I've gone behind your back,' I explained.

'Do it, Pat, that's fine.' David was really down and getting criticism from everywhere. He needed support from the people who could help him, the players.

We held that meeting at Carrington and everyone aired their opinions. The players admitted that they weren't performing to their abilities but that they didn't have full faith in the manager. Too many of them blamed the manager, but I still felt that it was a frank and productive meeting. Team meetings can be a good way of clearing the air, man to man, but they shouldn't be held all the time. Any more than three a year and they lose their effect.

We won away at West Brom in the first game after Olympiakos, but then we lost 3-0 at home to Liverpool, a disastrous result. The United fans were magnificent that day and kept singing until the end, even though their team was losing 3-0 against their biggest rivals. David called a meeting of the defenders the following day at Carrington. Nemanja Vidic was coming back from his big injury and it was common knowledge that he was leaving for Inter Milan at the end of the season. David went through all the defensive players in the meeting and picked out Nemanja and Phil Jones for criticism for their positioning. Suddenly, Nemanja started swearing in Serbian.

'Sorry, do you have a problem?' David asked a visibly emotional Nemanja.

'We have to defend one against one, but Rafael and Patrice are always high, they think they are strikers, they need to stay back.'

I disputed that, shouting: 'You have to take your responsibility, Nemanja!' We were now both angry with each other. Really angry. We stood up and argued, unable to hear each other above each other's shouts. We started to square up and then I pushed him. David was going mad, telling me to calm down. David's assistants were now keeping us apart as I shouted at Nemanja: 'I'll wait for you after training.' It escalated in no time. Nemanja wasn't scared; I wasn't scared. Neither of us did fear and those qualities had led us to playing for the best team in the world. We were frightened of nobody – including each other!

My plan was to wait for Nemanja and fight him after training because David's assistants wouldn't let me get near him at the club. I would see him in the car park and we could fight there and then, man to man. As I was thinking my plan through, one of the coaches told me that the manager wanted to see me in his office.

I walked up the stairs to the manager's office. David was shocked – I don't think he'd seen two players fight like that before. I told the manager that I was sorry, that I shouldn't have pushed Nemanja.

'Where did that strength come from, Pat?' he replied, surprised and laughing. 'But seriously, you cannot fall out with Nemanja like that. You are both teammates.'

'I know,' I replied. 'I respected him and I'm hurting because Vida was there for me at the start of my United career.'

I was still really angry, though, and went back home and planned how I was going to punch Vida the next day. I'd barely calmed down the next morning when I arrived at training and changed, but I didn't see Vida all day. David told me not to do anything stupid and I promised him that I wouldn't.

After that, Vida and I simply didn't speak to each other, not even in matches when we played alongside each other. There were games when Rio was switched to play alongside me rather than Vida. That suited Vida as he was right-footed. We didn't speak for weeks and I became sad about the situation. We'd be in the same dressing room day after day, on the same coaches, trains and planes or in the same hotels and we wouldn't speak. We were both too proud to back down, two strong personalities. We'd brush past each other on a train or plane and just ignore each other.

It changed in one game when I made a good pass and heard: 'Well done, Pat.' It was Vida! I was delighted to hear this, I was singing inside and because of those few words, I knew the war between us was over. After the game, I said: 'Well done, Vida,' in the dressing room. A big roar went up among the other players.

'They're best mates again now!' shouted one, probably Giggsy. We weren't best mates and something had been broken in our relationship by that argument, but Ryan had made people smile. He was always important in the dressing room, always taking the piss but always setting high standards. I apologised to Vida. We'd had a difference of opinion, but my respect for him is massive. In all my career of international and club football, Vida and Rio formed the best central-defensive partnership that I played alongside.

In the meantime, we faced Olympiakos at home, needing to come back from 2-0 down and effectively save the season. It was my turn to talk to the media amid speculation that it could be my last Champions League game for United. I was out of contract and hadn't signed a new deal.

'It is not a good day to talk about my future because the most important thing is Manchester United's future, not mine,' I told the press. 'When I put on a Manchester United shirt, I will give everything, no matter what my future is. I am not going to tell you we are going to qualify, but I promise we are going to fight and the fans will be proud of us after the game.' I meant that, too.

David told me that I'd said exactly what he wanted to hear and that he could tell my words weren't hollow. They weren't – we gave it everything and won 3-0 to reach the quarter-finals of the Champions League. That was the minimum expectation for United and that victory seemed to spark us into getting a bit of rhythm going, beating West Ham away, but it was all too fragile. Once again our world came crashing down as we lost 3-0 at home to City in the derby. This was worse than the 1-6 defeat for me personally. In the 1-6, my head wasn't right because my brother had died and I didn't really register the result.

City were very, very good, a class apart from us. They sensed our weakness, our fragility of mind, and exploited it. That's what the best teams do. After those 3-0 home defeats to Liverpool and City, we knew that we had major, major problems at Old Trafford. I felt the mood of the fans – you can sense the atmosphere from the pitch, from what people say to you as you go into the stadium and leave – that they'd had enough of David Moyes.

You can feel it in the atmosphere inside the stadium too. People have been critical of the Old Trafford atmosphere, yet that surge when the team attacks is the most beautiful, natural sound. It's not staged, not organised, not accompanied by a drumbeat. It's a roar from fans happy that their team are attacking. And it had gone because we'd been convincingly beaten 3-0 in two successive home games by our main rivals. The mood was changing, and while it was harsh on the manager – a good man and a good manager – he knew that the results were nowhere near good enough for Manchester United.

We drew 1-1 with Bayern Munich at Old Trafford in the last eight of the Champions League. I was suspended and Buttner in my place did a good job against Arjen Robben. Then we went to Newcastle away and won 4-0 and I played, but I was irritated when the other players wound me up by saying that Buttner was going to take my place. I shouldn't have been wound up because they were only having a laugh, but none of us were ourselves around that time. There was too much tension in the air.

Wazza was the main voice in the dressing room at that time, a player happier now he was the main striker again. After a super first season, Robin was the striker who was unhappy because he was now playing second fiddle to Wayne. This is absolutely normal for strikers and would have happened whoever was the manager.

We travelled to Munich for the second leg and visited the memorial site close to the 1958 air disaster. It was a massive deal for me. I prayed at the memorial for those who died, including all those great young players. I took photos, I spoke to United fans doing the same and I just felt it. Back in my hotel room, I prayed again. Normally I say thank you to God and ask for his protection for my family, but this time I asked God to protect the Busby Babes and if I could score a goal for them to say thank you. I was playing this game for them, part of the same United family as me, young boys who died doing what I do and realising their dream. Our team travelled together on planes all the time and you take for granted that it will be safe.

Our form had been inconsistent going into the game against Bayern, one of the great clubs in world football, but it was 0-0 at half-time. We still needed to score to go through as they'd got an away goal, and David had named an attacking line-up with Wayne Rooney, Danny Welbeck, Shinji Kagawa and Antonio Valencia up front. It worked and we created chances in the first half and Antonio had a goal disallowed for offside. The four strikers were doing well, but they needed a hand – from me.

I decided to move more upfield and was in position when 'The Beast' Valencia put in a great cross from the right after 57 minutes. I hit a left-foot rocket from outside the area, which flew into the top corner, bouncing down from the underside of the bar. It was without doubt one of the best goals I've ever scored. I knew I should have been a striker! I was overcome with emotion as I celebrated and kissed the United badge and thought about the Busby Babes. High on the top tier, the travelling United fans bounced around, singing 'United! United! United!' They always followed us in big numbers around Europe and now they were making the only noise in Munich. I ran to the side and could see the relief in David Moyes' face. He later said that he wanted the game to end there and then, but the relief lasted all of 73 seconds.

Bayern scored three times and I was blamed for two of the goals, but I was only at fault for one of them, when Mandzukic got in front of me for a header. We were also playing a very good Bayern side who were the reigning European champions, but the Champions League was the only competition that we'd had left and now we were out.

Manchester United's season was over at the start of April, the worst at the club since 1989. The mood changed drastically after Munich, and David lost almost all support from within the club. Everyone started to think that not only would he be changed at the end of the season, but that he would be fortunate if he lasted that long. He was barely ten months into a six-year contract and Europe had kept him alive. Nobody said anything in public because the media would have been all over it. I'm amazed at how little of the discontent was picked up on the outside, but when players spoke to the media – and few did – they reverted to stating the obvious about trying their best and wanting to win games.

I was dropped for the next game away at Everton, David's former club. 'Patrice, you were too emotional after Bayern,' said my manager when he came to see me in the hotel before the game. 'I can see you are down.'

We lost 2–0 and a fan dressed as the grim reaper stood behind David Moyes during the game. Giggsy, who was also dropped, went mad after that match when Everton fans surrounded our bus outside the main stand and started abusing us. One of them threw something that bounced off the coach window. Giggsy stood up on the coach and shouted: 'Fucking Everton fans are now taking the piss out of us. Enough is enough.' He was right.

The next day, the senior players – myself, Vida, Wayne, Giggsy, Rio and Michael Carrick – were summoned to Ed Woodward's office at Carrington. I think David knew what was happening. Ed spoke to us players separately so he could get our individual opinions. I was last to go in.

'Is David Moyes still the man to lead this team?' he asked.

'The players are the first people who are responsible,' I replied. 'We are to blame more than the manager, but the dressing room is not a happy place. I will defend David, but there are problems here.'

'I know,' said Ed. 'Thank you for your honesty. We will see what decision we take.'

I knew then that Woodward had lost faith in David, and was not surprised at all when he was sacked. I went to see my manager – I don't know of any other player who did – as he packed up his stuff to leave his office.

'Boss, I'm sorry for you,' I said.

'Thank you for what you have done for me, Patrice,' he replied. He was frustrated and angry not just at how things had worked out at United, but that he'd found out he was losing his job from the media, not from the man who had employed him.

Nobody had wanted it to work out like this at Old Trafford, not David, the players, the fans or Ed Woodward. It was a very difficult job for anyone, but so many things had gone wrong in such a short space of time. The happiness and enthusiasm that I'd seen in David's face when I'd first met him in the canteen almost a year earlier had gone, but I knew someone with his qualities would come back from it.

Ryan Giggs was named caretaker manager until the end of the season for four next-to-nothing games. But the mood shot up in the dressing room, like the real United was back. I was disgusted that people who weren't prepared to give everything for David were now prepared to do anything for Giggsy.

Ryan impressed me from the start. I called him 'boss' in training.

'Are you crazy?' he laughed. 'I'm Giggsy.'

'Ryan, I'm calling you boss.' Other players called him Giggsy and that annoyed me, but he didn't care as long as they did what he said, which they did.

We had a meeting to prepare for a game against Norwich, which we won 4-0. Giggsy came across like he'd been a coach for 20 years. He'd already completed his pro coaching licences and was confident when taking charge of training and in pre-senting analysis.

'I can feel Ferguson's blood in you,' I told him after he'd spoken so well to try and motivate the team. He brought Scholesy in to train with the lads, and as soon as Paul crossed the ball you could tell he was still better than anyone else. Everyone was buzzing and Ed Woodward asked to speak to me at the end of the season, to ask who I thought should be manager. I didn't have to think for a second. 'Giggsy. He's won everything, the players really respect him. He is Man United.'

Woodward took everything on board but he had a big deci-sion to make. I did too, because I was soon to be out of contract and I'd mentally started preparing myself to leave the club at the end of the season.

If Giggsy made one error, it was that he didn't choose his strongest team in the games he played, because he said he would give everyone a chance, which meant that one of those games was lost and another drawn.

I was out of the final home game against Hull City when a couple of young players – James Wilson and Tom Lawrence – were given their debuts. I didn't even go to Old Trafford to see it, which was wrong of me, but I couldn't come to terms with the fact that I was leaving United and didn't want to torment myself further by spending hours hanging around there.

My wife had told me that she wouldn't make my decision for me, but she was still not at home in a city that she associated with so many negative things. She wanted to be in Paris close to her family and said that she couldn't cope being away from them.

My mind was a mess and I'd started to weigh up whether I should stay or not. It felt like the end of an era with Ferguson going, yet I liked the idea of playing under Giggsy. It was a blow to me when Louis van Gaal was made manager because it meant Giggsy hadn't got the job, but Ryan later called me to say that he was going to be the assistant and that I should stay at United.

At the club's end-of-season Player of the Year awards for a team that finished seventh, I'd spoken to Ed Woodward about my future and explained the situation with my wife. I'd always got on well with Ed and made suggestions to him, such as he should visit the dressing room after games and shake players' hands as David Gill had done. Ed had said that wasn't his style, that he liked to give the players and manager their own space, but I insisted that it was right that the players saw him regularly, and he accepted that. I respected him, more so when Ed told me that the club wouldn't exercise the option on my contract that I'd signed under Ferguson and would let me go for free as a thanks for my service. Everything Ed said was right, yet I felt pain because he and I were talking about me leaving United. I wanted to feel wanted, for him to say: 'Stay, stay, stay.'

We took a family holiday to Dubai at the end of the season. I was enjoying a birthday meal at Zuma, a Japanese restaurant in Dubai, when my agent texted me to ask where I was. I told him I was having a meal. He insisted that I went somewhere private where I could talk without being overheard.

'I'm having a meal, can we talk later?'

'No, it's really urgent.'

'Text me to tell me what it's about first.'

He sent me a message from United that said they were going to offer me a one-year contract extension. I was furious, that was not what I'd understood. I felt betrayed as I went back to my room in the hotel to call Ed.

'Hello,' said Ed cheerily.

I went crazy at him, swearing and calling him every name under the sun. I threatened him, accused him of not being a man, of not respecting me. The Patrice from the street was back. I hung up on him. Ten minutes later, I called Ed again. No answer. I called him at least 20 times. And 20 times he didn't answer. On the 21st time, Ed answered and said: 'Patrice, if you swear again I won't talk to you.'

I tried to gather my composure – and not to swear. 'How can you do this to me?' I asked him. 'You told me that we will not renew the option to sign.'

'But, Patrice, you are too important to the club. The new manager wants you and I can't let you go.'

'It's not about money, it's about trust and respecting my decision to leave,' I went on, before I started shouting again and, I'm ashamed to say, threatening Ed and telling him what I was going to do if I met him. He put the phone down and he didn't pick it up again.

Now, I understand Ed's position completely. The club were about to lose four senior players in me, Giggs, Rio and Nemanja. He was putting Manchester United first and wanted me to stay after talking to Louis van Gaal. They wanted to create an obstacle to stop me leaving, but I didn't appreciate all this when I called him from Dubai.

Giggsy called me the following day. I was still determined to leave and regretted that the fans would think I was deserting United when they needed me the most. Ed had told Giggs about our phone calls and the threats I'd made. Giggsy knew just how to handle me. 'Come on, Pat, don't leave this club,' he said. 'I know you love this club. We need you here, we want you here.'

Giggsy calmed me down but I also knew that Juventus were interested. Months earlier, I'd instructed my agent: 'I want to stay at United, but find me another club because I want to test myself.'

Juventus quickly said they would be interested and I was told that Antonio Conte wanted me to play for him.

Then United announced that they had activated a clause to extend my contract by a year. I received a constant stream of messages of congratulations from friends and family for staying at United, which started the minute United made their offer public. With each one, my heart sank as I thought: 'What are the fans going to think of me now when I leave?'

With all this swirling around in my mind, I joined up with the France team for the 2014 World Cup finals in Brazil. I was happy to be playing for France again in the World Cup, a finals free of the problems of four years previously. While I was there, the Juventus coach Conte called me four times, telling me that everything was ready for me in Turin, but that I had to sign the contract. I told him that I'd make my decision after the World Cup, but I gave him every indication that I wanted to play for him at Juventus.

Paul Pogba was my France teammate and he knew that Juventus wanted me. He would come to my room and say: 'Come on, Uncle Pat, we want you in Turin. Come and follow me.' Carlos Tevez, who'd signed for them a year before, was the same. 'Come!' he'd text. I started to feel the excitement. These guys were my friends. It would be a new start after a confused and frustrating season, and it would make things so much better at home.

Finally, France had a good World Cup. We needed to beat Ukraine in a play-off to reach the finals and we lost the first leg 2-0 away before winning 3-0 at home. I was the regular left back and really enjoying playing for Deschamps. Deschamps had everything working for the 2014 World Cup in Brazil. The team spirit was better than I'd ever known for France. We beat Honduras 3-0 and Switzerland 5-2 before drawing 0-0 with Ecuador. We beat Nigeria 2-0 in Brasilia to set up a quarter-final tie with Germany in Maracana, one of football's most legendary stadiums. While it no longer held 200,000, it was packed with 76,000 fans. We lost 1-0 to the team who'd become champions of the world but, unlike previous tournaments, we left that game full of love for the France shirt.

Now I just needed to know which shirt I would be loving next in club football – if I could love another team at all after more than eight years at Manchester United.

CHAPTER 14

Turin

I took another holiday in Los Angeles with my family after the 2014 World Cup. Officially, I was still a Manchester United player. Coincidentally, United were also in the city and the new manager Louis van Gaal wanted to see me. Ed Woodward had been generous, even after I shouted at him so badly, and offered me a two-year contract, which was unusual for a player over 30, plus a testimonial as I would have been at Old Trafford for ten years had I stayed until 2016. He also said I would be considered as team captain and offered me a continuation of my £4.5 million a year wages – £1 million more than Juventus were offering. Normally, older players see their pay reduced.

'It's too late, Ed,' I told him, even though I'd not given my word to Andrea Agnelli, the president of Juventus. A day later, I went to see my United teammates who were staying at the Beverly Hilton. I told my wife that I was going to say goodbye.

'Don't change your mind,' were her parting words.

There were United fans outside the hotel opposite Rodeo Drive and they shouted my name. 'Please don't give me that love,' I thought. I saw Luke Shaw, the new signing in my position. I wished him well and told him that it wasn't going to be easy for him but that he'd been bought because of his talent. It was great to see them all laughing and smiling, Wazza and Ash setting the mood. I felt terrible that I was going to leave all this behind.

Giggsy spotted me and said that the new manager was ready to see me. Ed had told me that van Gaal wanted to speak to me but didn't want to call me during the World Cup out of respect for me being with France. Ironically, had he called me then, I think it would have made a difference to my mindset. Van Gaal was really pleasant and told me that he'd heard positive things about me from the people at United and that he thought I should stay. 'Come on!' he said in a jovial manner. 'It's not too late.'

The Dutchman explained that he would sometimes play three at the back and that I would be an option to be one of those. I could feel myself being reeled back into my marriage to Manchester United Football Club, but then van Gaal said: 'I'm not happy with Ed Woodward for offering you two years. It's up to me if you deserve a second year.'

To my mind, that was a mixed message and it tipped me back again. When I got back to our rented villa my wife was waiting for me. 'What now?' she said, seeing my expression as I came through the door. I said nothing, which made things worse. I'd told her we were going to Turin and she was looking forward to it, now I was wobbling and couldn't pull myself free of my addiction to a football club in the north-west of England, a city and country I wasn't even from.

I'd taken too many selfish decisions and it was time that I took one that made her happy. I decided to join Juventus, grabbed her and told her that we were going to Italy. I called Agnelli and announced: 'Forza Juve!'

There had been a few twists in the negotiations with Juventus in the previous weeks. Paul Pogba called me to say that the coach, Antonio Conte, who'd just led them to a third consecutive Serie A title, was leaving only a day after pre-season training had started. When I heard that, I told Sandra that we had to stay in Manchester, but Juventus quickly appointed the respected coach Massimiliano Allegri and he was the first person to call me after I'd spoken to Agnelli. Juventus legend and ambassador Pavel Nedved also called me; star players Andrea Pirlo and Gianluigi Buffon sent me congratulatory texts. They didn't know me, but I felt wanted in Turin and I appreciated the touch.

United had reluctantly accepted that I was going and Juventus were happy to pay a small fee of €2 million. I had a two-year deal ready to sign, and after eight years with United and a messy departure – in part because I made it messy – it was time for a new chapter in my life at the age of 33.

'After a great deal of thought I have decided the time is right for me to leave,' I said in a statement. It sounded so orderly, when in reality my head was all over the place. 'It is the biggest decision of my career as this club is, and will always remain, in my heart. An immense thank you to Sir Alex for making it all possible, for giving me the privilege to be a captain and to understand that nobody is bigger than the club. My biggest thanks go to the fans. We have had some fantastic times together and every single time I stepped out in that shirt I knew I was playing for a very special club.'

I would continue to doubt my decision to leave, despite the certainty of this official farewell.

I arrived in Turin on the same day as Paul Pogba, who had been given the same return date as me after playing for France in the World Cup. At my first meeting, Juventus told me that we would have ten days of training in Turin before going to Australia for a pre-season tour. At Juventus' Vinovo training ground south-west of the city, I immediately felt very welcome, like I could feel the love from every single person there, like they were waiting for me to complete the jigsaw of their team. I did my public presentation where I said how happy I was to sign for Juventus, then it was straight into what I was told was 'a little training' at the Juventus Centre.

There was nothing little about the training – it was very, very hard. After doing a lot of running, I took a shower and was heading back to my hotel in the city when I saw that I was the only player without a big bag. 'Why do you all have these big bags?' I asked.

'We're in a hotel for ten days,' came the reply.

I couldn't understand why Juventus stayed in a hotel in Turin pre-season when everyone lived in Turin, but it was the norm for the club. So I got my clothes and computer from my hotel and went to the team hotel 20 minutes from the training ground.

Each day, we would train in the morning and the afternoon before spending the evening in the hotel. The club did this to monitor players closely and you had no choice what you ate in those ten days, with each portion of really healthy food weighed out for you. I looked for pasta in the canteen and the players started laughing at me because it wasn't on the menu. Paul told me to look in the kitchen, where I saw photos of every player with colours around them according to the portions of food we'd be served. Green was normal, orange was half-portion and red was like Ramadan. Paul and I, fortunately, were down for green.

The club wanted every player to be at their optimum weight and fitness after those ten days. I'd never had a problem with my weight as a footballer, but it was a strict regime, which was difficult for me because I'd not known anything like it. With respect to Manchester United, the training there was like being on holiday compared to Juventus. I did win everything on that 'holiday' schedule so I'm not complaining, but I don't think there's a team in the world that works as hard as Juventus.

It wasn't just me who found myself working harder than ever before. Between the whole squad, we could draw on our experiences at a lot of the world's best clubs. Even Mario Mandzukic, who'd been at Diego Simeone's hard-working Atlético Madrid, said Juventus was tougher. I saw an interview with Zinedine Zidane where he said he'd trained so hard at Juventus that he vomited. That was nothing new, for I saw midfielder Claudio Marchisio doing exactly that in an early session. He wasn't feeling well and he stopped running for a while to be given replacement fluids, before carrying on. At the end of the session Marchisio was called back to finish the running he'd missed. It was an extreme intensity.

The methods used were different from my other clubs too. We'd play eleven against zero, where you have movement but no opponent. Carlos Queiroz had once suggested this at Carrington, and Paul Scholes simply kicked the ball away and said: 'You can't have a game against nobody.'

I felt that football was a job in those first weeks in Turin – a good job where you earn a lot of money, but one where the work never stopped. The club gave me a nice car from their sponsors Jeep, but I didn't want to use it because it felt like a work car, like the club had complete control over me. We would have one day off once a month at Juventus – that's it.

At United, the day after a game we'd do light training and then take a massage. There was light training through the week, and Thursday was a 'free day' for football, tennis or practising finishing against a goalkeeper. Friday was the most intense, with those tough practice games, because Ferguson wanted you to get into the competitive mindset a day or two before the match. At Juventus, training was heavier and I've never run so much in my life; there was also more emphasis on tactics. We even trained at the stadium on the day of the game. I wanted to punch Tevez and Pogba because they'd mentioned nothing about this.

'Why didn't you tell me?' I asked Carlito after training.

'Because I want someone to die with me,' he replied, smiling.

In training I started to neigh like a horse as we ran around because I felt we were being trained like racehorses on the gallops. My teammates laughed, but it wasn't meant to be funny. There were three-dimensional scans to measure your body fat and other tests most days. We were like lab rats and I felt knackered every day. I've always loved music, but I felt too tired to listen to it. As soon as I stepped back in my room, I fell asleep.

At United, we wore monitors in training. At Juventus, we wore them all the time including when we slept. The club wanted to know everything about us and they even gave us a blood test after our monthly day off to see what we'd eaten. The idea was to rest on your day off rather than, say, go to Paris to see your family. I didn't even see the beautiful centre of Turin, with its baroque architecture set against the backdrop of the Alps. I didn't even dare drink a Coca-Cola because they probably had a cola-detecting machine at the club. If training was this hard, what was it going to be like actually playing for Juventus?

We flew to Australia via Indonesia, where we stopped en route in Jakarta. Juventus fans were waiting for us in the airport, which surprised and impressed me. I knew United were a global club, but Juventus were also huge. I fell asleep on the team bus from the airport and woke to see that we were outside a stadium. Another training session. 'Why are they punishing us like this?' I asked Pogba. He laughed at me. He wasn't laughing when we did non-stop running in that session.

We played a game in Jakarta and I was pleased as we won 8-1. I felt fit and it was nice to play some football rather than run. That was what I was paid to do, yet one of the club fitness coaches had a word with me. 'We're going to have to do some real work, Patrice,' he said. 'You're not fit enough.' I couldn't believe it. And there was me thinking that I had been doing okay.

We played an A-League All Stars team featuring former Juventus hero Alessandro Del Piero in Sydney and 80,000 people attended. Juventus had huge support in Australia, where there is a big Italian expat community. It didn't feel like so much of a step down from United.

It was during our stay in Australia that we were actually given a half-day off, from 5 pm to 10 pm. I've never cherished free time as much in my life. Paul and I went to a restaurant, where Paul ordered three main courses and ate them all. I ordered a steak and a Coke and it tasted so good. I felt free, that I was getting revenge against the regime, knowing that they were not able to do blood tests on us every day while we were on tour.

I was tired after that tour, mentally and physically, but we were rewarded with two days off. People would ask me how Turin was and I'd reply: 'I don't know.' My life consisted of hotel, training and church once a week. In hindsight, I was suffering from depression. I kept calling Sandra and my agent to complain all the time. It wasn't me, I'm not a negative person and I know I've been lucky to have the jobs I've had. But I was cross with Sandra and said: 'You've brought us here, I don't want you to complain about anything.' Instead I did the complaining – about our small apartment as it had only three bedrooms and was very small when compared with my big house – and tree – in Manchester.

I was kept out of the first league game of the season because pre-season was so tough, but was promised by the coach that I'd make my debut against Udinese in the first home game. Before that match, I pulled the Juventus shirt on for the first time in a proper game and went to the toilet, where I looked at myself. There was a problem – the shirt wasn't red.

'This isn't you, you're lying to yourself,' I said.

I went out and settled in well as a left-winger in a very offensive 4–4–2 formation where you have to run a lot more than as a left back. I enjoyed that role, but Conte had made a point of telling me that he planned to play 4–3–3. Allegri had also told me this and we'd played 4–3–3 in pre-season. However, we conceded too many chances and the coach changed to three at the back when the season started. That change came from the influential players suggesting that it would be better to start the season with a 3–5–2.

Pavel Nedved, who salutes the fans before every game on the pitch, came to me after my debut. 'You played really well, but you don't look happy,' he said. 'You look like someone has died.'

He was stating the obvious.

We won away at AC Milan in our third game, but I was on the bench. I had gone right into a strong, winning side aiming to win Serie A for a fourth straight season, but I was unhappy and angry. I couldn't understand why we needed to be in a hotel two days before a home game, why we needed to train on the day of the match. I was depressed and miserable and it wasn't just Nedved who could see it.

'We know you won everything at Manchester,' a fitness coach said to me one day, 'but this isn't Manchester, it's Juventus and this is how we work here. Our priority is not for you to play well, but for you to be an athlete, to be healthy and to run more than you did in Manchester. This is the Juventus way.'

'Okay, guys, I appreciate your honesty,' I replied, 'but if we don't win anything at the end of this season then I'll go crazy with you.'

I spoke to Allegri. 'Even though we are winning, I feel like I'm not enjoying my football here,' I said. 'If you want a player to control like he's in a PlayStation game that's fine, but I'm not like that. I like to receive the ball, to go deep to get it. At

Juventus you want the full back really high alongside the striker. I've not played like this, and you told me before you signed me that you wanted me to play in a 4–3–3 system.'

'Patrice, you have to understand that I have to look after the team,' Allegri explained patiently.

I respected his point of view, but I replied: 'Until you play with four at the back, please don't play me.'

Maybe I'd come to regret saying that, maybe I was being impulsive and immature, just like I'd been in Monza all those years before, but I wasn't happy and wanted to tell my boss why. All the time, I looked to see how United were doing in England. After they'd lost 3–5 at Leicester, I called my agent and said I wanted to go back to Manchester. He told me not to be stupid. I felt like the *Titanic* was sinking in Manchester and I wanted to be Leonardo DiCaprio, the man who stays until the end.

'You're mad,' said my agent. 'You're first in the league, you're in a great team and you've only just joined.'

'I don't care!' I shouted. 'I'd be happier to be relegated with Manchester United than win the league with Juventus.'

He ignored me.

We went to play a Champions League away tie at Olympiakos, and Allegri heeded my words and didn't pick me, going instead for Kwadwo Asamoah in a 3–5–2. We lost 1–0, the second time in eight months that I'd seen a defeat at Olympiakos. It was also Juve's second consecutive defeat in the Champions League following a 1–0 loss in Madrid against Atlético. We'd actually played well in that game against an excellent side who were the Spanish champions and who'd been a minute from being European champions four months before.

That Olympiakos defeat was a surprise for me, though. When I'd arrived at Juventus the directors had told me that winning the league was normal, but it was really important to give a better image of Juventus in the Champions League. They said that the target was to reach the quarter-finals. I'd replied that they should be aiming higher and they were laughing at my confidence. I was not laughing after getting home from Olympiakos at 4 am to be told that we'd be training at 10 am. I was so angry that I didn't sleep, but I dragged myself to training. Those players who hadn't played were sent to run laps and I was in a stinking mood.

The fitness coach Simeone told me to run faster because I was last. 'Look, Simeone,' I replied, 'I'm not a robot and when I don't sleep or don't get enough sleep, I'm vulnerable to getting injured.' I've always taken my sleep seriously and tried to get eight hours, or seven now I'm a little older. I then reacted to Simeone's instruction by running faster until I was at the front. My legs were hard and stiff after that.

The next day, we trained again but when I turned for a ball, I felt a 'pop' in the back of one of my legs. I told the doctor what had happened. 'Did you feel a release?' he asked. 'Or was it just a surge of cramp?'

I'd only had cramp once in my whole career, but I told him that it was cramp and that I'd carry on. The doctor, taking no chances, stopped me from training immediately and took me for a scan in Juventus' medical lab, the Ferrari of football's medical facilities.

'I see some blood,' he said. 'You won't be able to play tomorrow.'

'I will play tomorrow,' I replied.

'It's better that you don't,' came the reply. I was pissed off but woke up the next morning, saying that I was going to play. There was a problem: I couldn't lift one of my legs because of a pain in my hamstring. I spoke to the club doctor and fitness coach and told them how fed up I was, that I'd been playing 50 games a season for United without getting injuries, yet I'd been in Italy for a few months, felt exhausted and was already injured. They understood my perspective and felt sorry for me, more so when they told me that I was going to be out for eight weeks.

I was now really depressed and didn't want to speak to anyone, not my wife, my agent, my friends. One Juventus fitness coach, Marco, helped me out of my depression. He empathised with me and told me not to worry.

'I can't do anything, so I'll go and take a break for a week,' I said. 'Probably Dubai.' Marco started laughing, but I was serious.

'You have to come here every day,' he said. That annoyed me even more and I had a tough month of rehabilitation. I thought I was fine after one month, when I could run and sprint at 70 per cent, and told Marco I was ready to play. He shook his head and we carried on doing fitness work. When Marco felt I was ready, another fitness doctor came to test me and the power in my legs. I passed and was selected for the Turin derby against Torino.

'I'll make you happy,' Allegri explained to me. 'We're playing four at the back.' I started smiling – briefly – but my optimism faded after playing against the Brazilian Bruno Peres, who was really fast. He scored a brilliant solo goal where I struggled to catch him, but we won 2-1 with Andrea Pirlo scoring the winner in the 93rd minute. I was so glad of that goal because I would have been slaughtered if we'd not won.

I kept my place in the team for a 0-0 draw at Fiorentina. The feeling among the media and the directors – one of them told my agent – was: 'Yes, he played better in this match, but this isn't the Patrice Evra from Manchester.' They were right because I'd hidden all my qualities. I'd showed none of my leadership skills and not been vocal enough before, during and after games.

I went back to my apartment, where I'd not unpacked any of my boxes from Manchester, probably in case I needed to move back there. I didn't want to be in Turin, so why should I make it my home? That night, I put some music on and had a serious word with myself, my good angel talking to my devil.

'Patrice, when you were young you slept with two or three people on a mattress for one. Now you are crying like a baby because you miss your big house in Manchester and moaning about playing for Juventus, one of the greatest football clubs in the world. Why are you unhappy? You need to show them the real Patrice, and you start tomorrow.'

The next day, I began to train with a smile on my face. People began to take notice, but the only place they'd really take notice would be out on the pitch. It had the right effect, and I felt happier and started to fall for Juventus, the shirt, the stadium and the fans.

Another test of my personality came when the captain Buffon, Tevez and I called a players' meeting after a home draw to Inter, who were 11th in Serie A, in January 2015. It was such a poor result for us that many of the players were blaming Allegri, who they accused of being too soft in comparison with Conte, who shouted a lot.

I listened to what they had to say before standing up to address them, speaking from the heart. 'I'm sorry because I've been moody and haven't been myself since I arrived. I apologise for that. Maybe I was missing Manchester and complaining too much, but you won't hear any more complaints from me. I promise I will die for this great club now. I care a lot about Juventus and I think you're making a big mistake here. I've seen it all with David Moyes at United last season. You're talking about Conte like the United players talked about Ferguson. It means that Conte is the real boss here, not the man who has got us to the top of the league, a man who is very good at his job. Conte is not coming back and you are looking for problems that barely exist.'

I think most of the players were with me. We played a huge

game that same month away at Napoli, the second-best team in Italy for most of the time I was there. We'd lost 8-7 on penalties to them the previous month in Qatar in the Supercoppa Italiana, contested between the league and Coppa Italia winners. Napoli's Gonzalo Higuain scored an equaliser after 118 minutes to take that game to penalties, his second goal of the match. The Argentina striker was a magnificent player who always played with hate against Juventus. Napoli fans loved him and we saw that love when we travelled there this time, with their songs and banners singing his praises.

For a visiting player, a trip to Napoli is like no other in Italy. On the team coach to the Stadio San Paulo, I asked players why we needed so much security as we were surrounded by police cars, motorbikes and vans. They told me that I'd soon see why. As the coach neared the stadium, eggs and stones started to thud against the sides and windows of the bus. We won 3-1, with goals from Arturo Vidal, Pogba and Martin Caceres. The goals were set up by Andrea Pirlo, Fernando Llorente and then Alvaro Morata, who came on for Llorente to play alongside Tevez. As you can see, we had some truly great big-game players at Juventus, and that match was played in one of the best atmospheres that I've experienced.

I had read that, unlike in the Premier League, the stadiums were half-empty in Serie A. That wasn't my experience at Juventus, where all 40,000 seats were usually full for home games and we attracted the best crowds away from home. Juventus have fans all over Italy and it showed. We could be at a hotel in Cagliari or Udine and would be greeted by hundreds of local Juventus fans. The *tifosi* at home in the Stadio delle Alpi, which had been redeveloped to bring the stands closer to the pitch, were always so loud and well organised, with flags and songs. They had a song for me. True, there were crazy elements among them, but in a good way.

I vomited several times during that win at Napoli, with the manager and director asking me if was sure I was okay. I said I was fine, but I had a pain as if someone was putting a knife into my stomach. It was the sort of pain I'd never had before and told the doctor, so when we were back in Turin they did some tests on me where they gave me an injection to put me to sleep. I woke up naked, wondering where I was. A doctor was looking down at me.

'Why am I here?' I asked. 'And I hope nobody touched me!' The doctor started laughing as he explained that they'd put a camera inside me and found an ulcer. He said that the stomach wall was open, but it wasn't bleeding. The pain had come from inflammation. They also did a full analysis where they found I had a partial allergy to eggs and milk. I'd eaten eggs most mornings in Manchester. The gastric problems that had plagued me for so long could now be managed.

On the pitch, Serie A football was like a chess game where you had to think about every move. You needed to be very fit to play this way and fill every space; otherwise you'd be exploited. By contrast, English football is two heavyweight boxers punching each other, and I think it does make for the best show in football. Italian football is more tactical and men-tally draining, with less adrenalin. At the end of matches in England, I felt like I couldn't play another game, that I'd need ice on an injury. In Italy, I felt like I could play the game all over again. There were fewer heavy challenges, which meant fewer contact injuries.

With all the quality that we had, I started to believe that we could prosper in the Champions League, yet that belief was not shared. Tevez had told me that the players who were so good in Serie A would start to shake and be scared in the big Champions League games. I was feeling more confident in the dressing room, and before the last-16 game at home to Borussia

Dortmund, I said: 'Guys, we're going to the Champions League final.'

Vidal laughed at me. 'Guys, trust me, we have a good team. I've been in this competition many times and there's not one team who can run like we run.'

We didn't play well but beat Dortmund 2-1 at home, an expected result. The key was the difficult away leg. I was calm, but nothing like as calm as Allegri. In the pre-match meeting, the Juventus coach told us: 'Guys, we're going to play a friendly game and beat them easy. I've watched them closely, so let's have some fun, but remember we have a game to prepare for at home to Genoa.'

The players couldn't believe what they were hearing. Dortmund was a huge game and he was treating it like a pre-season friendly. Then Allegri showed us the video of how we were to beat the Germans and, for the first time in my life, it was like déjà vu when we walked onto the pitch. We had already seen the game – and Dortmund's weaknesses that had been pointed out so clearly by our boss. Even though they had top players including Marco Reus, Ilkay Gundogan, Pierre-Emerick Aubameyang and Mats Hummels, we knew everything about the way Dortmund would play, and whenever I received the ball I felt like I had three options of what to do with it. We took the lead after three minutes through Tevez and then we destroyed them.

It was such a pleasure to play in that game in their superb stadium, and our confidence soared. We won 3-0 in Germany and were applauded off by the home fans. I began to realise that Allegri was a master tactician.

Juventus had talent in every position. Gianluigi Buffon was our captain, our goalkeeper and the most experienced player at the club. He didn't give grand speeches every day, which meant that when he did speak we all took notice. Gianluigi would train as hard as everyone, but he was friendly with a warm and caring personality. He'd relax with a cigarette every day in the showers after training, like a footballer from the 1940s. I'm sure the Juventus regime didn't like it, but what could they say? He was one of the best goalkeepers in the world and he was in love with Juventus. The feeling was mutual and I felt he respected me when he saw I was committed to his club.

Central defender Giorgio Chiellini was another with a Juventus obsession. Like me, he'd had problems with Luis Suarez, but while we laughed about it, we never really spoke about the Uruguayan. Chiellini is an intelligent, humble man with a deep interest in current affairs and social issues. He knew more about France than me and was of the opinion that France's struggles with the national team were influenced by our different origins.

He would also say: 'Patrice, I'm not a good footballer compared to these guys here. I can't do those long balls that Pirlo does.' He didn't believe in himself at times, yet he worked harder than any player to improve. And he was a warrior, the type you always want in your team. He would cover for me on the pitch and we had the right understanding.

Leonardo Bonucci played alongside Chiellini at the back of one of the best defences in world football. Bonucci was a one-man show for the fans and he wanted to be in charge of the team, but he was already surrounded by leaders. He told me how Juventus fans had booed him when he joined and how he'd come through that. Bonucci had balls.

Pogba played just in front of me on the left – the French connection. We had a lot of fun together on and off the pitch at a club where fun was frowned upon. He would come into my room a lot when we were away, both for the national team and Juventus. We became really close, like family, as we had started to do at United. Paul started to love my funny personality and I felt that I could be completely open with him, even if that meant saying: 'Paul, you're playing shit today. Come on.'

'Sorry, Uncle Pat,' he'd say. He told a journalist in an interview that I was called Uncle Pat and it stuck. Paul was incredibly talented, but he received a lot of criticism from fans who wanted him to play more simply. Instead, Paul insisted on his own style within the Juventus system. He was also his own man with his individual way of dressing and haircuts, which drew criticism from players and the media.

We were given beautiful Trussardi suits by Juventus to wear for matches – and Paul tucked his trousers into his sports socks, wearing trainers instead of shoes. People blamed me for being a bad influence on him because I wouldn't tell him off, but Paul is an eccentric who does things his way. I would never want him to change, and besides, as I told the other players, he was there to play football and was delivering on the pitch. Paul had a big heart and every single player liked him. They knew that when we went to the biggest games, in Naples or Milan or Rome, he wouldn't be found wanting.

If Paul was the giant, Marchisio was our little prince. He was the local boy who had come through the academy, whose family were all season-ticket holders. He would call me Martin Luther King and say that my speeches motivated him but that I took football too seriously. I was a serious joker, if that's not a contradiction.

Andrea Pirlo was an inspirational maestro. He inspired me to be more relaxed on the ball. People think that Pirlo walks around, receives a pass and then hits a long ball. But he actually never stops running, he just runs slowly, moving like a shark waiting for his chance to make his move, to attack. His foot was like a magic wand; he could put the ball anywhere he wanted. He would drop deep into defence, pick up the ball and then accurately ping it forward like a quarterback in American football. He'd signal to me to stay high, that he'd already seen me and knew where I was going to be – not where I was. For a wide man like me, playing with Pirlo was as beautiful as playing with Paul Scholes.

People think Pirlo's a shy guy, but he's funny once you know him. I called him Picasso because I considered him an artist. He didn't do convention and would dress individually like Paul Pogba, with a brown or green jacket and trousers that didn't reach his shoes.

I called Arturo Vidal, another attack-minded midfielder, 'the volcano'. He was quite a character, with too much energy and a brain that was incapable of taking life seriously. He was a pitbull on the pitch, a top player.

My old friend Carlos Tevez was another pitbull, but the difference between him in Manchester and Turin was that he had far more maturity now. He told me himself that he was less impulsive, more calm, more of a family man. He knew exactly what he had to do on the pitch, where he was so clever. He still didn't give 100 per cent in training and would simply say: 'My knee is sore so I can't do what you want me to do,' or: 'I'm too tired to train.' Juventus had little choice but to indulge him because he was such an important player, one who never let his team down on the pitch.

Kingsley Coman was my little French compatriot, a powerful, fast attacker who liked to run at players. Juventus killed Kingsley's style of football because they wanted him to be more tactical. He wasn't getting enough minutes and decided to leave.

Fernando Llorente was a really good striker and an important player – strong, good in the air and he scored goals. He was the nicest person on earth, too nice for football's cynical world. Carlito is a hard bastard who knows who his friends are and trusts them and few others; Fernando is a gentle soul and played up front with Carlito, who would shout at him. 'Carlito, you can't shout at me like that,' he'd say. Carlos couldn't understand that. On one trip, I was trying to sleep on a plane when I heard someone crying. I looked around and saw Fernando with his headphones on. We were in the air so he couldn't have received bad news from his phone.

'Nando, are you okay?' I asked.

'Yes, Pat. But every time I watch this film I cry. It's the second time I've watched it and the second time I've cried.'

I then did something that I shouldn't have done – I told Carlito when we were in the queue for passport control. 'I'm going to tell everyone,' he said gleefully.

'Patrice told everyone that you were crying on the plane from watching a movie,' he said out loud to Nando. Everyone laughed.

'It's true!' said Nando, not in the slightest bit bothered. 'Every time I've watched this movie I've cried.'

Stephan Lichtsteiner was the other full back. I'd argue with him every day. If he had a problem he told you face to face. So we could be two bulls in the same pen. Stephan moaned about everything, yet we needed him on the pitch because he worked his balls off, he was a soldier.

After beating Dortmund, we met my old club Monaco in the quarter-finals. We won a tough game at home in the first leg 1-0. As is often the case, Monaco had a very talented young team, with Bernardo Silva, Anthony Martial, Yannick Carrasco, Fabinho, Geoffrey Kondogbia and my old compatriot, Jérémy Toulalan. They also had another of my old teammates, Dimitar Berbatov. Monaco was a good place for him to end up and I bet he was still the coolest man in the principality. We all couldn't help but notice Martial because he was so fast and skilful – Chiellini escaped a red card for a challenge on him. I told some of the Monaco players that 'we won against you because you don't believe that you can beat us.' French teams would have the 'we're going to try and win' attitude rather than 'we're going to win.'

Our hotel had such a stunning view over the Mediterranean and Monaco that Matteo, who travelled with the team and was in charge of logistics, closed the curtains in the room where we were all eating. 'The manager says that we'll feel like we're on holiday with this view,' he explained. He had a point, not that I could eat well because I was still vomiting as it was taking a while for my gastric problems to settle down. Tevez was also fucked with heavy flu. We both had a painkilling injection into our butts. I wondered how we'd play the game and wasn't confident because I knew the magic that could come when Monaco were playing well at home. I'd been there against Real Madrid.

Christian Campi, an old friend from Monaco, came to see me at the team hotel. He'd helped me buy a place in Monaco when I lived there and we had stayed close friends. He was in his sixties with terminal cancer and would die only a few weeks later, but he still came to see me at the hotel. He'd been told not to drive, so he rode there on his scooter. He'd lost a lot of weight and I joked that he looked better than ever, but I was shocked and upset. You can live in a bubble as a footballer where you're surrounded by all these ultra-fit men – not that Carlito and I were feeling that great – in the physical prime of their life.

Martial was on form in the second leg as Monaco attacked and attacked, but our defence was so good that we just soaked it all up and kept the score at 0-0. We could have played for another two hours and Monaco wouldn't have scored. We started with 3-5-2, then switched to four at the back to suffocate Monaco by making them think they were in charge, yet we were actually in charge because they were never going to score. Chiellini was magnificent, putting his head where it hurt all the time. Like a man possessed and obsessed with the Old

Lady, Chiellini refused to let Juventus concede a goal. He would have died for the team. How could Monaco compete with that?

I went to the away dressing room after the game and gave my shirt to Prince Albert, who was pleased to see me but not pleased that we'd knocked his team out. The Monaco players were upset, but admitted: 'You gave us the possession and we thought that we were in control, but you were in control.'

I told Martial that I was proud of him, especially as he comes from Les Ulis. Tshimen, who still coaches young footballers in Les Ulis and is a very respected member of the community, had coached Martial when he was younger and he turned up once when we were filming an advert for Nike. Tshimen had told me before the Monaco game: 'Remember that little kid with his dad from the commercial. He's now at Monaco.'

Tshimen has a signed shirt from me and Martial above his desk at Les Ulis. The stadium is next to the garage with the shop where we used to steal chocolate bars, acting in tandem to confuse the people working there.

Real Madrid, the holders, were our opponents in the semi-final. The players cheered, especially Chiellini. 'Fuck that, guys, it's Madrid!' I said.

'We know how to deal with them,' came the consensus. 'We're their black cat.'

I saw no fear in the Juventus players, only complete conviction that we would beat them and reach the final. What a turnaround from the previous spirit at Juventus. We beat Madrid 2-1 at home with goals from Alvaro Morata, who was on loan from Madrid. Alvaro played unbelievably well in the Champions League but it was more difficult for him in Serie A, where it was more tactical. He needs space, but his finishing is brilliant, he can be strong when he wants and he's powerful. He can run over distance and in short bursts, and he had slowly started to take the place of Llorente, but he also always had

Tevez on his case, saying: 'You're still a kid, you have to learn.' Alvaro had a lot of respect for Tevez and ran his balls off in that attack. Allegri would tell Alvaro that he was just a kid every day and that he needed to grow up and listen to instructions, to develop as a player. Alvaro would react and say: 'I'm not a kid,' but Allegri kept tapping away at him. Morata needed love, too.

Allegri was so relaxed. Even when I saw him being animated on the sidelines, I thought it was a show for the Juve fans, who always demand passion. That wasn't really Allegri's style, he was smoother than that.

We went to the Bernabeu for the second leg and drew 1-1. It was another incredible defensive display from us where I saw the collective power of the Juventus rearguard. It was nice to see Cristiano again in Madrid, and we agreed to swap shirts after the match but he was so pissed off that he didn't show. Chicharito, another of my former United teammates, came on as a sub. Allegri later said that my experience in dealing with Chicha had been very important in the game. I'd challenged him and there had been appeals for a penalty, but it wasn't a foul. I'd just put my body in front of him and we both fell inside the box. That was experience.

'That was a penalty, Pat!' he said.

'No, it was not,' I replied in Spanish, before laughing.

To the delight of the Juventus defenders, Karim Benzema hadn't played in the first leg. He played really well in the second and was a handful. I found it easier to play against Gareth Bale – the key with him is not to give him space and to stay tight with him. I was pleased with how I played, and we held out and resisted the white storm that Madrid subjects every opponent to. Paul Pogba and I had a little dance after the game. Another Paul – Scholes – who was commentating on the game for British TV, texted me to say how well I'd done. Rio Ferdinand said he couldn't believe I was still playing to that level. I was so proud to reach the final, proud that after leaving United, I'd not gone away to be quiet as some people suspected, but was playing in a team that was one of the best in the world. We were now on target to win Serie A, the Coppa Italia and the Champions League.

I felt an important member of the team, too. I didn't play in a Juventus side that lost a league game my entire first season. We'd carried on winning in the league and confirmed the title with four games to spare after beating Sampdoria away at the start of May before the first Madrid game.

After that game in Madrid, my beautiful wife had a message for me: 'Are you going to say thanks?' she asked.

'Even if I win three Champions League medals with Juventus, it will never replace playing for Manchester United,' I replied. It was too strong an answer, but I still had some anger about the way I'd left United and I'd yet to fully fall in love with Juventus. I'm sorry, but I couldn't force my feelings.

We played Inter away a few days later and won as we closed in on another Serie A title. That game showed Juventus' strength, since several players were rested knowing that we'd have a home game against second-placed Napoli and a Coppa Italia final against Lazio within four days. Plus we knew we'd be in the Champions League final, where Barcelona would be our opponents in Berlin.

We beat Napoli at home in the league and then faced Lazio in the Coppa final in Rome's Olimpico, the usual final venue but also Lazio's own home. We did well to be in the final after losing the first leg of the semi-final at home to Fiorentina. They had a young Egyptian striker called Mohamed Salah and he scored both of their goals in the Juventus Stadium. No other team beat us at home that season. I was one of several players rested for that game but brought back for the second leg in Florence. We won 3–0 and Salah had a quieter time against the stronger Juventus defence.

The Coppa final in Rome was brought forward because we'd reached the Champions League final. Morata was suspended after being sent off in the semi-final, Marchisio was also suspended, and Buffon was out. Chiellini was captain and scored our equaliser after 11 minutes. That came when Pirlo sent a free kick over the box, which I headed down for Chiellini to score. I was more advanced than usual as we played a 3-5-2, but we couldn't get a second against a physical and technically sound Lazio side. Not until Alessandro Matri, a veteran striker who came on loan from Milan for the second half of the season, got one for us in the 97th minute. We'd won the double and finished 17 points clear of second-placed Roma. Now we had to win the treble against the best team in the world.

I was calm in the days before as I'd been to four previous finals, winning only one of them. 'Come on, Patrice,' I would say to myself. 'You can't lose again, that will be a disaster.'

People were saying that I'd be up against Luis Suarez again, but it wasn't a big deal to me. I saw Neymar and Messi in the tunnel and went to shake their hands. Suarez was next to them and I shook his hand too. 'Good luck,' he said in Spanish. He was a gentleman and I felt it was a positive moment.

'Good luck,' I replied in Spanish. He had served his punishment for the racist word he used against me.

The referee, Cuneyt Cakir, was the man who'd sent Nani off at Old Trafford. I would have preferred anyone to ref the game but him, and my fears were confirmed when he didn't award us a clear penalty in the first half. Barcelona had scored early after four minutes through Ivan Rakitic. Morata equalised after 55 minutes and we had other chances through Carlos Tevez, our top goalscorer, to make it 2-1. Then Luis Suarez scored after 68 minutes.

Barcelona got a third after 97 minutes through Neymar, the best player on the pitch. Everything he did was accurate, he was amazing. He played simply and made difficult moves look easy. His control, touch and passing were all perfect. I played really well that night in Berlin, but sometimes that isn't enough in football. Pirlo was crying on the pitch, the other players were really sad, but my thought was: 'I'm fucking sick of this competition and fucking sick of Barcelona.' They were and are such a great team and I was fated to come up against them in such unbeatable form so many times.

CHAPTER 15

Dancing in Turin

I began to relax for my second season, 2015-16, at Juventus. After a year of feeling tired, Manchester-homesick, unhappy and moody, I became the old Patrice, focused and professional and driven to succeed.

The happier side of my personality reasserted itself too. I'd always held off from joining social-media sites, probably because I wanted to concentrate entirely on my football and because to me the word 'media' meant interviews. But I started to make online videos for fun, to make people smile. My first videos came as a bit of a shock to many at Juventus. It's quite a conservative club and here I was dancing around in a costume or singing Bob Marley songs, but soon they could see that they were a genuine expression of my *joie de vivre*. I was not going on video to analyse games or criticise the coach. The club realised most of my videos were stupid and fun, so where was the harm in that? Agnelli, who was a serious man, smiled as he told me that he watched my videos on Instagram.

We were drawn in a Champions League group with Manchester City, which meant a first trip back to Manchester for our first group game. I felt dizzy as we travelled along those roads I'd known so well. We stayed at the Lowry Hotel, which had been United's first-choice hotel for so long. The people there knew me and gave me the same room I'd always had. It was a painful experience. The clean break from my marriage to United had helped me, but my recovery had not been easy and now I had no choice but to be back in the city. At least I could see my old barber and get my hair cut. At the Etihad everyone was friendly with me too, which they didn't need to be. I was equally polite, though I did hum '20 times' – the number of United's league titles – as I walked up the tunnel past them.

Chiellini scored an own goal, but then we grabbed two in the last 20 minutes. When Morata scored our second, which turned out to be the winner, we all slid across the wet Manchester grass to celebrate in front of the travelling fans. A picture of that moment hangs on the wall at Juventus' training ground and I was doubly proud because we beat City, United's rival.

Paul Pogba and I did a little dance after that goal and it was all smiles for me. I felt like a leader, I had found my feet and a love for Juve, yet the team were struggling in Serie A and we really needed that win at City. We'd had a terrible start to the season, much worse than Moyes's start at United, and dropped as low as 15th in the table. For a team that had won the previous four Serie A titles, this was not acceptable.

Our first two league games ended in defeat against Udinese and Roma. We lost four of our opening ten games, including losing 2-1 at Napoli in September. Juventus were unheard of 12th by the end of October, although we did beat Torino 2-1 in the derby.

The following game was at Empoli, one of the smallest clubs in Serie A. Rumours were swirling around that Allegri would be sacked if we didn't win and our coach looked so sad the day before the game. It was as if he knew he was going to lose his job and, in truth, many people wanted him to lose it – fans, people in the media and, I suspected, some players.

I spoke to our captain Buffon.

'Gigi, we need a team meeting.'

'We don't need to talk,' he replied.

'I don't care what you think,' I said. 'The way we're training, the way players are laughing behind the manager's back mean we should have a meeting.'

Gigi finally agreed, but he wasn't convinced. He opened the players' meeting with the words: 'Maybe the coach will be sacked if we lose, but we need to play for ourselves.'

'Whoa, wait a minute,' I interrupted. 'We didn't call this meeting for that. We called it because there are people here who don't respect the Juventus shirt. Teams now think they can beat us. I have respect for Napoli, Inter and our other rivals, but I will be ashamed if we don't retain the league with this team. We have more than enough quality here. We won the league by 17 points last season and now we're not even in the top half of the table.'

Other players offered their opinions.

'We're like this because we're missing some players,' was a common theme. It was true. Carlos Tevez had gone back home to Boca Juniors and I missed him a lot, as did the team. Arturo Vidal, Fernando Llorente, Kingsley Coman and playmaker Andrea Pirlo had all left as well. But left back Alex Sandro, midfielders Sami Khedira and Pablo Dybala, and strikers Mario Mandzukic and Simone Zaza had been bought to replace them. All are very good players, yet, as one of the Juve directors told me, the black and white shirt was 'heavy', meaning that it came with a big responsibility. Collectively, we were failing.

When we went a goal down at Empoli after 19 minutes, Allegri – in the eyes of many in Italy and maybe some of the Juventus players – was on his way out. But I wanted to repay my boss, as did others. Mario Mandzukic, our new centre forward, equalised after 33 minutes. The Croat was a warrior and a fine goalscorer who I called 'Mr No Good'. If I asked him how I was doing, he'd always say: 'No good.' But who was I to talk? I had hardly been the happiest person in the dressing room the previous season.

Five minutes later, I scored with a header from 12 yards out to give us the lead. The goal meant a huge amount to me but also to the team. Dybala then made it 3-1. He needed that goal. At his former club Palermo he had scored plenty, but Juventus is a bigger stage, especially for a 20-year-old who looked like a child. People had begun to question his quality and he'd struggled to handle the pressure of being a Juventus player, but I could see his talent in training, if not his personality or confidence.

I sat down with him – we sat down a lot together on the bench – and explained that I'd played with some of the best in the world and that he had the talent and the magic touch to be one of them. The quality and speed of his touch was amazing, the accuracy of his shots too with that left foot, but I told him he needed the personality to become a top player. Yet he was also putting too much pressure on himself by wanting to be the main man. All he had to do was play his natural game. I think he appreciated my feedback and I'm glad he continued to improve.

That victory at Empoli was only our second away win of the season from the six we'd played. We then went on a winning run for 15 straight league matches and rapidly rose up the table from 12th to first. And when the 15-match run ended in a draw at Bologna, we responded by winning the next ten league games – 25 wins and a draw from 26 games. The Scudetto was ours again.

We also faced AC Milan in the final of the Coppa Italia.

Both teams visited the Vatican to see the Pope before the

game – a tradition for the finalists. The players from both teams wait in a room, meet the Pope and have a picture taken. It was all a bit rushed, the people around him moving him on so that you don't even have time to smile at him. The Pope, a fan of Argentinian side San Lorenzo, wished both teams good luck and his speech was really nice, but I was disappointed with the whole experience and felt negative rather than positive energy when I walked around the Vatican, where expensive products were on sale. I paid €3,000 for a holy cross, but as a Catholic I was hoping for a deeper religious experience.

We beat Milan 1-0 in extra time, thanks to Morata, who came on from the bench and scored in the 110th minute with only his third touch of the ball. We didn't reach another Champions League final in 2015-16, but we did beat Man City home and away in the group stage before being paired with Bayern Munich in the last 16. These were huge games for us.

We drew 2-2 at home in the first leg after being 2-0 down. In Munich, we played better in the first half than in any other first half during my time in Turin. We were 2-0 up after 38 minutes, with goals from Pogba and Juan Cuadrado. Robert Lewandowski netted after 73 minutes for Bayern, but the score was still enough to send us through on aggregate. Then, in the 91st minute, Thomas Muller grabbed an equaliser to make it 4-4 on aggregate. That goal was like having a knife stuck into your body. I was partly to blame because Paul and I had a misunderstanding. We could have kept possession but lost the ball.

Bayern were better in extra time and scored twice – including a fourth by Coman, who was on loan from Juventus. That hurt. For the second time in three seasons, I was in a team knocked out of the Champions League in Munich.

Still, that season was a huge success from unpromising beginnings as we won a second league and Coppa Italia double, adding to the Supercoppa Italiana that we had won the previous August with two goals against Lazio.

Napoli had been our most consistent recent domestic challenger. So what did we do? We bought their best player, the striker Gonzalo Higuain, for an Italian record fee of €90 million.

On holiday, I celebrated the news in a video by dancing around a table-tennis table with my agent's son and Tshimen's son to 'My Boo' by Ghost Town DJs and shouting '*Forza* Juve!' I really did love this game in moments like that, my delight was genuine.

I'd had a great connection with every Argentinian I'd played with. Higuain was one of the best strikers in the world and he was coming to play with me. Why not celebrate with a little dance?

When he arrived at Juve, he came straight over to me and thanked me for the video.

'It touched me,' he said, 'I felt that the club wanted me.'

Life was fine at Juventus and I signed a new two-year contract on the same money, which would keep me in Turin until 2018. The club had pushed for that, which was deeply flattering. I felt so much respect from Juventus and the feeling was mutual.

I went to Euro 2016 in a happy mood. France needed a lift. The Paris terrorist attacks the previous November had killed lots of innocent people and the main attacks happened during the evening when I was playing for France against Germany at the Stade de France.

There had been the sound of a small explosion outside, which most people ignored as it sounded like a firecracker. I was actually on the ball around 20 minutes into the game when I heard a second big, dull bang. Again, I thought it might be a firecracker, similar to the type lit every week by ultras in Italy, but I soon began to suspect all was not well.

The game continued in a surreal atmosphere. News was kept

from the players about the dreadful events outside. Both the coaches and the officials had been told that there was an incident, but decided to continue with the game because it was not known then how serious the situation was. Their tension on the bench was obvious and unsettling.

François Hollande, the president of France, was at the game but was evacuated from the stadium at half-time. None of the players knew about this or any of the explosions until after the game.

We won and were then taken into the dressing room while the fans were ordered onto the pitch. Some of the players watched the news coverage on the TVs in the tunnel as stories started filtering in of explosions near the stadium and then of attacks in the centre of Paris.

We learned that an attacker wearing a suicide vest had tried to enter the stadium while we were playing. Security found the vest and it was detonated. Two other bombers were near the stadium and detonated their bombs.

The French players were kept in the stadium until the early hours of the morning when we were driven out of the ground to the Clairefontaine training centre outside Paris. As there had already been a bomb threat to the German team hotel earlier in the day, they were kept at the stadium until 7 am, before being driven straight to the airport in minivans as the team coach had writing on it that identified it and might become a target for any further attacks. Some of the German players tried to sleep in the corridors near the dressing room. I spoke to Sami Khedira, my Juventus teammate who was frightened for his family who'd travelled to Paris to attend the game.

By that time, 130 innocent people had been killed, including 89 at a concert in the Bataclan theatre. Antoine Griezmann's sister was at the concert and he was desperately trying to find out if she was safe. We heard the death toll going up and up. It was the deadliest attack on France since the Second World

War. I felt sick, shocked, that anyone could set out to do that to innocent people.

When we played against England at Wembley a few days later, Wembley sang 'La Marseillaise' as every player, including the substitutes, lined up for France's national anthem. The arch above the stadium was lit up in the colours of the French flag. It was very emotional.

I was on the bench that night and we lost the game 2-0, but I played in every other game up to Euro 2016. Deschamps had pulled the national team together and put it back on track. When the tournament started amid concerns over security, we had a chance to become European champions in our home country, to make France a little happier.

Two important players, Karim Benzema and Mathieu Valbuena, were left out because of a scandal surrounding a sex tape and disputed allegations of blackmail – a decision I disagreed with and told the French Federation so. Despite this, we went into the competition feeling like the country was behind us and with no big problems with the media. That was not a normal situation for the national team.

We had seven matches in that competition and I played every minute. We beat Romania 2-1 in the opener and my performance was very poor. The lead-up to the match had not been ideal – and it was my fault. I arrived late for the pre-match video analysis because I didn't know that the time for the team meeting had been changed. I hate being late and wasn't happy with myself. Deschamps wasn't impressed either, but didn't say anything.

Giroud gave us the lead with a header, before I gave a penalty away for Romania to equalise. It was Dimitri Payet's amazing 89th-minute goal that not only saved France, but saved me from a lot of criticism. Thank you, Payet, the man whose tears when he scored won French hearts.

Our next game, in Marseille, was hard fought against a very

tough and well-organised Albanian team, with 20,000 travelling fans. They all played like they would do anything for their country. Even without their captain Lorik Cana – who I knew from playing against him in France, England and Italy – Albania made life so difficult for us that we didn't score until the 90th minute when Griezmann headed us in front. Payet got another deep into stoppage time in the city where he's adored.

We'd won twice but had needed goals in the last minute of each game to beat Romania and Albania – teams who were not among the favourites. The inevitable grumbling started in the French media, the suggestions that this wasn't a top French team. When we drew 0–0 with Switzerland in our third game, the griping continued, yet the mood inside the team couldn't have been better. Yes, we would have liked to have played better, but sometimes you have to grind out results, especially in major tournaments.

The Republic of Ireland, who we faced next, wanted revenge after controversially missing out on the 2010 World Cup finals because of Gallas's goal from Thierry's handball. We played Ireland in Lyon – what a game! The atmosphere was electric on a hot afternoon in late June, the Irish fans singing and drinking everywhere. It felt like carnival time – and shouldn't tournaments always be like this, with fans having a good time? Robbie Brady gave Ireland the lead in the first minute and we spent most of the next hour chasing an equaliser, which Griezmann got after 57 minutes.

Griezmann – or Grizzle to me – had a reputation similar to Paul Pogba's in that he was considered to be one of the best young players in the world. Both had been presented beforehand as potential stars of the tournament and expectations were high, yet they were on the end of unfair criticism as we struggled to overcome teams in the group stage.

Griezmann silenced his critics by scoring a second goal

four minutes later – 2-1 to France. Both he and Paul were linked with moves from Juventus and Atlético and I spoke to Paul about leaving. When he discussed whether to go to Real Madrid or Manchester United, I told him, naturally, that he should go back to Old Trafford.

We were leading Ireland 2-1 and pushing for a third. We won a corner, but Deschamps told me from the sidelines to stay back rather than go forward. Without thinking, in the heat of the moment, I said 'Fuck off' and moved forward. My manager looked at me like he was annoyed. He was.

Back in the dressing room. Deschamps came in, congratulated us, adding that 'even if I have tension with players sometimes'. I put my hand up like a schoolboy and apologised to Deschamps in front of my teammates for my reaction. They gave me a loud round of applause to embarrass me still further.

The next day, Deschamps called me over for a quiet word.

'If you ever say that to me again, you'll never play for me again,' he said. And he meant it. He was correct and I accepted that. We were soon smiling again.

I genuinely felt for Ireland and my old teammate John O'Shea. Their fans were amazing, their players too. They choose from a population of five million, one-twelfth the size of France. Their players were so down and the assistant manager Roy Keane was really pissed off when I shook his hand.

But if Ireland was a small country compared to France, our next opponents were tiny. Iceland had spectacularly beaten England and we played them back at the Stade de France in the quarter-finals. I should thank England because Iceland's victory made us focus and stopped us from underestimating them. We knew they'd be good.

I played at the back along Samuel Umtiti, a defender I'd barely heard of before the championships. He was only called up because of an injury to Jérémy Mathieu.

'Trust me, he's good,' Pogba assured me of the player who would join Barcelona that summer from Lyon. Umtiti was indeed excellent, as was Paul who scored in a 5–2 win. We were on top throughout that game.

Deschamps and I would chat before every game and he'd ask for my opinions on his decisions. I enjoyed these chats, they showed that Deschamps trusted my knowledge and judgement, but he wasn't afraid to criticise me. In the group stage, he felt that I wasn't at the top of my game and he asked me: 'What's wrong, Patrice? It's like you're feeling the pressure. You're not playing so well. I need you to show me something. If you don't show me something then I will drop you.'

'Okay,' I said to him, 'you think I can't handle pressure? Are you taking the piss?'

It had the desired effect, as I began to show what I could do – for myself, my team, for France and for the great Mr Didier Deschamps.

Germany were our next opponents in Marseille's Vélodrome. Life is worth living for moments like this.

'We must become a nation of winners once again and the only way to do that is to end this tournament with the trophy,' I'd told the media. 'I have never won anything with the France team and it would feel like a failure for me, a blot on my career, if it stayed like that. But we have a chance now. I am proud of all my teammates. They're doing their utmost to try to make me cry by winning the European Championship.'

I delivered a very different message to my fellow players.

'Guys,' I said the day before the game in our hotel two kilometres from the stadium, 'Germany is the team that knocked us out of the World Cup in Brazil. We want revenge.'

Some players were scared because they knew that Germany usually beat France, but I wasn't having any of that.

In the dressing room I laid it on the line as we changed. 'We have to play with heart,' I said. 'We have to play for France. They cannot be more passionate than us when we take to the field, we have to fight for this shirt. It has to be a pleasure to defend. When we recover the ball we're going to have to hurt them. Everyone must give everything. We can't be tired today. We need a trophy at the end. It's too beautiful what we're doing.'

The players applauded me when I finished.

We knew that Angela Merkel, the German Chancellor, was at the game, and another player said something that struck a chord with me: 'I don't want to see Angela Merkel shaking hands with everyone at the end of the game with that little smile on her face because she has beaten us French people.' None of us wanted to see that and every France player was as fired up as a mad dog when we walked onto that pitch. The stadium, so beautiful with a new roof and 65,000 fans, was at boiling point. Several players said it was the best atmosphere they'd ever experienced. I tried to hold the tears back when 'La Marseillaise' was played before the game and I thought: 'I would love to play here for Marseille.'

I started alongside Umtiti.

'I'm going with the kids,' Deschamps had told me before the game. We beat Germany 2-0, with Griezmann scoring both goals.

After the game, while I was being interviewed for TV, Paul Pogba grabbed the microphone and started to interview me in Italian. It was fantastic.

We returned to our base at Clairefontaine and had a little celebration, a little dance. The team spirit was better than I'd ever known with France.

That win set us up with a final against Portugal in the Stade de France. The venue was a mistake. Marseille was a cauldron, the stadium full of true football fans. By contrast, the Stade de France, with its stands distanced from the field, was for business people in suits who could afford the more expensive tickets.

There was no atmosphere before the game, with fans taking selfies to boast that they were at the final. Where's the passion in that? It was bullshit, but it wasn't a new problem. The France team had experienced the same in 1998.

Still, we were sure that we'd beat Portugal, no one more convinced than me. Like my teammates, I could already see us celebrating on the Champs-Élysées. None of us were scared of Cristiano Ronaldo. I spoke to Nani before the game – on Instagram.

We were heavy-legged when the game started. The atmosphere was strange, the July air hot. There were butterflies all over the stadium. Some players were nervous, others like me were too confident.

When Ronaldo got injured and went off after 25 minutes, the French crowd cheered.

'That cheer is going to kill us,' I thought. 'That's all the motivation Portugal need.'

And I was right, as Portugal raised their game, especially my friend Nani. They fought for every ball, while we missed some chances. Griezmann missed one, but it would get even worse. In the 92nd minute, I gave the ball to our substitute André-Pierre Gignac, who turned past Pepe and shot. The ball looked like it was going in but hit the inside of the post before rolling across the goalmouth. More than one France player said that the Portuguese had performed voodoo for that to happen. This will haunt Gignac for life.

We paused before extra time and took drinks on the pitch.

'We will be okay if we keep on playing like this,' said Deschamps.

'No, we're shitting ourselves,' I replied. 'We're playing too slow, missing chances. We have to play quicker. We're in a trap here.'

We had worked so hard to get to this final. I gave every part of myself in that tournament, I was on a mission where

I couldn't fail, but I could sense that the situation was going to turn bad.

In extra time Eder, who was on loan at Lille and not even a regular, came on for Portugal and scored with a shot from 25 yards along the ground.

What a shit night it turned out to be. Everyone was angry and upset in the dressing room afterwards. I was so pissed off I went straight into the dressing room without saying goodbye to the fans. I felt the fans didn't deserve our thanks; they'd not given us enough support as they had done in Marseille, but in reality there was no one to blame but ourselves for the defeat.

I was slumped in the dressing room when Lucas Digne, the 22-year-old substitute left back who was about to join Barcelona, came up to me.

'I respect you, Pat,' he said, 'but you have to say thanks to the fans. Please, Pat. Come with me.'

I went out with Lucas. He was very mature in that situ-ation. Euro 2016 had been a magnificent tournament for us, one spoiled with that final. We received our shit losers' medals and, as usual, I don't know where mine is.

I spoke to my mum after the game.

'I'm very proud of you,' she said. She'd been at that game. At every major final that one of my parents had attended, I had lost. Part of me thought it was better that they didn't come.

'I'm not proud of me,' I replied.

I returned for my third season in Turin, this time with-out Paul Pogba, who had taken my advice about Manchester United. After four years in Turin he wanted a new challenge. He'd won leagues and cups, he loved Juventus, but he wanted something different. I think he loved the idea of moving to Barcelona or Madrid to improve his football, but when the offer from Manchester came it was the natural choice as he had a lot of unfinished business there.

I didn't feel like I'd had a break and I was very tired when I returned to pre-season, with all the hard running that is entailed at Juventus.

I didn't start the first game, with Alex Sandro chosen ahead of me. I was fine with that, it was the first game. Alex, as I said earlier, had signed in 2015 and had a difficult time because I was playing every week. People had assumed that he was going to take my place but I was determined he wouldn't. Alex is a top guy, a strong and powerful player. I wanted to help him all I could and congratulated him when he played well. I just didn't want him to take my place.

I came on for the last six minutes in a win against Fiorentina, but didn't start in any of the next six league games. I did play in the Champions League matches, but I was concerned and went to see the coach.

'Boss, what's going on here?' I asked Allegri, with whom I had a good relationship. 'You've asked me to sign for two years and now you don't play me. I didn't sign to sit on a bench.'

'Patrice, you need to play only in the important games now,' he replied.

'No, boss, I'm not that kind of player. I want to play when I'm fit.'

Allegri stood firm: 'You'll play in the Champions League.' I understood his perspective and that he wanted to play Alex, but I didn't have to agree with it.

We did prosper in the Champions League, winning four and drawing two of our six group games. My teammates called me 'Champions League Man', which I laughed at but was uneasy about deep down. I wasn't happy about missing so many games at Juventus and began to think: 'If I'm not happy somewhere then I should leave.' My family had gone to live back in Paris because being exposed to so many different languages was starting to confuse my children. Our youngest, my daughter

Maona, arrived in 2012. She had been born in Paris. She had already lived in England, Italy and France in a short period of time. As she was having some learning issues, we took professional advice to settle on one language. We wanted both her and Lenny to be educated in French for the first time after English and American schools.

So I was living alone in Turin and not playing every week. Life became difficult. I'd pray in the morning and evening. I used to go to church every Thursday, but I started to doubt the church because of the child sex-abuse scandals that were being revealed around the world.

I'd grown up in a house with a picture of the Pope on the wall, and had once asked my dad: 'Why do we have a picture of this old man who we don't know in our house?' My dad nearly broke the table as he leapt up and said: 'If you say that again I will slap your face.'

My religion is to be the best human being that I can, but I still pray – with Muslim people, with Christian people. I respect every religion.

With my family away, I started to become good friends with Higuain. He was single at the time and we'd eat together. Even though he was born in France, we'd speak in Spanish and got on really well.

Gonzalo was a well-educated man who tried to make good jokes, but his jokes were never funny – which made him even funnier. He knew how to score, but not how to tell jokes. It was a shame we played so few games together because he was a top man and an amazing player, but he came to Juventus – for a huge €90 million fee – to win trophies and he didn't disappoint.

I've never seen a player so concerned about goalscoring; he'd eat his nails away during the week if he wasn't scoring. Not scoring makes him sick, he needs goals. If he doesn't score in game, he's not happy. Critics said he was fat but he'd score more goals when he had a little red wine during the week. He was a goal machine.

Gonzalo tried to keep my spirits high, but he wasn't the one sitting on the bench. I wanted to play against Palermo and Genoa too, and became unhappy when I didn't. This negative energy was not part of my nature.

I went to see Allegri again.

'Boss, I like you, I love this team and this club, but if the situation doesn't change then I'll leave in the January transfer window.'

'You're crazy,' he said. 'We love you here.'

'I love you too, but I'm not happy when I'm not playing. The club and the fans deserve better.'

Buffon, Chiellini and others didn't think I'd leave, but my mind was being made up more all the time.

Two days before Christmas 2016, we had a game against Milan in the final of the Supercoppa Italiana in Qatar. Alex Sandro had been injured and I expected to start, especially as I was doing so well in training. But Alex came back and I was on the bench. I was so disappointed as I'd played all the cup games so far that season.

For the first time in my career as a footballer, I was mentally unprepared to come off the bench because I was so down. Normally when I don't play I still speak in the dressing room before the game. Not this time; I said nothing.

Alex was injured after 33 minutes, meaning that I had to come on with barely any warm-up and little preparation. I was close to saying that I didn't want to go on the pitch – I didn't want to play.

I did go on, but didn't defend well. It was 1-1 after extra time, then we lost on penalties, 5-4. I barely slept that night in Qatar, maybe an hour at most. I'd tried my best at Juventus but it wasn't enough. I felt rejected, down and sad. I didn't accept that I was finished as a top-flight player, and I thought long and hard about my future in the short break we had after that game. I stayed in the area and went to Dubai for a holiday with my family.

When we returned to Turin after Christmas, I went to see Allegri.

'Boss, I respect you but I'm sorry because I let myself down. I didn't want to play that game against Milan. I don't think Juventus fans or my teammates deserve that. I don't think I deserve it myself, and I want to leave the club. I've not spoken to any other club and nor has my agent.'

'You're crazy,' Allegri told me, 'but I like the way you won't accept playing less. I appreciate that honesty. What do you want to do now?'

'I want to train and I'll try and do my best if you pick me,' I replied.

'You have two or three weeks to rest,' he replied. 'I think you're psychologically down.'

Word seeped out and my teammates were sad. Chiellini thought I was mad for wanting to leave Juventus.

I was six months into a two-year contract and I wanted to leave. That surprised the Juventus directors, especially as I didn't want to be paid up. I just wanted to go and play football every week somewhere else. Everyone thought I had another club lined up, but I didn't.

I continued training with Juventus throughout January 2017. I asked my agent to speak to Manchester United again and I exchanged texts with Jose Mourinho. Jose liked the idea of me going back to Old Trafford to help Luke Shaw develop as a left back.

I started to believe that I was going back home to United. The fans who sing in J Stand at Old Trafford held a flag up with my face on it and '3 is the magic number' underneath. Rio

Ferdinand said something about me going back to Old Trafford on his social media, asking me if it was the truth.

The next day, Ed Woodward texted my agent to say that any deal was off. I suspect the club wasn't comfortable with how my returning to Old Trafford would go down with Luke Shaw, maybe it would seem like a step back. It was a massive disappointment. Jose apologised to me and Ed texted me to say that, although we couldn't do a deal as a player, I'd always be welcome at United.

Rejection is never nice, but it's also part of life.

My agent told me that I should stay at Juventus, that I was crazy for wanting to leave a great club where I'd been a success, that we'd win the league again and play more Champions League football. I certainly had a lot to lose – and not just financially – by leaving Juventus.

I answered anyone who advised me to stay at Juventus that I preferred my happiness to winning the league title in a team I wouldn't play in. I had enough trophies and didn't want to sit back on a contract and not do enough. That's not me.

When my agent had established that I was serious about leaving, he told me that Marseille were interested in signing me. I was immediately keen to join such a historic club, the only French team to win the European Cup, the team who played in the Stade Vélodrome, which had been on fire when we'd played there for France in Euro 2016.

Within a day, Andoni Zubizarreta, the legendary Barcelona and Spain goalkeeper who was the sporting director at Marseille, had driven to see me in Turin. That impressed me – it's a five-hour drive through the Alps. He came to my apartment, we ordered pizza and spoke about football for four hours in French and Spanish. He's a huge, gentle man with such a love of football and ambition to rebuild Marseille. He was realistic, too. He knew Marseille weren't going to win the Champions League like Barcelona had done while he was their sporting director, but he wanted Marseille to have a high profile in Europe.

By midnight, I was saying that it was maybe time for him to go as I needed to sleep. He wanted an answer that night. I told him that I appreciated him driving to see me to outline his offer and that I thought my answer was probably going to be positive. We didn't speak about money.

'Come on, are you definitely coming to Marseille?' he pushed.

I asked for one more night to consider, said goodbye and then went to training with Juventus the next day in a good mood. After training, I called Deschamps and told him about Marseille's interest.

'The place is on fire, they live football there,' said Deschamps. 'You have to be ready to play there, but with your personality I wouldn't be worried.' He also said: 'When you make your decision, wake up the next day and say "I am a Marseille player." See what you feel then.'

I did what he suggested and felt happy, so I texted Marseille's manager Rudi Garcia and Zubizarreta and told them that I wanted to join. I also joked with Garcia that I'd always beaten his Roma team when I played for Juventus. I told my agent to make the deal and went to training, where I felt a little pain in my hamstring. The medical staff told me there was a one-centimetre tear. I didn't tell anyone.

I finished training and went to a sushi restaurant not far from the training ground with Buffon, the veteran defender Andrea Barzagli and Marchisio, who owned the place.

I received a call from my agent to say that I had to catch a plane to Marseille in two hours.

'I have to leave, guys,' I said before giving them a hug and leaving to pick up my bag from my apartment. The players looked surprised that I was going, but deep down I hope they understood why I was leaving Juventus.

'Patrice had a great two and a half seasons with us,' Allegri told the media. 'He's a great champion, a great professional and I'm sorry he's left. But we talked and we came to this decision. I have only positive things to say about Evra. He played for ten years at Manchester United, he came to Juventus and was a very important player for us.'

I could have stayed and won another league title and a cup and played in (and probably lost) another Champions League final, which Juventus reached in May 2017 against Real Madrid after knocking out Barcelona, Porto and Monaco on the way. But my decision was made.

I drove to my apartment and then to the airport, leaving the keys on the wheel of the car for someone else to collect.

As I looked out the window of the plane towards the snow-capped Alps, it was already getting dark. My wonderful dancing days in Turin with Juventus were over.

CHAPTER 16

From Marseille to Moyes

'Patrice, you have something there on your hamstring,' said the Marseille doctor conducting my medical.

'I've had it there for a long time,' I lied.

'But it looks like there's some fresh blood and maybe a tear of one centimetre,' he replied, correctly.

'It's fine, it's fine,' I reassured him, but it was far from fine.

The doctors were dubious, but I didn't give them the choice to express their doubts. I was a new player, a big-name signing for Marseille. Nobody wanted to spoil that, especially as I was due to make my debut against Montpellier the following day. Nobody would stop me going out on the pitch. Marseille were seventh in the league and there was little positivity among their fans. My signing was supposed to lift the mood.

'I know Evra well from the French team,' said Marseille midfielder Rémy Cabella. 'He's a captain who binds the group together and talks a lot. He's a great player.'

The crowd was only 28,527 for my first Ligue 1 game for my new club. That beautiful football stadium had held over twice as many people when I'd last played there for France against Germany. Marseille fans know how to make some noise and so, even though the stadium was only half-full, it was loud. They started chanting my name from the minute I touched the ball in the warm-up. What a feeling!

Marseille were the heroes of France when they became the first French team to win the European Cup in 1993. My friends had wanted to be like the English winger Chris Waddle after that game. I thought Waddle would be considered a huge star when I came to England, but he's just a huge star in Marseille where he'd done so well. Abedi Pele, Jean-Pierre Papin and Basile Boli were also big heroes and I saw them all in the first few weeks in Marseille. I like how Marseille keep their former players close to them. I preferred Monaco as a kid, but Marseille were big time and big news, with their larger-than-life president Bernard Tapie. Marseille were afraid of nobody and their fans were so proud, but in recent years people accused them of living in the past.

On 27 January 2017, we were definitely living in the present as we hammered Montpellier 5-1. I asked to be taken off after 72 minutes because my hamstring was sore. The newspaper headlines were glowing the following day, people talked of the 'Evra effect' and Marseille getting back on track.

We played Lyon in the Coupe de France four days later and won 2-1 after extra time. We were leading 1-0 when I had to come off after 48 minutes. The crowd was 53,502, a huge increase on the previous game. There was more talk of the Evra effect. I was so frustrated and angry because due to my injury I couldn't train and couldn't travel to Metz, who were 18th in the league, for the next game. We lost 1-0.

When you win in Marseille you're a hero, but when you lose it's a big drama. Our manager Rudi Garcia asked to see me.

'About your injury,' he said. 'I know you've done a lot for the team in such a short time, but I think you need to calm down.' I agreed I wouldn't be part of the team for the next game at

Guingamp, which we won 2-0, but I said I was ready for the following match away at Nantes. Still injured, I played on one leg – I was 50 per cent fit – but lasted for 90 minutes.

I was made Marseille captain at home to Rennes, the club I'd trialled for as a kid. We won 2-0 and I managed 75 minutes, although it was a struggle – one I kept hidden. We had a bigger test against Paris Saint-Germain, the league leaders. I said publicly that they may have been favourites, but if we showed the form we had against Rennes, we could get something out of the game.

I had a scan on my hamstring beforehand – the tear had grown to two centimetres. I've never seen a physio so worried for me. The physio said I shouldn't play, the club doctor said that I shouldn't play. Stupid Patrice Evra said that he was definitely playing.

The doctor laid it on the line: 'Patrice, the first sprint that you do, your leg will open like a ham being sliced by a knife.' I ignored him; I wanted to play for a Marseille team that destroyed PSG. I wanted the fans to have their greatest moment of the season, to show why they were France's greatest club. If my leg was going to split open then maybe that was my destiny, to shed my blood on the field fighting for Olympique de Marseille.

I strapped up my leg so much that I looked like an Egyptian mummy. I took two anti-inflammatory tablets before training – after I'd sworn that I wouldn't take any more because they made me sick. I was in a kind of frenzy. I wanted to sacrifice myself if needed for the team, to show that I'd do anything for the shirt. I wanted to be a hero.

The Vélodrome was full for the first time all season, with all 65,000 seats sold – not that anyone ever sits down in the Virage Sud or Virage Nord. We were 2-0 down after 16 minutes, with goals from Marquinhos and Cavani. I didn't manage a single sprint. I told the manager as I walked down the tunnel at half-time that I couldn't go back on, to my bitter, bitter disappointment, and we lost 5–1. I was killed in the media, even though it was 2–0 when I left the pitch. They said I was taken off because I was so shit. That wasn't true.

The coach did some straight talking to me, spelling out that I needed to rest for six weeks to get over my injury, that I was not a robot, but I still felt I was letting my team down. I needn't have worried. The team started winning in my absence and, when I came back, continued winning. We were on a roll.

My family were settled back in Paris and I moved into Marseille's best hotel, a beautiful suite in the Inter Continental overlooking Marseille's Vieux Port, the Mediterranean and the church of Basilique Notre-Dame de la Garde. It looked like paradise and the hotel staff couldn't have done any more for me. I felt like the king of the city at the start, but not for long. A hotel is not a home; you have to ask for everything, for food, to wash your clothes. It's not a real existence.

I'd not been to Marseille before, apart from for football matches. It's France's second-biggest city and has a big rivalry with Paris but also a negative reputation in much of France. Yet I couldn't understand why that should be so – it's a beautiful place with good weather. There's one negative: the Mistral, the wind that comes down the Rhone Valley from the north. It's so strong that you think it can lift you up and make you fly. As you can imagine, it would affect our training sessions.

Steve Mandanda was our captain and goalkeeper, a Marseille legend. He'd die for the club, and loved being the main man. He gone to Crystal Palace in 2016–17 and things hadn't gone well. He'd been at Marseille for eight years before that and was desperate to get back from London to Marseille. Dimitri Payet was the same. He was a hero at West Ham, but he loved Marseille so much that he had to come home. Marseille has that pull, that spirit.

The club had been taken over by American businessman Frank McCourt in 2016 and the arrival of myself, Payet and Mandanda in the next year would be part of his 'OM Champions Project'. I arrived in the first transfer window under the new owner. Marseille also wanted to buy some of the best young French talent, and central midfielder Morgan Sanson signed from Montpellier a week before me for €9 million. Another midfielder, 27-year-old Grégory Sertic, came from Bordeaux at the same time as me. Marseille weren't spending the type of money that PSG were – nobody was in world football – but there was serious investment in making the team better and bringing characters to the dressing room.

Winger Florian Thauvin was talented and had a bright future. Adil Rami was an experienced central defender who came from Sevilla, as was the Portuguese defender Rolando who hailed from Cape Verde, like my mother.

One of my best friends was Rod Fanni from nearby Martigues, who had a strong local accent. We were the same age; we'd played a couple of games together for France and he made me laugh more than anyone. He told me that the previous coach Marcelo Bielsa had sent him to train with the reserves, yet Rod was an experienced battler who'd do anything for Marseille. I called him 'the fireman' because he'd put out any problem on the pitch.

As the 2016–17 season finished I featured in all the last seven league games. We won four and drew three, ending up fifth. I scored the winning goal against my old club Nice at home, heading a move that started with Payet's no-look pass. I celebrated by doing press–ups. Life was good.

I had really positive feedback from Marseille fans who knew I wanted the club to succeed. They'd watched some of my speeches in the dressing room, which had been filmed by the club's TV channel. I didn't feel comfortable with it; I felt it was an intrusion and could be a double-edged sword if we lost. The dressing room should be a sanctuary, but at least those clips went down well.

The next season began positively with wins in the opening two games of the season – home to Dijon then away at Nantes – and I started both games. I didn't play in the third and fourth, which we drew and lost, the fourth a humiliating 1-6 defeat at Monaco.

Marseille had bought a new left back, Jordan Amavi from Aston Villa, a good player and one I tried to help and encourage, just as I'd done with Alex Sandro at Juventus. I made a video the next day talking about motivation and coming back from defeat. The media put the responsibility for the defeat on me, when I didn't even play. Footballers, according to some, are supposed to keep their heads down in defeat, not appear bright and optimistic the next day.

I was in the team the following week against Rennes and did an interview for *La Provence*, the most important newspaper in Marseille. It was my first proper interview since joining the club. I talked about the need to bounce back against Rennes, but couldn't put those words into actions. I played badly, as did the rest of my teammates. We lost 3-1 at home, a terrible result as Rennes were 19th in the table. I received so much criticism, but I still did my normal video on the Monday after the game.

The French media attacked me for my Instagram videos. I was told that I should focus on my club football instead, yet the videos only took me a couple of minutes to make. Losing is part of football and without the ability to get over adversity you cannot succeed as a footballer. It's not pleasant to lose, it hurts, but you have to be as positive as you can.

I know players who keep a low profile when their team has lost. I understand that, as fans are passionate and don't want to see players enjoying themselves after they've lost a game. But that is not my style. I filmed myself giving food to homeless people as I wanted to highlight the problem of homelessness in France. My intention was clear because I felt I was in a good position, with a high profile, to publicise it. But I was hammered for it in France, with people accusing me of doing it to take the attention away from our defeat against Rennes. It hurt me a lot as my motives were entirely genuine.

There was actually a debate on television about it, where I was accused of using homeless people to seek self-publicity. In the face of this barrage of criticism and declining results, Marseille fans fell out of love with me. They didn't sing my name any more inside the stadium. It got inside my head. I suspected that the French media were thinking: 'Finally, we've got him!' They were laughing at me, saying I was finished, past it, too old to play football. I was far from in the best form of my life, but it's amazing how much pleasure others can take from your misfortune. And they did it cleverly, too, saying that I didn't respect Marseille fans. Sadly, some Marseille fans bought that, even though it was bullshit.

Even when I played well in Europa League games where I was captain, my mistakes would be highlighted. I would only play one more league game for Marseille after that Rennes defeat – for 80 minutes away at Lille, where we won 1-0.

On 2 November 2017, we played a Europa League away game at Guimaraes in Portugal. The preparation was normal, but I heard some of the travelling Marseille fans shouting out the names of players with insulting comments as we practised in front of them.

'Patrice, son of a bitch!' I heard a few times.

We'd just won at Lille and the game had yet to start, but the fans were already on our backs.

I saw a loose ball close to those fans and I went to pick it up. Maybe it was a mistake to do that, but I wanted to hear what they were saying close up. One of the Marseille coaches warned me: 'Don't listen to them.' But I went over and they shouted: 'Patrice! Give us the ball!'

I said to one of them: 'You're shouting abuse at the players and you want me to give you a ball.'

'Yes, I want a ball for my son.'

A sudden burst of anger flared up inside me. 'I'm not your bitch,' I told him. Then I demanded to know who had been calling me a son of a bitch. Nobody answered, until one shouted: 'Calm your voice down.'

'I won't calm my voice down,' I replied. 'And I'm not scared of any one of you,' I said, gesturing towards some of the ultras.

'You want to play tough?' one of them bellowed. 'You will see when we come down.' They were a few rows back in the stand. I was by the edge of the pitch. They were starting to move forward in front of me.

'Stop doing the fucking monkey!' another taunted me. I didn't pay any attention to that comment, I've heard far worse, but I couldn't ignore what followed.

'When we're in Marseille we're going to kill your family!' one shouted. 'We'll kill your wife and kids!'

I exploded, kicking the ball against the glass partition. Behind that, the fans had already climbed over one small wall towards me. Then some of the fans jumped over the glass partition and down to pitch level. They thought I would be scared, but I stood my ground. All that separated us now were the advertising hoardings.

'We're going to kill you!' one of them threatened.

'Come and do it now, then!' I replied. 'I'm going nowhere.' He came towards me and I tried to punch him but was pulled back. The Marseille players rushed over and tried to tell the other fans to go back and get me to move away.

'Leave them!' I said. 'I like to fight, it's not a problem.'

'Come on, Patrice,' said one teammate – I don't know who it was – 'come inside.'

Then I saw one of the fans run at me. I paused, as if I was going to punch him with the right fist so that he would move to the left. He did that and I was waiting to kick him with a high left foot. *Boom!* It felt like a good connection.

The players and the fans were stunned – there was a shocked roar. Rolando took me to the dressing room. At first, I didn't feel like I was in trouble. I felt that the fans had jumped over two barriers to approach me and I'd not left the pitch.

Once I was in the dressing room, Rudi Garcia came to see me.

'What happened, Patrice?' he asked calmly.

'Boss, I fucked up,' I replied. 'This is my personality. If someone threatens me or my family, I will stand up to them.'

'An experienced player like you shouldn't be doing this,' he replied. 'You have to rise above it. Did he say something racist?'

'Yes, but it wasn't that,' I replied. 'I lost it when they threatened my wife and kids.'

'Fucking hell, they shouldn't say that,' he replied, 'but come on.' He was very disappointed with me.

I told him that I was prepared to take full responsibility, though I didn't know how bad things were going to be. Indeed, when the team returned to the dressing room after the warm-up, I still thought I was going to play and lined up with the team, when an official from UEFA told me that I'd been given a red card by the referee.

'Really, when the game hasn't started yet?' was all I could say. I went back to the dressing room, took a shower and watched from the stand. Fans asked for pictures with me and I happily obliged. We lost the game 1–0 and stayed overnight in Portugal.

My son Lenny called me the following morning.

'Daddy, why did you kick that fan?' he asked.

'He was threatening me and the family,' I explained.

'Then you should kick him,' he said.

I liked that, but I told him that you should never kick some-one. I need to take my own advice.

We trained well in the morning, but outside of our little bubble the news was everywhere and on the front page of newspapers around the world. I was thinking: 'I bet the French media are delighted that they've finally got me.' They made me out to be worse than Bin Laden, but I didn't feel like a criminal, I didn't have any anxiety because I felt I had had justification for my actions.

Not everyone shared my confidence. 'We're going to have a meeting when we get back to Marseille,' my coach told me. 'I'm worried about the situation and for you.'

Marseille's security on the plane said I would need to increase my personal security and that when I landed in Marseille I'd need to be smuggled out of the airport because there was the likeli-hood of angry fans waiting. I was having none of that. I wanted no special treatment and so said I would go the normal way like everyone else, although it was through a private terminal that Marseille's team had access to because they flew to games on a pri-vate charter plane. My big brother Dom had driven to the airport in my car and was waiting for me. He wouldn't be scared either.

I walked through Arrivals and there were a lot of journalists waiting. I walked past the clicking cameras, saw Dom and got in the car. Dom was angry about everything that had happened, that I was front-page news. I suggested that we go for a pizza in the middle of Marseille.

'That's going too far,' he said.

'I want to eat pizza,' I replied. 'I will eat pizza.'

I walked through my hotel. Everyone looked at me. Everyone was stunned when they saw me walk out of the hotel, but that's what I did. I found a pizzeria close by and ate a pizza with my brother. People stared at us, but nobody attacked us. I then said I wanted to go to the cinema.

'No chance,' Dom told me. 'You'll end up fighting with a fan.'

He had a point and we went back to the hotel. Not a single Marseille fan gave me the slightest bit of abuse in the rest of my time there. It shows the disconnect between what the media say and what people say in real life when they see you. Maybe if someone has a problem they are more inclined to abuse you anonymously, but I could only judge by my experience of meeting people in the street. And what people said to me is that some of the ultras were not representative of most fans. The ultras have a lot of power, though, too much power.

I loved the support, noise and colour that make the Vélodrome one of the most atmospheric stadiums in the world, but there's a flip side, an intimidating side where players have been threatened for not playing well. Several players from various clubs thanked me for what I'd done. They felt they'd been bullied by ultras, pressured into supplying tickets or even handing over gifts. One player was even bullied into buying a pair of Christian Louboutin boots for one of them. When I arrived in Marseille, a few of the players warned me about the situation. But I'd told them that, although a player should always respect the fans, he should not be afraid of them.

In response to the incident, my manager told the media: 'Pat has experience and he must not react, it's obvious. You can't respond to insults, as bad as they are and as incredible as they might be. He must learn to keep his cool.'

I understood that, but the level and type of provocation was unacceptable to me. After training the following day, when Marseille's club president Jacques-Henri Eyraud came to see me in my hotel room, he got straight to the point.

'What happened in Portugal is inexcusable. To protect the club, we're going to suspend you for two weeks.'

'I am a man, I will take it,' I replied. 'If you think that is for the best of the club, I will take it. I don't want to cause problems for the club. I'm sorry if I hurt anyone at the club.'

He said something that I didn't like about protecting me from the media, who wanted to destroy me when I was playing at Marseille.

'I don't need your protection, I'm not a baby,' I replied. 'I can deal with the media after what happened in South Africa with France.'

There were calls for me to be banned for life and I trained alone for a week or so. I think Marseille were waiting to see what sanction UEFA gave me before they decided fully what to do. UEFA said that I would be banned for the rest of the season from all their competitions and fined €10,000. I would still be able to play in league games, but Marseille received so much pressure from the media that they announced their suspension one day before UEFA.

I sent my lawyer to meet with the club's lawyer. My instruction was that I didn't want to damage the club by staying around, bringing pressure on them and negative energy. We agreed mutually to terminate my contract and Marseille said they would pay me for two more months. I thought Marseille handled it professionally, and when I look back on my ten months there, the good memories far outweigh the bad. I'm glad I went there. I would recommend any player to play for OM. The staff are fantastic, the vast majority of the fans too.

I was 36 but hadn't given up on football. I didn't want to stop playing, but I didn't have a club. I went to Dubai, where I knew I would be able to train in the warm weather. Dominique and Tshimen came with me. I knew a personal trainer, Shaun, an English guy who worked with two English assistants, Lee and Mike, who put me through my paces. One of the princes said that I could use the facilities like it was my own house, including his masseur and doctor. Those facilities were incredible, with recovery chambers and equipment that was better than most top-level football teams.

I was determined to be as fit as possible and find a new club. I put harsh demands on myself and trained twice as hard, often from 10 am to 5 pm. I knew it would be difficult training alone and it was. I made regular videos, to motivate people to come through hard times by working hard, but I wasn't completely happy. My family were still in Paris and I was being difficult with people around me. I usually get angry rather than depressed and I wasn't very pleasant with Dom and Tshimen. They did nothing but support me, yet I'd lash out at them, ask them why they even bothered being with me in Dubai. They just laughed at me.

'You're happy when I go to restaurants and pay the bills,' I said. 'You're not so happy when I ask you to train with me. You're lazy.' They both told me that they weren't lazy and would start training with me the next morning. I had so much fun with them when they did because they weren't out of shape but they weren't quite athletes.

I began to get interest from clubs. Galatasaray were my first choice and I flew to Istanbul and spoke to Igor Tudor, the coach. He asked me if I was still fit and told me that he wanted me. I spoke to Bafétimbi Gomis, who was playing there. He kept telling me to come and I was waiting on the offer from Galatasaray.

Galatasaray fans started contacting me on Instagram, urging me to join them. The offer was agreed with my agent, the same money as I'd been on at Marseille. That wasn't as important to me as playing football again. I didn't want to end my career by kicking someone. I was on call and prepared to fly back to Istanbul from Dubai. I trained more carefully and didn't push myself too hard because I didn't want to get injured.

My agent told me to book my flight to Istanbul.

'Should I pay for the ticket myself?' I asked. Normally a club takes care of those details. He told me to reserve a ticket but not pay for it.

As we were waiting for a fax to confirm everything, Galatasaray surprisingly sacked Tudor, who had been doing well. Fatih Terim, the legendary Galatasaray boss who returned to coach the club for a fourth time, still wanted me. Galatasaray met my agent in Paris and they also said they wanted to sign another of his players, Kwadwo Asamoah.

'Asamoah will stay at Juventus,' he explained. 'I thought we were here to talk about Patrice.' Galatasaray said they wanted more time. I had to wait, yet time was running out as the transfer window closed on 31 January. By 25 January, I told my agent that Galatasaray were messing us around. I was given Fatih Terim's number and called him, leaving a voice message.

'I want to join Galatasaray,' I said. 'Just give me a yes or a no. I don't want to waste my or your time.' He didn't answer me, but I was told by one of his friends that he got the message. I was also told that he would do the opposite of what everyone was telling him to do. I was promised an answer on 28 January.

In the end, Fatih Terim decided on Yuto Nagatomo from Inter. One of the guys from Galatasaray called to say sorry. I was disappointed, my pride was hurt, but I replied: 'You don't have to say sorry. It's destiny. If it's not meant to be then it's not meant to be.'

I also messaged Terim again to wish him well and say that I hoped Galatasaray won the league. I didn't receive a reply and all interest from Galatasaray disappeared.

I continued training – with anger. Instead of becoming disheartened by the rejection, I became more determined. Shaun couldn't believe my stats and asked me what I was eating. I was careful about every aspect of my lifestyle, including going to bed early. A goalkeeper and a couple of players were brought in so I could play more with the ball. I was training harder than at any time in my career and my GPS readings were proving that, but I missed my family and my teammates and I wondered where I would go next. I thought about the MLS in America or the CSL in China. On 31 January my agent called me and said: 'I'm sorry we didn't find you anything, Patrice.' There was a pause before he said: 'I need to check, but I think you can still sign for a club even if the window has closed as you'll be a free agent.' He was right and I relaxed a little while planning to go to Paris to see my family.

Before I left Dubai, I decided to skydive. I'd not done it before but I was so excited – despite Dom begging me not to do it in case I got injured.

'There will be no injury if something goes wrong,' I replied, 'I'll just die.'

I was asked to say my final words to a camera on the plane in case something happened to me – they do it to scare you a bit. I had no fear when I jumped and felt like a bird, free in the sky. Adrenalin flooded through me and continued when I landed.

I was on my way to afternoon training when my agent called.

'You have to be in London in the morning,' he said. 'West Ham. David Moyes. They want to do tests on you in the morning.'

'How can I be in London at such short notice?'

'Don't fucking play with me,' he replied. 'Don't train and go and find a plane.'

I thought about calling the skydive man, flying to London and jumping out of the plane onto West Ham's training ground, like a paratrooper ready to save West Ham. Then I re-entered the real world. There was one plane left at 2 am to London, which would get me in at 6 am local time. I hardly slept on the flight and grabbed a car to the training ground, where Moyes was waiting to greet me and show me around.

'I've brought my stuff to do the fitness tests,' I said.

'I trust you,' he replied. 'If you tell me that you're fit then you're fit.' He'd also seen my records from Dubai, which had been sent to West Ham the day before to show that I was in great condition.

I passed the medical and Moyes said: 'It's down to David Sullivan, the chairman. I want you here because our left back is suspended for six games. Maybe you won't play one game, maybe you'll play more, but don't make my life harder. I know and respect you, but you have to give me that respect.'

Of course I respected him. We had to go to David Sullivan's house. It was the best meeting I'd ever had to sign a contract – it was all done in five minutes.

'I know all about you and respect you,' said Sullivan, 'but you're older now.'

'I'm not coming here begging you for money,' I replied. 'I just want to play football, I miss it.'

'Let's go to the kitchen,' he said. 'And write down on that paper what you want.'

'I want the same as what I earned in Marseille,' I said.

'I can't give you that,' he replied. It was about £40,000 a week.

My agent wrote down on the paper a figure a little less than I'd been on, plus bonuses if West Ham stayed up.

'We're staying up,' said Sullivan, who agreed to the lower sum. And just like that, I was a West Ham player.

Training the following morning was such a joy. It was freezing, but I preferred that to being alone in the Dubai sun. Just playing again was like one of the best days of my life. The training ground was nothing like at Man United, and Moyes apologised for that, but I wasn't bothered – I just wanted to play.

Moyes watched and was pleased with me. He saw that I was bringing a positive energy to the club. We played Watford and won 2-0, though I was on the bench and David had explained that, as I'd only been at the club a few days, I wouldn't play. He wanted me around, though, and I wanted to be around footballers preparing for a game.

'Are you ready for Liverpool, Pat?' asked Moyes. I was told I was going to make my West Ham debut against them. I arrived at Anfield, which had completely changed since my last visit, with a huge new main stand. The atmosphere wasn't as intense as visiting with Manchester United, but that didn't matter as I said thank you to God over and over again for giving me the opportunity.

The Liverpool fans booed me non-stop on the pitch but I didn't mind, I had missed it. It was a good game, and I did myself justice, but we fell apart in the second half and lost 1-4. I also suffered a very bad tackle from Trent Alexander-Arnold near the end. He hammered me and the resulting wound would need five stitches. The crowd cheered when I limped, but I carried on playing as the blood began to soak into my socks. They jeered me until the end and as I left the pitch. I smiled at some of them and they smiled back.

The doctor looked alarmed when he saw my cut and quickly sewed it up. I'd been delighted to play, gutted to lose and to be injured because I knew it would mess up my West Ham progress.

I didn't train for three days and our next game was at Swansea, a relegation battle that we were due to fly to, but the bad weather meant we went by coach, a seven-hour drive in heavy traffic. There was talk of the game being cancelled but it went ahead. I had to go on as all the central defenders were injured. I took painkillers and was heavily strapped up, but every time I got a knock the pain was horrendous. I tried to hide that I was suffering but the pain was too strong and I only lasted 45 minutes. We were 2-0 down at half-time, a bad performance all round and a terrible result.

We lost the next game at home to Burnley, 3-0. West Ham's

fans were furious and a handful came onto the pitch to protest. That was their right, but I hoped they wouldn't start fighting with the players as I didn't want to end up fighting with fans again. And I respected those fans, knew that they were proper fans of a proper club with roots among the working class in the East End of London.

Nobody starts following West Ham because they think they'll win trophies; they do it because they follow their family and friends in supporting a club they're deeply proud of. But they weren't proud of the team as Burnley battered us. The West Ham fans near the bench where I was sitting were all shouting. I told the security to let them express their anger since they weren't threatening anyone. Their anger was directed towards the club rather than any individual players. They missed their old stadium at Upton Park and they let their feelings be known. I looked into the crowd and saw a young fan crying. His dad looked at the players, pointed to his son and said: 'You see what you are doing?'

I watched the son rather than the match. I smiled at him and he smiled back. At the end of the game I went to see the kid, who was about nine, and gave him my shirt.

'I promise you that we won't get relegated,' I said.

We needed to get out of the poisonous environment around West Ham and had decided to go to Miami for serious warm-weather training during the international break. Several players thought this was a bad idea as it would look as if we were taking a holiday when the club was up against it.

I decided to speak up.

'We're in the shit,' I said. 'I need you more than I need family at the moment. I need to get to know you. We can have a change of scene and work hard away from the bullshit.'

Maybe some agreed, maybe some didn't. We went and certainly worked hard, Moyes made sure of that, with added classes of spinning just to finish us off. It was like pre-season again.

'If I see one picture of you drinking alcohol or with a girl then I'll fine you.' There was one picture of the West Ham players looking at an American swimwear model doing a photo shoot on South Beach, but we were only walking past and the boss allowed us that one.

Moyes organised a dinner at a superb restaurant and told every player to find a song to sing. It was a fine idea. I sang Bob Marley's 'Three Little Birds'. A couple of the players were very nervous about singing, but the rest of us urged them on, said that we were in it together and had to be united. Cheikhou Kouyate sang Shakira's 'Waka Waka' and set the room on fire. We had a brilliant time in Miami – apart from those gruelling training sessions. We returned to London full of positive energy and beat Southampton 3-0. I was on the bench for that game, but then I came on for the last half an hour of Chelsea away. We were a goal down when Chicharito, my old United teammate, came on and scored an equaliser, a huge point for us, and the Little Pea and I celebrated together as we had done at Old Trafford. Moyes was delighted with us.

After a boring 1-1 stalemate at Stoke, where I was really upset not to start, we travelled to the Emirates a few days after the announcement that Arsène Wenger would be leaving the club after 22 years. I went over to him in the warm-up and said sincerely: 'Thank you for everything you have done for football.'

'Thank you for the things you've done,' he replied. We lost 1-4 and I didn't get off the bench.

We lost by the same scoreline the following week against Manchester City, when I started at centre back. City came to us looking like champions; they wanted the ball more than any team I'd played against, whereas our minds were on the Leicester City game a few days later, which annoyed me. We had to beat Leicester away and we did – 2-0. The atmosphere was superb because we knew we'd be staying up. Then I learned that Sir Alex Ferguson was in intensive care after a stroke and my happiness dissolved. I sent him a message: 'I love you.' That was it.

Alex's son Jason Ferguson called me a few days later to say that his dad was awake and talking. People have criticised me for not posting any public statement about Sir Alex, but does everything have to be public? I felt it too deeply to comment on social media.

And then for the first time in my life I had the chance of playing against Manchester United, but I wasn't selected and I was fine with that. I didn't want to come on in a nothing game, it didn't feel right. I don't even think the away fans noticed I was there. I didn't want to fight against that badge and I felt nothing but pain when I spoke to all the staff and players after the game for so long that they nearly missed their flight.

Moyes did all that was asked of him and kept West Ham up. He arrived when the team was 18th and carrying a large number of injuries, and he left them in 13th. He always faced the media and he didn't have a lot of money to bring new players in. But he wasn't asked to stay on at West Ham – and that is football, which gives so many wonderful things but takes them away as well.

CHAPTER 17

Meeting Margaux

My contract at West Ham expired in May 2018 and I thought that maybe I'd start living what I believed was a normal life. I'd spent my entire adult life in the bubble of being a footballer, of being trapped like a robot and told where to go and what to do. That's the sacrifice you make when you are a professional footballer, and I have no regrets, but I still had the rest of my life to look forward to.

I'd not definitely decided to stop playing, but I felt I wanted to do different things. I started to learn about myself, and I discovered the world in a different way as I took my first job on television covering the 2018 World Cup finals in Russia.

France struggled in the group stage and the coach, my old boss Didier Deschamps, invited me to see the France team and speak to all the players at their team hotel. I had lunch with them and felt privileged to enjoy the moment because, from my experience, they go so fast. As a player you only see the inside, not the thousands of fans on the streets having a party or in the airports like I was now seeing. I could see the outside and Moscow's Red Square full of fans from around the world, with the bars and restaurants packed. But I could also see a little of the inside.

I spent time with Paul Pogba and Kylian Mbappé in their hotel rooms and they seemed relaxed and happy. Both had the potential to be stars of the tournament. The players gave me a new France national shirt with my name and number on and I left the hotel feeling proud of France, hoping that I'd brought some positivity to the camp.

Then I went back to my hotel where I was spending two weeks with the other commentators, Roy Keane, Ian Wright, Ryan Giggs, Eni Aluko and Gary Neville. I'd never been around Roy, someone I respected because he was a Manchester United great. We're both big characters and there was a mutual respect. I'd played in Roy's testimonial but hadn't spoken properly with him before. We talked a lot over breakfasts and dinners and agreed on the importance of sacrificing yourself for your team, of playing through pain of injury if it helped the team win. We had a nice connection and we shared another trait: we wanted to be on time for everything.

I found that out when we agreed to go for lunch with Ian Wright and arranged to meet in the lobby at noon. Roy said he liked Ian and his charisma, even though he was a Gunner. That was good enough for me and I got there early, even before Roy. He approved of this and told me he liked me even more for being early. His happy mood didn't last long and by 11.58, Roy started to become agitated. By five past 12 I started to see the crazy Roy Keane that people talked about.

'This is ridiculous, Patrice,' he said. 'Ian Wright is not respecting us. I don't know why we gave so much credit to a fucking Gunner. We're on time because we're United. That's why we won trophies!'

Ian arrived ten minutes late. Roy gave him the hairdryer, shouting at him and asking him who on earth he thought he was keeping us waiting. Ian was laughing at the start, but not after Roy carried on telling him where to go. Then Roy left because he didn't want to wait around with Ian any more. Ian stood there and I felt sorry for him, but I also thought: 'This is Keano; small details matter to him.'

On another day before a game we were both working at, Roy heard me opening my hotel-room door. He was next door to me and he ran out because he didn't want to be later than me. Except there was a problem which Roy realised when we were in the lift: he'd left his glasses in the hotel room and he needed them to watch the game properly. I told Roy that he had time to get them. Roy refused to go back to retrieve them because he'd be late. It was a funny experience.

There were a lot of former United lads there. I did gym sessions with Giggsy, I'd have breakfast with Gary. On screen, I also had a crazy experience with Eni Aluko. I clapped her because I was impressed with her analysis. Actually, I was asked by the female presenter to rate Eni's analysis after her first appearance. This threw me – no one asks me to do that for the men I work with. I had to respond and I did. A newspaper accused me of being sexist. Eni was surprised at this, because I'm not. BT, who I was working for, asked me what I wanted to do and if I wanted to continue working. Of course I did. I told them that I would wear a wig if the newspaper kept talking trash.

They told me not to put more oil on the fire. I joke, but it wasn't a nice experience. I don't like it when people talk about me that way, but I realised you have to be careful what you say on television. When someone is good, I clap. Eni was very good and knows football. It was unfair to say I was patronising because I know the strength of women. My mum had 13 kids and educated every single one. Even when she lost her leg she became stronger. My mum is my hero. So I want to do so much to promote women in football.

I was so proud when France won the World Cup. I was a fan there watching from the outside, but I was delighted when Paul and Didier face-timed me from the dressing room straight after they had beaten Croatia in a superb final game. They said their success was about continuity after the European Championships, even though we had lost in that final. I saw my old teammates on the screen and they said nice things to me, about my influence on them. After that call, I felt like I'd won the World Cup too. The new generation has given us strong talent throughout. Deschamps deserves so much credit because he knew how to build a group to win. He was a huge part of France's success.

A few weeks later, Deschamps invited me to his house close to Monaco. He'd won the World Cup as a player and a manager and I wanted a piece of his magic as I thought about my own future. If you want to find out about the road ahead, it's good to speak to someone who has been on it.

We talked about the World Cup. Didier felt Paul had matured because of my influence. We discussed Didier's tactics. He'd been under heavy media pressure to play with three strikers but he was convinced that he would get more balance with two and using Olivier Giroud at the front. He was right, even though Giroud wasn't scoring. Giroud was a big part in that success, the man in front of Antoine Griezmann, Kylian and Ousmane Dembélé. Deschamps told me that so many journalists who'd criticised him now wanted to be friends with him after he'd won the World Cup. He'd seen it before with Aimé Jacquet in the 1998 World Cup.

Deschamps asked me if I was angry with him because he'd left me out of the squad. I said I was not, but his wife had criticised him for not selecting me in front of both of us. Thank you, Mrs Deschamps! Benjamin Mendy was supposed to play in my position but he was injured and Lucas Hernandez stepped in and did well.

If I'd done better with West Ham maybe I could have made

the squad, but I was not the player in 2018 that I'd been two years earlier and I was not playing every week, let alone performing well. The timing was unfortunate, but I had played 81 times for France over 12 years and 11 times for France Under-21s.

I'd watched that final in London, my new home. My life was changing. In the weeks after the World Cup, I found it enjoyable not to be a professional footballer, not being stressed and being able to sleep a little longer and not go to training, but I'd not made the final decision to retire. I'd not announced anything.

I still trained by myself every day and started pre-season with West Ham and stayed there, even with Manuel Pellegrini as manager after David Moyes left. I had interest to continue playing in America, in Asia, in England and at one point Pellegrini asked me if I still wanted to play for West Ham. Even though I was no longer getting paid, I was going to training and enjoying it for month after month. It gave me some focus in my life, some structure. I even sat in on team meetings, but where was it all going? I didn't know.

I spoke to Thierry Henry. 'Patrice, you will never retire if you don't stop training with West Ham, even though they are not paying you,' he said. 'Try to have two weeks when you don't go to the training ground.'

I listened to Thierry's advice and after three days I still felt okay not going to the training ground. I didn't miss it. Life carried on. It's unusual that you do something every day for almost all your life and then you just stop doing it. More unusual, though, was that I didn't miss playing one bit. In fact, it was a year or two before I started to think: 'I'd like to play a game of football.' Maybe every player has to go through this and has to adjust to their new reality out of the dressing room. I know many find it difficult and the rates for depression and divorce among recently retired footballers are high. They lose the structure in their life, but I tried to keep a structure to mine. I was still doing my cross-fit, just not putting my football boots on. I'm still fit to this day and weigh 72 kilos, three less than when I played. I eat healthily and take care of myself. I'm proud of my body and how I look.

I started doing the things I'd not been able to do. I went to restaurants with my brothers, to nightclubs in London, too. I started to enjoy life a little more, but it was all a little odd to me seeing people drinking alcohol and partying. It didn't suit my personality and I felt conflicted and guilty going out. Friends told me that I didn't need to be a robot any more. I'd never drunk alcohol and I felt a little sick after one glass of wine because my body wasn't used to it. It felt like poison in my body. I don't think nightclubs are for me.

I started to wonder what I was doing with my life, but my brother and friends told me to relax and enjoy what I'd been missing out on for so long when I'd preferred to train as hard as possible to be as consistent as possible. But I also felt free and happy, and maybe that was because of who I met. My marriage had ended and the divorce proceedings had already started. Sandra and I had been together for 25 years and we have two children. But after some difficult times we were no longer sharing the same roof. We would meet only around family moments. I'd been living in London for two years without my family and I'd not lived with them properly for seven years since leaving Manchester. It's never nice when a relationship ends and a divorce follows, but our story was over.

Things changed when I went for dinner with my brother Benjamin in London in October 2019. It was late and I saw a beautiful girl at the end of the VQ restaurant in Chelsea very close to Stamford Bridge. It's not glamorous. My brother Ben went to her and said: 'You should meet my brother, Patrice.' She said she didn't know who he or I was.

When I left the restaurant, I saw my brother talking with her. I grabbed the opportunity to introduce myself.

'Oh, hello, nice to meet you,' I said.

'Hello, nice to meet you.' She asked my name, but was obviously confused – in a good way.

'Why did your brother approach me in such a weird way saying I had to meet you?!' she asked, smiling. 'Who are you?'

'I'm nobody, I just like to make people happy,' I replied. We talked a little more. It felt natural. We exchanged numbers.

I texted her and said we should meet. She replied and asked why her friends had wanted a picture with me. She'd not Googled me or anything. I invited her to the cinema. I was wearing my gym clothes because I was also going to the gym. Margaux was impressed with the idea of watching me in the gym and to be fair I don't know what I was thinking. Maybe I wanted to show that I was strong. She still jokes with me about this now.

We watched a war film, *Midway*. It went well, the film and the date. Then we went for a lunch and next I invited her for lunch at my house. She came and saw a picture of me with a Man United shirt on and asked if I was a footballer player. She said that, after she followed me on Instagram and saw me jumping around and laughing in my posts, she got the idea that I was some kind of comedian or blogger or some IG personality. It's weird for me to meet someone who doesn't know who I am, but I liked it.

We had a nice lunch. We couldn't meet a lot in the weeks after because she was travelling a lot in her work as a model, but every time we met each other I felt a strong connection. I felt happy. I missed her when I was wasn't with her. Margaux gave me assurance. She said that I didn't need to force myself to go to nightclubs if that wasn't my world, but it was still a shock for me to be a footballer every day and then not be a footballer every day. She lived the opposite kind of life, loving to cook at home, to go to the cinema, to the gym or for a run. Life's simple pleasures, like going for a walk and appreciating nature, and she brought that to me.

We became serious and Margaux, who had her own flat, came to live with me. She moved in three days before lock-down. I understand that a lot of people felt trapped in lockdown and that's why I tried to make people smile with my videos in a difficult time. Some of the videos were so popular that people who didn't even know I'd been a footballer watched them and loved them. I hope these can be used as a force for good, for positivity. Truthfully, the first lockdown was not so bad for me because it meant I could wake up next to her every day and our love could grow.

This is a woman who has shown me that crying is not a weakness, but a strength. She taught me to calm down, to be soft, to share my emotions and feelings. As she got to know me, she suspected that because I'm so lovely at times and yet so tense at others maybe I had been traumatised in the past and haven't made peace with an element in my life.

This is difficult for me, but I explained to her what happened when I was younger – what I wrote about at the start of this book. I cried all day when I did this, like everything was coming out. I had not cried for 20 years. Family members had died, but I hadn't cried because I felt I had to be strong. I was always the guy at the funerals telling people to smile and not cry.

I had not told anyone in any detail about what had happened and what you read at the start of this book was the first time I discussed it. It's an important part of my life and I needed to get it out. I now understand that I hadn't been weak and that the abuse wasn't in some way my fault. I also understand that I don't always have to protect my image, the famous, always-smiling, full-of-positive-energy footballer Patrice Evra who is strong and makes other people happy.

I could have revealed the truth to the police about what happened earlier and I reproach myself about it, but I was still the frightened boy lying in the dark, waiting for his abuser. I will always be that boy in some respects but I have allowed him to tell his secret and that is a start. I have walked into the light as a man.

As for the future, I'm not walking away from football. It still calls me. I am doing my coaching badges and enjoying that. I spent some time at Manchester United, with the Under-16s, the Under-13s, and I watched the women's team. United asked me if I was interested in an ambassadorial role. I'm unsure what comes next. I love football; football made me and I was fortunate to have an incredible career, to win the biggest trophies, to play in Italy, France and England. But I also speak to managers and I don't know many who enjoy the job or watching the game. When I watch football, I want to enjoy it.

I have done some television work and it was fun and a challenge. It was while working for Sky that Jamie Carragher apologised to me on live television for what had gone on with Luis Suarez all those years ago. It came from his heart and I respected that. Liverpool's CEO Peter Moore also wrote to me, apologising and expressing humanity. I greatly appreciated this. They were big enough to hold their hands up, admit a mistake and try to make the world a better place where racists are kicked out. It was better late than never. I forgive and have more respect for Liverpool.

Where Manchester United is concerned, I will never be fake with the fans. I speak from the heart and that might sometimes upset the club, but I only want what is best for the club, a club I sacrificed so much for. When I spoke out on television about United it was because I was concerned about the commercial priority that I felt the club was taking. There was some talk of me being a director of football at the club and I sat next to Ed Woodward at a couple of games. We don't always have to agree on everything, but we get on fine. I've enjoyed watching United too, the best being against Paris Saint-Germain in March 2019. I sat with Eric Cantona properly for the first time in my life. We'd said little hellos, but this time I could thank him for leaving the door open for French players at United.

'If I opened the door, you smashed the door open,' said Eric. I was delighted to hear this from the man I had an image of when I lifted the League Cup for United in 2006. We kept in touch and met in Monte Carlo after. We follow each other on Instagram and make each other laugh. We have other things in common: he kicked a fan and I kicked a fan. Neither of us regret it.

In Paris, we also saw our old boss, Sir Alex, and new boss Ole Gunnar Solskjær invited us to the pre-match team meal. There, I told striker Romelu Lukaku that he was going to score two goals. He said that if he did, then he'd give me his boots. Romelu scored twice, United had a great win and I didn't need his boots.

In the stand, the injured Paul Pogba and I sat together and celebrated – and those celebrations were misinterpreted in the media. We sat in the stands and a French politician was behind us. As PSG dominated, he kept saying 'Ici c'est Paris!' ('Here is Paris') or 'Evra, we can't hear you any more.' Paul always wanted to answer him back, but I kept saying, 'Wait until the end, United can still win this.' That's what happened and we did a celebration saying 'Here is Manchester!'

We weren't laughing at PSG but at the politician, who I kept out of the film which I put on social media, because I didn't want him going to his lawyer or whatever. Some PSG fans went crazy at me, maybe because I'd said they had been beaten by United's D team – by some of the kids who used to clean my boots, players who didn't even have sperm yet! Okay, I went a bit far, but I was having fun. There was some pressure for me to apologise, but I'd spoken to PSG CEO Nasser Al-Khelaifi after the game and we were fine.

As for my own life, I know I will have to make a choice. I know players and managers who have asked me to be their assistant. I have knowledge and experience, but when I do this I want to be 100 per cent and give whoever I work with the full me.

We have started a family with baby Lilas Latyr Evra, who was born on 3 May 2021. That's where my focus is, enjoying our truly special love. Margaux is my soulmate, my best friend, my everything. I miss her even when she's next to me. I love this woman and, of course, I Love This Game.

ACKNOWLEDGEMENTS

I'd like to thank my parents, Juliette Rigal and Cyprien Evra.

Plus my many brothers and sisters and cousins. Most are listed at the start of the book.

My childhood friends from the street Les Ulis, especially Tshimen Buhanga, my best friend.

My Senegalese Angel from Milan Central train station. I am sorry I don't know your name.

Every teammate I played with and played against. Respect.

The special coaches: Sandro Salvioni, Didier Deschamps, Sir Alex Ferguson, Massimo Allegri.

My football agents: Frederico Pastorello and Luca Bascherini.

The fans.

Andy Mitten. For having to patience to follow me in Turin, Marseille, London, Paris and Manchester. It was long and at times stressful. I hope it was worth it.

My manager, Napper, and all his team from One House and my PR team, Outside.

My publisher, Ian Marshall, and all at Simon & Schuster.

INDEX

The initials PE indicate Patrice Evra.